LONDON RECORD SOCIETY
PUBLICATIONS

VOLUME XIX
FOR THE YEAR 1983

TRINITY HOUSE OF DEPTFORD TRANSACTIONS, 1609–35

EDITED BY
G. G. HARRIS

LONDON RECORD SOCIETY
1983

The publication of this volume has been
assisted by a grant from the Twenty-Seven
Foundation.

Phototypeset by
Wyvern Typesetting Ltd, Bristol
Printed in Great Britain by
The Thetford Press Ltd, Norfolk

CONTENTS

ABBREVIATIONS

Anderson	R. C. Anderson, *List of English men-of-war, 1509–1649* (Society for Nautical Research, occasional publications, no. 7) (1959)
APC	*Acts of the Privy Council of England*
BL	British Library
C 66	Public Record Office, Patent rolls
CD	*Commons Debates, 1621*, ed. W. Notestein, F. H. Relf and H. Simpson (7 vols, 1935)
CSPD	*Calendar of State Papers, Domestic series*
CSP Ven.	*Calendar of State Papers, Venetian*
DCB	*Dictionary of Canadian Biography*, vol. 1, ed. G. W. Brown and M. Trudel (1966)
def.	defendant
DNB	*Dictionary of National Biography*
HCA 3	Public Record Office, High court of admiralty, act books
Monson	*The naval tracts of Sir William Monson*, ed. M. Oppenheim (Navy Records Society, 5 vols, 1902–14)
Oppenheim	M. Oppenheim, *A history of the administration of the Royal Navy* (1896)
PC 2	Public Record Office, Register of the privy council
Pett	P. Pett, *Autobiography*, ed. W. G. Perrin (Navy Records Society, 1918)
pl.	plaintiff
PRO	Public Record Office
Proc.	*Tudor and Stuart proclamations*, ed. R. Steele (2 vols, 1910)
Rem.	City of London Records Office, Remembrancia
Rem.	W. H. & H. C. Overall, *Analytical index to the . . . Remembrancia of the City of London, 1579–1664* (1878)
Scott	W. R. Scott, *The constitution and finance of the English, Scottish and Irish joint stock companies to 1720* (3 vols, 1910–12)
SP 14	Public Record Office, State papers, James I
SP 16	Public Record Office, State papers, Charles I
Statutes	*The Statutes of the realm* (10 vols, 1810–28)
THD	G. G. Harris, *The Trinity House of Deptford, 1514–1660* (1969)

INTRODUCTION

On 20 May 1514, letters patent were granted to the Trinity House of Deptford which conferred upon the corporation two main responsibilities: the superintendence of pilotage in the Thames and the maintenance of an almshouse at Deptford.[1] By the early seventeenth century, as a result of a statute of 1566 (8 Eliz. c. 13), further letters patent of 1594,[2] and the growth of usage, the corporation was also concerned with the conservation of the river and the administration of the ballastage supply for shipping there; beaconage, buoyage and lighthouses; licensing of indigent seamen and their wives and widows to beg; authorising watermen for the river; arbitration in maritime disputes; provision of ordnance to merchant ships for self-defence; and advice on merchant shipping, the construction of the king's ships and sea defence. These and other maritime topics constitute the subject matter of the Transactions published in the present volume.

Constitution
The charter of Henry VIII was confirmed by his three successors, but in 1604 James I made a new grant which confirmed and extended the rights and powers of Trinity House but was primarily concerned with the government of the corporation. Formal recognition was given by the new charter to the division of the brethren of Trinity House into two classes, the elder and the younger brothers. The elder brethren, thirty-one in number, constituted the governing body of the corporation and within their ranks was an inner group consisting of the master, four wardens and eight assistants. The master and the wardens were elected from the elder brethren by the whole membership, younger as well as elder brethren, for a year in the case of the master, and two years in that of the wardens. Assistants were appointed for life by the master, wardens and assistants who had reserved to themselves a number of important functions, including the selection of elder and younger brothers and the issue of most formal documents. Prior to 1604, the assistants seem to have been chosen annually.[3] According to a report by Sir Robert Cotton, annexed to the findings of the commission of enquiry into the navy set up in 1608, the change to life appointments resulted in mismanagement: revenues were let out for less than their true value for private benefit; aliens were

1. For a fuller history of Trinity House before the Restoration, see G. G. Harris, *The Trinity House of Deptford, 1514–1660* (1969). For the early history, see A. A. Ruddock, 'The Trinity House at Deptford in the sixteenth century', *English Historical Review*, lxv (1950), 458–76; *THD*, 19–30.
2. C 66/1410, mm. 11–12.
3. C 66/1651; *THD*, 28–9.

allowed to practise pilotage in the Thames; the house fell into debt; the recruitment of new members was neglected; and the poor were left without relief. Cotton went on to say that James I had secured the appointment of Hugh Merrit (a principal master of the navy) as master, and that the affairs of the corporation had then quickly improved, for revenues were raised 'from the proportion of £150 to £750' yearly, debts had been reduced, and as many new members, all of them shipmasters and the greater part shipowners, were admitted in his term of office as in the preceding seven years. It all sounds too good to be true.[4]

Premises and officials

By the early seventeenth century, the effective headquarters of Trinity House had moved from Deptford to Ratcliff, then a mariners' hamlet in the parish of Stepney (**3**), probably because it was here or nearby that more important members of the corporation lived; it may also have been regarded as more accessible. After the Restoration, however, there was a further move to Water Lane, close to the present site of Trinity House on Tower Hill, because Ratcliff was considered to be too remote. Nevertheless, the brethren returned to Deptford for their annual Trinity Monday meeting. What was believed to be the old hall, which stood close to Deptford church, was not demolished until 1786.[5] The premises at Ratcliff have not been identified, but the later ballast office which stood on the riverside near Ratcliff Cross may have been the site.[6]

Richard Nottingham (d. 1626), clerk of Trinity House, was living at Ratcliff in 1610 and 1613 (**5, 38**), perhaps in or adjacent to the headquarters of the corporation. By the early 1630s, Josias Best, son of one prominent elder brother and son-in-law of another, was clerk and held the office until his resignation in 1641. Best engaged in private trading ventures as a part-time activity, and some of his personal commercial correspondence is entered in a later volume of Trinity House Transactions. The clerk must have had—as was certainly the case in the early sixteenth century—at least one servant or assistant.[7] There was also an 'officer' (**113**), lighthouse and buoy keepers (**172, 325–6, 332**) and collectors of the corporation dues (**172, 177, 180**).

Encroachment on privileges

Two major privileges of the corporation acquired during the sixteenth century were successfully challenged under the early Stuarts. First, Trinity House lost their monopoly to provide lighthouses. The elder brethren had interpreted the statute of 1566 concerning seamarks as giving them sole power to erect lighthouses. In 1607–9, they had established four lights on the coasts of Norfolk and Suffolk in response to

4. SP 14/41, ff. 70–1. I was unaware of the references to Trinity House when *THD* was prepared.

5. *THD*, 46–7.

6. Sir H. Llewellyn Smith, *The history of East London* (1939), 227. The ballast office was probably close to the ballast wharf, which was near Ratcliff Cross, just SW. of the S. end of Schoolhouse Lane (J. Gascoyne, An actual survey of St Dunstans, Stepney, 1763 (BL, Maps, Crace, xvi 12)).

7. G. W. Hill and W. H. Frere, *Memorials of Stepney parish* (1890–1), 68; *THD*, 54–5.

petitions from shipmasters and owners who had offered to pay a toll to meet the cost. Letters were secured from the privy council authorising the levy (**256–8**). In 1615, however, they allowed a private projector, Sir Edward Howard, to obtain letters patent permitting him to maintain a lighthouse at Dungeness and to exact a levy. Since Howard was cupbearer to the king (**388**), they may have had no choice, but it was a tacit admission that their monopoly was not exclusive, and it was a precedent for a government always alert for means to reward hangers-on at court. Soon afterwards Sir John Meldrum and Sir William Erskine, both of whom had connections with the court, sought a patent for a lighthouse at Winterton on the dangerous Norfolk coast. The elder brethren, who had previously failed to respond to a petition by 300 shipmasters and owners for a light there, now argued that lights were unnecessary but nevertheless stated their intention to build lighthouses. The outcome was that Trinity House lost their monopoly and did not regain it until the nineteenth century.[8]

The second disputed privilege was that of ballastage in the Thames. There was an important link between ballastage and the conservation of the river. Silting in the harbour of Sandwich had destroyed the commerce of that port, and the government and the city aldermen feared a similar fate for London if the deterioration in the condition of the Thames was allowed to go unchecked. Such fears had foundation: in 1633, the elder brethren reported that during their lifetimes the depth of water in the Pool of London had been reduced from twelve or thirteen feet to eight or nine feet, and they considered that the river would soon not be navigable within six or eight miles of London (**414**). The deterioration was partly attributable to natural silting, but a major factor was seen to be the propensity of Londoners to use the river and streams flowing into it as a repository for rubbish.[9] Apart from measures against such dumping, the remedy was dredging. But that was an expensive operation and one way of cutting costs was to utilise the spoil (i.e. the product of dredging). It could be used for brickmaking, paving, and above all as ballast for ships. The spoil, even when left to dry, was not ideal as ballast; the scourings of a river which was used partially as a sewer were bound to be smelly and unhygienic, as well as damp.

Under the letters patent granted in 1594, Trinity House secured the office of ballastage in the Thames—indeed the elder brethren claimed in 1633 that they had been concerned with the ballast supply for 120 years (**425**), although there is no evidence to support their assertion.[10] Their tenure of office in the early seventeenth century proved to be very uneasy. In 1609 the aldermen of London complained to the government of the brethren's failure to use sand and gravel dredged from the river as ballast. It was certainly true that the agents of Trinity House rented land on the outskirts of London where ballast was quarried (**376, 413**). Trinity House exercised a monopoly of the sale of ballast on the basis of the grant of 1594, which must have been particularly irritating for the aldermen

8. *THD*, 183–213, 263.
9. *THD*, 128.
10. *THD*, 130.

because the government held them responsible for the deterioration of the Thames. The complaint was repeated in the House of Commons in 1621, and inevitably private projectors came forward. Although not the first in the field, Innocent Laniere and Alphonso Ferabosco, both court musicians, obtained a grant from James I for the cleansing of the Thames, and Trinity House were forced to accept them as tenants for the ballastage office. The relationship proved to be most unhappy (**169, 232–3**). Eventually the brethren freed themselves of the two partners, but other projectors, such as Edward or Edmund Needham, were almost as tiresome (**391, 393, 461**). Difficulties were also encountered with interlopers who supplied land ballast as opposed to sand and gravel dredged from the Thames. Perhaps the most troublesome of these was Miles Croxton, who sold ballast from Greenhithe, which he alleged was the best in the kingdom, much superior to the sandy ballast supplied by the main agents of Trinity House. The lawsuits, together with Croxton's allegation that he had been shot with poisoned bullets, are recited in his petition to the House of Commons (**331**). An altogether more fundamental issue was raised when it was claimed that the ballastage office conferred no right to a monopoly of the supply of ballast; the function of the office was held to be simply one of inspection. That contention was eventually accepted, and the right to supply ballast in the Thames was granted by letters patent to Thomas Smyth and others in June 1636. Trinity House consequently lost revenue. The brethren had to wait until the Restoration to recover their monopoly.[11]

Other activities

Matters other than silting concerning the Thames occupied the attention of Trinity House. They might be asked for advice about wharves upon the riverside which could be a hazard to navigation (**138, 157, 184, 501**). They commended a proposal in 1635 for the use of mooring chains instead of anchors, the arms of which might protrude and cause accidents (**485**). They supported a proposition to build houses for seamen at Blackwall because of the proximity of the East India 'works' and the number of ships lying there—seamen close at hand were needed in case of fire or storm (**156**). They were unenthusiastic about plans in 1633 to rebuild houses on London Bridge which had been destroyed by fire, for fear that soil from the houses would augment silting in the river (**414**).

From the time of their incorporation by Henry VIII, the supervision and provision of pilotage in the Thames had been one of the most important responsibilities of the brethren. Their role was supplemented by that of the Fellowship of Lodemanage of the Cinque Ports, operating mainly from Dover under licence from the lord warden of the Cinque Ports.[12] The Fellowship had the major part in providing a service for ships entering the Thames through the southern channels, and a working relationship was maintained between the two authorities (**283, 297–8**). There was no comparable organisation to deal with the northern approaches. While pilotage was the original reason for founding Trinity

11. *THD*, 132–5, 143–6, 262; C 66/1410, mm. 11–12.
12. *THD*, 81–2.

House, the brethren displayed no excessive zeal in carrying out their duties in the early seventeenth century, rather the contrary. Sir Henry Marten, the admiralty court judge, complained in 1621 about their toleration of unlicensed pilots (**178**), and Sir Robert Cotton had expressed similar views in 1608.[13] No trace has been found of any of the licences which were supposed to be obtained by pilots before they undertook the conduct of ships, although the explanation may be that there was a separate register, now lost. The corporation also opposed two projectors who wished to make pilotage of alien ships compulsory throughout the realm, so as to prevent strangers from learning the secrets of the channels: these projectors sought the right to appoint pilots for all alien ships, except in the Thames. Trinity House rejoined that a mariner needed pilotage into a harbour only once for him to be able to enter unaided for ever thereafter (**446**). Yet one of the original reasons for the foundation of Trinity House had been the exclusion of aliens.[14]

Two further activities of the corporation were the licensing of watermen for the Thames and the beaconage and buoyage of the river. Under the statute of 1566 (8 Eliz. c. 13), Trinity House had power to license watermen for the Thames,[15] although the Watermen's Company also had authority to do so. The formal right of the brethren to administer buoyage and beaconage in the river rested primarily upon the letters patent of 1594, but there are indications of their earlier involvement.[16] Problems encountered by the brethren in the installation and financing of a new buoy at the Gunfleet in the mouth of the Thames and their contacts in east coast ports and with the Trinity Houses of Newcastle and Hull (founded in 1536 and 1541 respectively)[17] are fully documented (**332–58**).

Trinity House were also concerned with the supply of ordnance to merchant ships for self defence. Ordnance made in England was still highly favoured by foreigners, who went to some lengths to secure possession of English guns for use in their ships. Regulations to control manufacture and exports were made by the privy council in 1574, 1588 and 1601, and revised in 1619.[18] Under the 1619 regulations, a certificate from Trinity House was required before ordnance could be issued to merchant ships in the Thames (or elsewhere) for self defence (**464**). Two volumes containing over 350 certificates are contained in state papers,[19] but there are no copies of certificates in the volumes of Transactions.[20] Several documents do, however, reflect the concern of the elder brethren that ordnance allegedly destined for English ships was in fact for alien use (e.g. **193–4**). The brethren sometimes advised on matters relating to the navy. Most notable are the detailed reports on ships being built for the king at dockyards on the Thames (e.g. **421**, **454**). Trinity House helped to choose ships and seamen for the king's service: in 1628 they prepared a

13. See above, pp. ix-x.
14. *THD*, 19.
15. **271** may be the beginning of a licence.
16. *THD*, 267–9.
17. *THD*, 27.
18. *THD*, 235.
19. SP 16/16; SP 16/17.
20. But **216** may contain the beginning of one.

list of over sixty ships in the Thames suitable for requisitioning, complete with details of tonnage and ordnance (**313–14**); in 1630 they prepared a report for the lord mayor about ships for convoy duties (**379**).

The shipment of coal from Newcastle to London, a trade made hazardous by navigational perils and the depredations of privateers, occupied their attention. A table of imports to London shows that the bulk was shipped in the summer when the domestic demand was lowest, but so was the risk of storms and fog (**1**). Shipowners were unenthusiastic about a proposal that convoy should be provided by the king, preferring to rely upon their own resources (**306**). In 1620 Trinity House opposed the suggestion that all coal for export overseas should be shipped from the Thames or Plymouth on the grounds that inconvenience to the city and the suburbs of London would be caused thereby, but their reasoning is obscure (**161–2**). Coal was measured in chaldrons, but there are difficulties over the definition of the term.[21]

It was common practice at this period for the civil courts to refer cases to experts for an opinion or for arbitration, and frequent use was made of Trinity House for this purpose by chancery, the admiralty court, and in a few instances, king's bench and the court of requests (e.g. **14**, **18–19**, **409**). Parties in a dispute were not always content to accept a reference to, or a decision by, Trinity House (e.g. **52**). On the other hand, the elder brethren were sometimes asked to arbitrate by the parties without formal reference from a court of law. Most of these disputes concerned wages, damage to ships, or maritime custom (e.g. **7**, **16**, **32–3**). A quick and easy way of settling wage disputes was desirable: seamen had neither the time nor the resources to pursue their complaints through the courts. In one case, the elder brethren pointed out that seamen who were cheated of their wages were forced to resort to piracy (**43**). On that occasion, the root of the problem was a disagreement between the merchant and the shipowner over freight. Only after the balance of freight had been paid (which was done apparently at a customary place, the Telling House on the west side of the Royal Exchange) (**15**) could seamen have their wages.

Another important task of Trinity House was certification of the misfortunes of seamen, and sometimes shipowners, in order to enable them to obtain licences to beg and not fall foul of the vagrancy statutes. But although documents concerned with that matter comprise a quarter of the first volume of Transactions, there are very few in the second. Some of the unfortunates, generally residents of London and its suburbs, suffered such a series of disasters that it is difficult to resist the suspicion that they were either accident-prone or incompetent. Fortunes could change quickly. The John Chaplin of Ipswich who signed a petition to Trinity House on behalf of William Androwes in 1610 was almost certainly identical with a man bearing the same name, also from Ipswich, who said that he was forced to sell his cloak from his back in order to buy victuals in Germany after an unfortunate voyage three years later (**12**, **36–7**). Captain Reynold Whitfield, gentleman, imprisoned for debt in

---

21. See J. U. Nef, *The rise of the British coal industry* (2 vols, 1932), ii. 367–8; **275**, **336**.

in *Acts of the Privy Council* receive very brief treatment but orders not entered in the registers, now in the Public Record Office (**256–8**, **313**, **365** and perhaps **68**) and therefore not appearing in the *Acts*, are calendared in full. Similarly, items adequately summarised in the *Calendar of State Papers Domestic* are treated briefly but where names or other details are lacking they have been supplied.

Christian names, place-names (including those which form part of titles), punctuation, the use of capitals and spelling have generally been modernised even where they form part of passages quoted verbatim. The original form of surnames has been retained. A few place-names have not been modernised, either because the seventeenth-century name is more familiar or because no modern equivalent has been found. The year has been taken as beginning on 1 January and not on 25 March. In supplying headings it has not been assumed that a document emanated from Trinity House unless there is positive evidence (e.g. the signatories being described as master, wardens and assistants); the fact that signatories were elder brethren has not, in itself, been regarded as adequate proof. The full title, Trinity House of Deptford, is only used when needed to distinguish it from the Trinity Houses of Hull and Newcastle. An asterisk shows that a term is included in the select glossary.

The index
Place-names have been identified wherever possible. County boundaries prior to the 1974 reorganisation of local government are used for English places. Offices held are given where necessary, and positions such as elder or younger brother of Trinity House are indicated. Two elder brothers, Walter and William Cooke, cannot always be distinguished: Walter first appears in 1621 (**172**); William, a principal master of the navy, was recommended by Charles I for election as elder brother in 1628 but may have been elected then or later.[25]

Acknowledgements
Dr Brian Dietz of the University of Glasgow, Dr A. P. McGowan of the National Maritime Museum, Mr John Bosomworth, my brother Philip Harris and my niece Clare Harris have helped in various ways. The Master, Wardens and Assistants of Trinity House gave me permission to publish the calendar. Successive principals of the Corporate Department of Trinity House, especially Mr V. G. Stamp, and members of the Corporate Department were unfailingly kind, helpful and hospitable on my visits to Trinity House, as have been the officials of the Public Record Office (especially Mr S. R. Bickell), the British Library Reference Division, and the City of London Records Office. Finally I owe a great debt to the late Captain W. R. Chaplin, formerly Warden of Trinity House, who generously gave me the benefit of his own deep knowledge of the history of the corporation, and Dr Alwyn Ruddock, formerly Reader in History at Birkbeck College, University of London, who first directed my research on Trinity House and who pioneered its early history.

25. *THD*, 34.

The errors[26] and obscurities which remain constitute the present writer's particular contribution.

26. Attention is drawn to four errors in the present writer's earlier work (*THD*): Humphrey Basse was not an elder brother; Peter Frobisher was the heir to, but not the son of, Sir Martin Frobisher; the grant of a patent for the Lizard lighthouse to Sir John Killigrewe occurred on 29 July, not June, 1619; and the fire at the Palace of Westminster occurred in 1834, not 1837.

TRANSACTIONS, VOL. I

1. [Unnumbered folio. *After 1629*] *Coal trade statistics*
Annual shipments of coal, expressed in chaldrons, from Newcastle and
Sunderland to places within the realm:

Year ending Christmas	Newcastle	Sunderland	Total
1621	118,950	10,478	129,428
1622	143,707	11,175	154,882
1623	124,455	11,423	135,878
1624	142,618	9,942	152,560
1625	82,124	9,216	91,340

Monthly shipments in 1629:

Jan.	3,211	May	6,383	Sept.	12,094
Feb.	3,298	June	6,884	Oct.	6,036
March	693	July	15,287	Nov.	5,089
Apr.	8,789	Aug.	5,112	Dec.	3,084

Annual total: 75,960

2. [f. 1] *9 Feb. 1610. Proposals made by London and Bristol merchants to
the privy council, referred to Trinity House*
The petitioners, having used the fishing trade of Newfoundland, are
confident that the country is habitable in winter because it is in latitude
47°, which is further south than any part of England and is the same as
Bordeaux. It is full of woodland and fair rivers stocked with fish, and
there are fowls and edible animals such as stags. The voyage from
England and Ireland takes only 3 weeks, with reasonable winds, and the
island is as near to England as it is to Spain. They seek to establish a
plantation with a few men to make trial thereof, especially since they
would not be molested because savages have not been seen there. The
following reasons may be considered: (a) 200 ships with about 6,000
mariners go there each year 'whereby great benefit accrueth not only to
many private persons, but also to the whole commonwealth by the
increase of navigation and trade in merchandise which ships going thither
to fish and in manner empty are fit to carry all matters for plantation'. (b)
If a foreign prince or state took possession of the land and erected
fortifications, thereby debarring the use of harbours and fishing, the
consequences would be very serious. Indeed, the French tried to winter
there in about 1580,[1] but by lack of foresight they all perished 'for want of
necessaries for plantation'. (c) If the plantation succeed, fishing would be
secure forever, and the commodity greater because of the probable
increase in the number of ships engaged in the trade, since planters could

1

fish in boats in places otherwise unusable for lack of harbours. (d) The settlers could provide supplies to the fishermen, care for the sick, and look after the boats. (e) The ground may be fit for tillage and pasturing cattle, and the woodland put to use. (f) The settlers will learn whaling for great profit, as the Biscayans already do on nearby coasts. [f.lv] (g) It is hoped that the country will afford furs, 'heath', pitch, turpentine, boards made from pine trees, masts and yards for small ships, soap-ashes [wood ash used in making soap], stags, skins, hawks of all kinds, seal skins, train oil and either copper or iron mines which in view of the woods and rivers might easily be very profitable. (h) The land lies on the direct route to Virginia and a plantation or fortification there would make it a serviceable rendezvous. Letters patent are sought for a small settlement in an area not previously occupied by christians, together with rights in respect of fishing and the use of the land.

1. French expeditions of 1578 and 1584 failed to reach Newfoundland (H.P. Biggar, *The early trading companies of New France* (1901), 38–9; *DCB*, 421).

3. *24 Feb. 1610. Trinity House to the privy council*
Mr John Slanye of London, Mr John Guye of Bristol, and other merchants brought the above proposal [2]. The corporation considered the plan at their meeting at Ratcliff today and concluded that people could live there and that a plantation would be valuable in view of the fishing trade and for other reasons, provided that there was no interference with the freedom of fishing now enjoyed.
Hugh Merritt, master; William Jones, William Bygate, Robert Rickman, William Jordan, William Hare, William Sims, Nicholas Diggens, John Goodlad, William Goodlad, Robert Kitchen.

4. [f.2–2v] *4 Aug. 1610. Bonds* [partly in Latin]
Thomas Silvester and others [listed in **5**], and Humphrey Basse and others, enter bonds to accept the arbitration of Trinity House to settle their dispute. Witnesses: William Allexander and Francis Pensax, servants to Thomas Hill, scrivener.

5. [f.3] *25 Aug. 1610. Award by Trinity House*
Humphrey Basse, girdler of London, Luke Barefoote and Tobias Johnson, mariners of London, on the one hand, and Thomas Silvester, Thomas Wilkenson, mariners of Ipswich, Samuel Cutler, merchant, Edward Man, vintner, Elizabeth Man, spinster, and John Sturgen, brewer of Ipswich, on the other, entered bonds [4] of £200 on 4 Aug. 1610 to accept the award of at least 6 members of Trinity House in respect of their dispute, provided that the award be made before 4 Sept. 1610. The award is as follows: (a) Silvester and his associates are to pay £47 to Basse and his associates. £21 is to be deposited at the house of Richard Nottingham in Ratcliff on 29 Sept., and the balance on 2 Nov. 1610. (b) Wilkenson is to pay £30 towards the cost of weighing the *Providence* of London in the Thames, of which Johnson was master. (c) The liability to pay the £47 [f.3v] and the cost of weighing the *Providence* over and above the £30 which Wilkenson himself has to pay is to be shared between

Silvester and his associates in proportion to their shares in the ownership of the *Sea Adventure* of Ipswich at the time of the weighing of the *Providence*. (d) On or before 10 Sept., both parties are to relinquish all claims on each other in respect of all disputes up to 4 Aug. 1610. Documents to this effect are to be deposited at the house of Nottingham by 12 Sept. 1610. (e) Both parties are to pay a fee of [blank] to Nottingham, clerk of Trinity House, for drawing up this award.
Hugh Merret, Robert Salmon, William Jurden, William Jones, Robert Kytchen, Robert Ryckman, Thomas Milton, Nicholas Dygens, Matthew Woodcot, William Byam, John Osborne, John Skinner.

6. [f.4] *11 Sept. 1610. Award by Trinity House*
Edmund Wynn, merchant of London, has withheld the wages of sundry mariners who served in the *Ellen and John* of London arrived from Virginia and sought to lay the burden of the insurance of his adventure in the ship on the crew. The mariners contradict. Both parties agreed to arbitration. The award is that since the ship reached the Thames safely as soon as her consort, and since the insurance seems to have been given out of fear, and not for any just cause, the crew have no liability. Since, however, a boat was lost through negligence, £7 is to be deducted from the wages and 'entertainment' of the master and the wages of the crew, divided up in proportion to earnings. The master must also pay £2 from his 'entertainment' as compensation to the owners because, after landing the passengers at Dartmouth, he went ashore, and commanded the crew to do likewise, whereby 'the owner received a day's hinderance in wages and victuals for their stay there'. No allowance is to be made for insurance, as is demanded.
Hugh Merryt, Robert Salmon, William Wye, William Jurden, Robert Kytchen, William Bygat, Thomas Milton, Nicholas Dygons, Matthew Woodcott, Robert Ryckman, Richard Chester, Thomas Norreys.

7. [f.4v] *9 Oct. 1610. Sir Thomas Smith, governor of the East India company, to Trinity House*
The company seek an opinion on the wages due, according to the right or custom of the sea, to mariners of the *Hector* and *Ascension*. On 3 Oct. 1608, 19 mariners of the *Hector* were captured by Portuguese frigates on a voyage from Surat with goods of great value. They admit not fighting, for which some blame the captain, but most say the fault was the gunner's for want of shot expended previously in 'creating a new captain' [? a gun salute]. Some of the 19 died before the return home of the *Hector*; some have come home; some are prisoners 'in the country' or at Lisbon; others are in the pay of the Portuguese or the grand mogul. The company wish to know whether any wages are due and, if so, whether payment should be made up to the date of their capture, their return to England, or the ship's return to England. The *Ascension* was cast away near Cambay. Elmer was put off her in a pinnace with 6 or 8 men and sailed to within 5 leagues of Surat. He then left the pinnace and travelled to Surat overland. He admits that he might have sold the pinnace for 300 rials, but alleges that he acted on the instructions of one of the factors at Surat. This is untrue

3

because the company has no factor there. By these means the pinnace was lost 'as also the ship out of which he was shipped' because it is said that he could not be awakened when he should have borne up sail. Consequently he lost contact with the *Ascension*.

8. [f.5] *9 Oct. 1610. Trinity House [to Sir Thomas Smith]*
Their opinion was sought [7] on the wages due to the mariners of the *Hector*, who were captured in the East Indies, and those of the *Ascension*, who were left alive when she perished, 'whether they come home before or after the return of the *Union*'. In the case of the *Hector*, the mariners who were taken prisoner should be paid up to the date of the return of the ship, whether they came home before or after her return, because, had they not been sent out of her for the benefit of the merchant, they might have come home in her if they had lived. Those who are still prisoners deserve consideration, but that is for the company to decide. Those who are now serving another nation voluntarily should be paid only up to the date of their capture. As for the crew of the *Ascension*, Trinity House have never known wages to be payable if a ship and her cargo are lost, because the money for wages is derived from freight. But it is understood that the mariners were engaged for the voyage of both vessels and not for one particular ship. If that is the case, and the *Union* returns, the crew of the *Ascension* should be paid up to the date of the *Union*'s return, because both ships were engaged on the discovery of a trade which may prove profitable to the company, and the men died because they were strangers to the area. But 'if the lading in both ships were so divided, as that the company of one ship should nor ought to have been ready at the general's dispose to have brought home the other ship if occasion had been offered', no wages are due in view of the loss of the *Ascension*. Those in the pinnace of the *Ascension*, which lost contact with the ship for want of sails and victuals (a fact known to the ship's master), did their utmost in the service of the company and deserve consideration.
Hugh Mearett, master; Robert Salmon, William Wye, William Bygatt, William Jones, Peter Hills, Robert Rickman, Nicholas Diggins, John Vassall, Matthew Woodcott, Thomas Norris, Robert Kytchen.

9. [f.5v] *6 March 1609. Algiers. Certificate by Richard Allen, consul [for the English at Algiers]*
The bearer, Thomas Nicols, gunner of the *Sara Jone*, Robert Rippon, master, was captured with the rest of the crew by the Bizerte galleys in the 'Gulf of Venice' [see **13**] on 31 Aug. 1608 and all were enslaved. The merchants, master and company of the *Dorcas* of London out of charity ransomed him when they called at Tunis and brought him hither. According to the testimony of those named below, Nichols has not engaged in piracy, but has asked merchants and shipmasters to secure his passage to his native country.
Endorsements (a) by Nicholas Keale and Hewet Staper that the above was written in Allen's hand; (b) of the truth of the above by Ralph Shotboulte, Walter Whiting, master, John Mootham, Richard Perston,

William Harris and John Daye, all of the *Dorcas*; (c) by Jo. King, master of the *Mathue* of London, that he brought the bearer to England.

10. *7 Aug. 1610. Trinity House to the king*
The bearer, Thomas Nichols, gunner, has asked for a certificate of his misfortunes. They know that the attached statement [9] is true. He was dispossessed of all he had, maimed in fighting the Turks, and was enslaved in their galleys. His ransom cost £50, for which his friends stand bond because he has nothing.
Hugh Merret, William Jones, William Jurden, Thomas Milton, Robert Ryckman, Robert Kytchen, Richard Chester, Nicholas Digens, Matthew Woodcott, John Kinge.

11. [f.6] *4 Nov. 1610. Trinity House to lord Ellesmere, lord chancellor*
At the request of John Fryer, the petitioner, they certify that he went to sea as master gunner of the *Gift of God* of London, about a year ago. Shortly afterwards, she sank in a storm on the Irish coast. All her cargo was lost and the crew barely escaped with their lives. Not long afterwards, the ship was recovered and was freighted again, but on 2 Feb. last was captured off Spain by Captain Parker, a pirate. Fryer and others, numbering 12 in all, were held prisoner for 4 months. Parker then took away 7, and turned Fryer and the others away, ransacked. On their way homewards, they were captured on about 2 July by another pirate, Captain Easton, who robbed them of the remainder of their estates, and maltreated them. All these misfortunes occurred within 11 months. Fryer has lost his entire estate of £300 and friends stand surety for part of his adventure.
Hugh Mearit, William Bygatt, Robert Salmon, William Hare, Robert Rickman, Thomas Best, Robert Kytchen, Thomas Norreis.

12. [f.6v] *8 Dec. 1610. Trinity House to the same*
William Androwes, the petitioner, and his neighbours of Ipswich have asked them to certify his misfortunes. Last March, the *Content*, of which he was master and part-owner, set out but owing to foul weather was wrecked at night on a rock off the Norwegian coast and sank in 10 fathoms. Eight of the crew were drowned, but 4 escaped miraculously by sitting in the maintop, which remained above water, until they were rescued by a fishing boat. He lost £300, which is more than his estate is worth, and he owes another £100 as part of his adventure, which he is unable to pay.
Hugh Meret, master; Robert Salmon, William Jurden, John Osborne, William Wye, wardens; William Joanes, Thomas Milton, Matthew Woodcott, William Hare, Nicholas Dygens, Robert Rickman, William Byam, Richard Chester, Thomas Beast, Robert Kytchen.
[Marginal note] By testimony of a letter from Ipswich under the hands of John Carnabye, John Chaplin, John Martin, Edmund Morgane, Richard Wade, Richard Birlingham, Robert Castone, John Hawkes.

13. [f.7] *16 July 1610. Tripoli. Samuel Harres to his father*
On the 15th day, 2 galleys of Tripoli and a frigate approached his ship off 'Cape Spartemint' [? Spartimento, now Palinuro, or Spartivento]. The master consulted the crew, but although most wanted to fight, others would not for fear of being enslaved. So the sails were struck, and Harres and all but 6 of his companions were taken aboard the galleys, while the ship was sent to Tripoli. The galleys made for the Gulf,[1] intending to sail to Valona, but since the wind was northwest, they had to go north of 'Sufelane' [? now Sazan], and there joined 5 galleys of Bizerte. When they put out to sea, the wind was southerly, so they sailed for Valona, but off 'Cape Lugo' [? now Kep-i-Lagit], they encountered 5 Venetian galleys which gave chase and captured the last of the Turkish galleys which was their consort and which had 6 of 'our' men aboard. Harres' galley escaped, and that night she took a ship of Ragusa, which had been laden at Corfu and was bound for Venice. The Turks took the men but released the ship. Harres arrived at Tripoli and found his ship and companions there. He was afraid of being enslaved because he had been made to row naked and had been beaten aboard the galley. He caught such a cold that he suffered from the 'blody flix' [dysentery] and is still unwell. His captors say that he and his companions will only have to serve for one or 2 voyages, and that then they will be released but he does not believe them. He beseeches his father to secure his release and to write if he is 'at Lant'. If his portion is due, it should be paid to his mother or used on his behalf. He asks his father to mediate for him if it is dangerous for him to come home for he 'must go perforce, and about 2 months hence'. He believes that his ship, which is the best, is going in a group of 4 to the west. He commends himself to his 'brother' William and Richard, his sisters, William Bull, and his friends. Randal Jesson commends himself to Harres' father and brother, William, and to 'fillup' [Philip].

1. ? Of Taranto. But the Adriatic was sometimes described as the Gulf of Venice (see, e.g., D. Howse and M. Sanderson, *Sea charts* (1973), plate 11).

14. [f.7v] *13 Dec. 1610. Westminster. Order in chancery to Hugh Merricke, master of Trinity House, Thomas Beast and William Bigott of Trinity House, Ralph Freeman, Humphrey Basse and Robert Bell, commissioners for assurance policies*
In a dispute in chancery between Robert Howe, Thomas Dennys, William French and others [John Falkner and Hugh French], pls., and William Jones, William Wye the elder, and John Barbor, defs., concerning the freight of a ship hired by the pls. from the defs. it appeared that 45 members of the crew had been unjustly deprived of their wages. Four or 5 of the addressees are to enquire and arbitrate by whose default the wages are unpaid and the amounts due. Upon certifying chancery, the mariners are to be paid forthwith. Or if agreement is not reached the suit is to return to chancery by [f.8] 20 Jan.
Brace [? Lord Bruce, master of the rolls].

15. *20 Dec. 1610. [Return to chancery. See **14**.]*
The voyage lasted for 15 months and a day, and the freight was £146 10s a

month. The pls. have not proved that the defs. broke the charter party. The voyage appears to have been completed properly and the freight, from which the mariners are paid, is therefore due. According to the custom of merchants and shipowners, half should have been paid within 4 or 5 days of the discharge of the ship at London so that the crew of 45 could receive their wages, which amount to £732 13s. The failure of the pls. to pay the freight (apart from £120 already received) is the reason why the crew are unpaid. The pls. should pay £732 13s to William Jones and William Wye the elder, 2 of the defs., or their assignees, on 10 Jan. at the Telling House on the west side of the Royal Exchange, which is the usual place for making such payments. The crew can then be paid. The pls. may yet be able to establish a stronger case, so the remainder of the freight should not be paid until witnesses have been examined. [f.8v] The writers can then either negotiate a settlement or certify their opinions. Hugh Mericke, Humphrey Basse, Thomas Beast, William Bygatt, Ralph Freeman, Robert Bell.
[Marginal note] Registered in the office of assurance on 13 Dec. 1610 and compared with the original, which is lodged in chancery, by Simon Cowell, servant to Richard Candeler, deputy register.

16. *1 Jan. 1611. Award by Trinity House*
By agreement of both parties, the dispute between John Davies, merchant, owner of the *Abigall* of Southampton, and Roger Newse and other mariners concerning wages for a voyage to Guinea was referred to Trinity House for settlement. The award is that the master, pilot and certain other members of the crew failed to do their utmost, contrary to the charter party dated 14 July 1610. Some mariners behaved in a factious and mutinous manner and no wages are due to them. They deserve a punishment greater than loss of wages, which is the only penalty which Trinity House can inflict upon them. Those who should lose their wages are Roger Newes, master, Thomas Adyson, pilot, John Adyson, master's mate, Matthew Sicklemore, boatswain, Thomas Mychenson [sic], Roger Stone, gunner, Henry King, Abraham Smith, Lawrence Teage, gunner's mate, and Thomas Mychenson [sic]. The rest of the crew should be paid. Hugh Merret, William Jurden, William Hare, Matthew Woodcott, Robert Rickman, Richard Chester, Thomas Best, William Jones.

17. [f.9. *? 8 x 28 Feb. 1610*] *Statement of wages* [*See* **18–20.**]
The monthly wages due for a voyage begun on 1 Jan. 1609 and ended at 'Candlemas last' [2 Feb. 1610]: Captain Holland, £10; John Anthony, £2 10s; Mr Cradle, £2 10s; Francis Warren, carpenter, £1 10s; Robert Morrey, surgeon, £3; Humphrey Crosser, boatswain, £1 6s; the gunner, £1; William Foster, £1; Peter Johnson, £1; the cooper, £1 5s; the boatswain's mate, £1; Andrew Tewell, 18s; Roger Stiles, steward, £1; the cook, £1; the cook's mate, 15s; Robert Parker, 15s; John Stricktson, 15s; William Downing, 15s; John the Indian, 15s; Rowland [blank], 15s; [total] £33 9s.
Monthly wages for the crew of the pinnace: the master, £2 10s; the mate, £2; the boatswain, £1; the gunner, £1; John Harper, £1; the carpenter,

18s; John of 'Sylly' [? Scilly Isles], £1; 'Pont' Shaner, 15s; [total] £10 13s [*recte* £10 3s].

18. [*26 x 28 Feb. 1610*] *Sir Daniel Dun, admiralty court judge, to the privy council* [*See* **17**, **19–20.**]
Captain Robert Holland of Dartmouth has complained that mariners and others are unpaid for a voyage to America because of his dispute with Captain Robert Harecourt. He was required to secure the assistance of Trinity House and either to settle the dispute or to [f.9v] express an opinion. He and Dr Treaver, admiralty court judges, obtained the help of Hugh Mearicke, master, and some of the most ancient members of Trinity House. They conclude that Holland hired the crew upon the instructions of Harecourt and that Harecourt agreed in writing to pay £46 10s a month in wages as from last Jan. 12-month. Harecourt has alleged that the greater part of the crew relinquished their claim upon him for wages in exchange for his bond to pay them upon a specified day; and that no account need be taken of Holland because he had been paid £50 beforehand and had taken the ship to a port other than that specified. Harecourt agreed to give a bond of £600 on or before the 12th of this month of February as surety for lodging £400 in the admiralty court on 1 March for the payment of wages. He also agreed that the remainder of the dispute concerning Holland's own allowance should be referred to Trinity House for examination and for a report by last Sunday, 25 Feb. Trinity House have reported that £43 a month is due to Holland and the mariners. Holland is content to accept this and to pay the mariners. There is no reason why this settlement should not be implemented, especially since Harecourt has neglected to give sureties contrary to his agreement. The mariners clamour for their wages. Holland insists, contrary to the allegation of Harecourt, that the voyage was well performed. Further proceedings are stayed, pending the instructions of the privy council.
Hugh Merret, master; William Bygate, William Joanes, Robert Kytchen.

19. [f.10][1] *June 1611. Trinity House to Sir Thomas Fleming and other justices of king's bench*
On Monday [27 May] the court referred the dispute [**18**] to them, the master and 4 ancients of Trinity House, for settlement or an opinion by the Saturday after the 'xviii of St Trinity' [? 8 June]. On Wednesday 29 May 2 men came on behalf of Harecourt to choose 4 brethren to hear the case and Holland accepted their selection. A day was appointed but Harecourt failed to appear and thrice subsequently although Holland did appear. That Harecourt is deliberately delaying proceedings appears to be confirmed by the fact that when the privy council referred the case on about 8 Feb. 1610 to Sir Daniel Don, admiralty court judge, and Trinity House, no settlement could be reached because of Harecourt's default. Holland has a copy of the certificate then given [**18**].

    1. xi is erased.

20. [f.10v] *11 June 1611. Trinity House to the same* [*See* **17–19.**]
[On 8 June] the court sought the views of the writers by next Wednesday,

the last day of term, according to their former order. Today Holland and 2 gentlemen on behalf of Harecourt appeared but the case is difficult and more time is needed. Both parties were asked to enter bonds to accept the award of Trinity House, but while Holland was prepared to do so, Harecourt's representatives deferred presumably to gain time.

Robert Ryckman, master; William Wye, warden; William Bygate, Matthew Woodcott, William Jurden, Thomas Milton.

21. *15 June 1611. Certificate by Trinity House*
In view of a patent dated 25 June 1571 for the confirmation of an act of parliament[1] concerning malmesies and other sweet wines of the Levant landed at Southampton, Robert Chambers of Southampton has asked what is the westernmost part of the Levant Sea. Their opinion is that it is the mouth of the Straits of Gibraltar, anciently called the 'Straites of Marocke'. It extends eastwards to all gulfs, ports and places in the 'middle earth sea'.

Robert Rickman, master; William Wye, John Osborne, wardens; Ro. Kytchen, Thomas Norres, wardens' deputies; William Bygate, Peter Hills, Thomas Milton, Jo. Vassal, William Hare, Hugh Merrit, assistants; Thomas Best, assistants' deputy; Nicholas Diggons, William Jurden, Richard Chester, Matthew Woodcot, William Goodlard, Robert Bradshewe, John King.

1. See *Letters patent of Southampton, 1415–1612*, vol. ii, ed. H. W. Gidden (Southampton Record Society, 1919), 120–5.

22. [f.11] *17 July 1611. Trinity House to the East India company*
The company sought their opinion on the wages due to the crew of the *Union*. Those who died on the outward or homeward voyage up to her arrival on 'our' coast should be paid up to the date of their death because they had done their best, the ship was laden, and she might still have reached home. Those who left the ship near the coast when she was in distress, taking money and goods of great value 'towards their satisfaction though not to the full', deserve no wages unless the company decide to have compassion upon them. Those who remained in the ship until she came ashore should be paid because they did their utmost, even though it was insufficient. Moreover it was not they who put the ship ashore. The French found her at sea in distress, pillaged her, and cast her away. The king of France has compensated the merchants.

Ro. Ryckman, master; John Osborne, William Wye, wardens; Robert Kytchen, Thomas Norres, deputies; William Jones, W. Bygate, Hugh Meret, Thomas Milton, Nicholas Dygens, John Vassall, Matthew Woodcott, William Jurdaine, Thomas Best, William Ivie, Robert Bradshew, John King.

23. [ff.11v–13] *24 and 26 Oct. 1611. Depositions and evidence relating to Henry Hudson's voyage in search of the Northwest Passage, and the opinion of Trinity House* [Printed in Historical Manuscripts Commission, *8th Report, Appendix*, i.236–7, but omitting details of the crew: (a) Turned adrift with Henry Hudson on 23 June: John Hudson, his son,

Arnold Ladley, John King, quartermaster, Michael Butt 'married', Thomas Woodhowse, a mathematician who was in deep distress when turned away, Adam Moore, Philip Staff, carpenter, Cyriack Fanner 'married'. (b) Died: John Williams (on 9 Oct.), Ivet (on the voyage home). (c) Killed: Henry Greene, William Wilson, John Thomas, Michael Peerce. (d) Returned home: Robert Billet, master, Abecocke Pricket, a landsman put in by the adventurers, Edward Wilson, surgeon, Francis Clemens, boatswain, Adrian Motter, Bennet Mathues, a landsman, Nicholas Syms, boy, Silas Bond, cooper. For Pricket's account of the voyage, see *Henry Hudson the navigator*, ed. G. M. Asher (Hakluyt Society, 1860).]

24. [f.13v] *1611. Trinity House to lord Elsmore, lord chancellor*
Thomasin Nelme, the petitioner, and her neighbours at Poplar have asked for a certificate of the misfortunes of her husband, William. He was master of a ship of 'Apsam' [? Topsham] in Devon which was unjustly arrested and taken by the Turks of Algiers while lying at anchor within the Straits at Cape Gata, not far from 'Cape Paule' [? Cape Palos]. He was thrown into prison, where he remains, the ship and her goods detained, and the crew enslaved in the galleys. Unless a ransom of £200 is paid, the crew are likely to perish, as will Nelme's wife and 5 small children, for want of sustenance.

25. [f.14] *11 March 1612. Philpot Lane [London. Sir] Thomas Smythe [treasurer of the Virginia company] to Trinity House*
Trinity House agreed with the Virginia company to contribute for 3 years towards the plantation in Virginia. The instalment for the first year was paid, but the second is now due. It is also requested that 3 members of Trinity House be nominated so that one of them can be chosen to assist on the committees charged with the management of the enterprise and to keep the corporation informed.

26. [*11 x 31*] *March 1612. Certificate by the Virginia company*
Certification of second annual payment of £50 by Trinity House [see **25**] to Sir Thomas Smith. Shares in lands, mines, minerals of gold, silver and other metals or treasure, pearls, precious stones, and other merchandise will be determined by the proportionate contribution. Sealed in the presence of Edward Maye.

27. [f.14v] *19 June 1612. York House [London]. T. [lord] Ellesmere, lord chancellor, [to Trinity House. See* **28–9**.]
The enclosed petition of one Adames for himself and some of his crew is referred to them.

28. *1 July 1612. Trinity House [to lord Ellesmere, lord chancellor]*
In reply to his letter [**27**] they have examined Adam Adams, late master of the *Greyhound* of London, and members of the crew, on the one side, and on the other, the shipowner, and Philip Barnardi on behalf of himself and John Francisco Soprain, the merchants. According to the charter

party and his own admission, Barnardi agreed to provide victuals, men, and wages for the voyage from the Thames to the Canaries, the return voyage to London, and for 7 days afterwards. On a number of occasions on the outward voyage the ship was surprised by pirates who took away the victuals and most of the mariners and their goods. The merchants apparently lost none of their goods. Nevertheless the ship reached the Islands where the master hired other men and loaded goods for the return voyage as the factor of the merchants directed [f.15] and then returned safely to London. Barnardi refuses to pay any wages or for the new victuals and also refuses to accept their award but determines 'to abide extremity of law', which the poor men are not able to endure.

29. *28 July 1612. Trinity House [to the same]*
Since their last report [28] Addams has informed them that their opinion was required as to what money was due to the mariners of the *Greyhownd*. Richard Davison, the master, who died in the Islands and those whom he hired should be paid £38 8s 6d by the merchants, Philip Barnardi and John Francisco Soprain, while the 5 whom Adams had to hire in the Islands to bring home the ship should have £25 15s. Such wages and more are usually paid.
William Byam, master; Christopher Newport, Michael Geere, William Goodlard, Robert Kytchen, William Bygate, Nicholas Diggons, Matthew Woodcott, William Ivie.

30. [f.15v] *8 Aug. 1612. Trinity House to the same*
Margery Larriman of Ratcliff and her neighbours have asked them to certify to him that her husband, George Larryman, had his ship, the *Blessing*, freighted with goods by the London merchants, Nicholas Leete and William Towerson, for the London plantation of Coleraine in Ireland. The merchants have certified in writing that the goods were duly delivered. The ship was then freighted in Ireland by William Barret, merchant, with goods for Malaga. On her voyage thither the ship was surprised while lying at anchor at the Southern Cape by the admiral of Spain. Larryman and 12 of his company are held prisoner in a galley of Spain for supposed misdemeanours. He is generally reputed to be a very honest man and his wife and 8 children are wholly dependent upon him.
William Byam, William Goodlad, Michael Geere, Robert Kytchen, William Bygate, Hugh Merit, Peter Hills, John Vassall, Nicholas Diggens, Matthew Woodcott, Robert Rickman, William Jurdaine.

31. [f.16] *14 Aug. 1612. Trinity House to the same*
David Mychell, mariner of Ratcliff, asked them to certify to the lord chancellor that he was master and part-owner of the *Gift of God* of London (about 80 tons) which was lost with all her cargo in foul weather in Sept. 1607, and that last March he was captured by pirates in the *Frindship*. He lost £300 by the loss of the *Gift of God* and £100 by that of the *Frindship* and is now impoverished.
William Byam, Christopher Newport, Michael Geare, Robert Kytchin,

William Bygate, Hugh Merrit, Nicholas Dygens, Matthew Woodcot, Robert Rickman, William Jurden.

32. *1 Aug. 1612. Award by Trinity House*
William Goodlard the elder, master of the *Hermet* of London, and Samuel Mower, master of the *Treasure* of London, referred to Trinity House for settlement their dispute over damage done by the *Treasure* to the *Hermet* while she lay at anchor within the 'Hound's sand'. The repair of the *Hermet* will cost £8 15s 11d of which Mower should pay £4 16s. Goodlard is to have the old bowsprit towards the other £4.
William Byam, master; Christopher Newport, Michael Geare, Robert Kitchyn, William Bygatt, Hugh Merrett, Matthew Woodcot, Peter Hills, Robert Rickman, Robert Salmon.

33. [f.16v] *6 Aug. 1612. Award by Trinity House*
Certain men of the *Greyhounde*, recently returned from 'Islande' [? Iceland], ascribe the overthrow of the voyage to the loss of the cables and anchors in foul weather and say that the master was left behind in 'Island' because of the failure of the ground tackle, whereby they were forced away with 1,800 or 1,900 fish. They demand their wages. Mr Bell the owner, says that their waste of victuals and their negligence has caused him damage. Both parties refer the matter to Trinity House who order that Bell should pay half the wages to the mariners including what they have already received; and that the mariners are to give a bond to Bell undertaking to accept a revised award by Trinity House if the master returns or if new evidence of negligence is forthcoming. If no new evidence is available by 27 Sept. 1612, a decision will then be given concerning the balance of the wages due.
William Byam, master; Christopher Newport, Michael Geare, William Goodled, Robert Kitchin, Thomas Milton, Hugh Merrit, Robert Rickman, Matthew Woodcot, Richard Chester, William Jurdaine, Roger Gunstone.

34. *10 Dec. 1612. Award [by Trinity House]*
The anchor and cable which Mr Jurden's men let slip is valued at £10. The Scotsman, who was mate, lost his wages having taken other employment, and when a sick man went ashore at [the Isle of] Wight, his replacement enabled a saving of a noble to be made in wages payable by the owner. The wages of the rest of the crew amounted to £35. There should be a deduction of 2s 6d in the £ from the earnings of every man and boy in the crew to pay for the damages. If the anchor and cable are recovered, the proceeds of the sale, after the deduction of charges, should be divided proportionately among those who paid for the damage. Seamen hired since the loss are not to contribute.
William Byam, master; Robert Kitchyn, Roger Gunston, Matthew Woodcott, Robert Rickman, William Ivie, Richard Chester, Robert Salmon, Robert Bradshawe, Andrew Shillinge.

35. [f.17] *4 Jan. 1613. Trinity House to lord Ellesmere, lord chancellor*
By virtue of his letter of 14 Dec., upon the petition of Daniel Palmer and

other mariners of the *Anne* of London, they have called before them Mr Goodlack and Mr Pratt, the ship's merchants. Pratt refused to come while Goodlack came but refused to submit to their censures. They therefore certify their findings. The mariners were hired by the month and the voyage lasted for 5 or 6 days short of a year when the *Anne* was sunk in the port of Lisbon. The men salvaged the ship, together with a great part of the goods and gold to the value, as Goodlack agrees, of over £1,000, besides the ship. It is considered that the crew should be paid for the period up to the time the ship was sunk, which is 12 months. Only the 12 petitioners out of the crew of 26 have yet reached home. Goodlacke refuses to pay because he has no notice from the master, who is still at Lisbon, what wages had been agreed. Nor had the petitioners the discretion to bring home a note from the master. Nevertheless, the wages which they say were agreed, amounting to £112 for the 12 months, are normal for such a voyage. The award, had Goodlack agreed, would have been that half the wages, amounting to £60, should be paid, and the remainder when the master returned.

William Byam, master; Michael Geare, Robert Kitchen, Roger Gunston, John Vassall, Matthew Woodcott, Robert Rickman, Robert Bradshew, Hugh Merrit, Nicholas Diggens, Thomas Milton, William Ivie, William Jurden, Richard Chester, Andrew Shillinge.

36. [f.17v. *Before 12 Jan. 1613*] *John Chaplyn to the farmers of the king's impost on sea coal* [*See* **37.**]
Three months ago at Newcastle he set sail, having loaded the *Maryan* of Ipswich with 76 chaldrons of coal for London. Owing to foul weather, the sails were blown away and the ship was driven to the 'Wezard' [river Weser] in Germany. To save the ship in the storm, he had to throw more than 30 chaldrons overboard. He had to wait 27 days at the 'Wezard' for a wind, and when at last he left, intending to sail direct to England, he was blown to Emden by a contrary wind. While at the 'Wezard', he had to sell the cloak from his back, together with some of the coal at below the market rate in order to buy victuals, and he had to give '6 months day of payment' against his will. He is ready to testify on oath. In view of his misfortunes and losses, he prays that he be discharged of the penalty of his bond.

37. *12 Jan. 1613. Certificate by Trinity House*
John Chaplyn of Ipswich, master of the *Maryan* and bearer of this certificate, appeared and testified on oath to the truth of his petition [**36**]. William Byam, master; Robert Kitchen, Richard Chester, Matthew Woodcott, Robert Rickman.

38. [f.18] *21 Jan. 1613. Award by William Byam, master of Trinity House*
Thomas Lanthorne, master of the *Gift of God* of St Andrews in Scotland, and Peter Pynder, ballastman of Ratcliff, on 15 Jan. 1613 entered bonds of £100 to accept the award of William Bygatt, Thomas Milton, Richard Chester and Robert Salmon, all of Trinity House, concerning damage to a ballast lighter belonging to Pinder which sank alongside the *Gift of God*

[in the Thames] and the great cost of weighing her. The award was to be made by 19 Jan., and if not, Byam was to deliver a decision by 21 Jan. Since the 4 arbitrators have not concluded the business in time, Byam's award is that although Lanthorne, the master or owner, 'received great spoil' to cordage and cables, as well as delay, reported to amount to above £30, he and the owners must bear it. The best estimate of the cost of weighing and eventually repairing the lighter is £11 16s, including the cost of the lost ballast. Lanthorne is to pay two thirds (£7 17s 4d) to Pinder by 23 Jan. Pinder is to bear the other third. This money is to be paid at the house of Richard Nottingham, 'our clerk', in Ratcliff and both parties are to acquit each other of all further liability. Since the business is unusual and to avoid precedents, it is fitting to record the reasons for this award. The master or owners must bear the cost of the damage to cables and cordage and part of the costs of the ballastman because Lanthorne tried to get the ballast aboard before he was ready for it and failed to control the crew to ensure that it was brought aboard quickly. The crew should pay half what is due to Pinder, if they have agreed to do so or if Lanthorne can deduct it from their wages, because they had failed to prevent the accident by getting the ballast aboard, throwing it overboard, or mooring the lighter. Pinder should pay his share because the accident is not wholly attributable to negligence. [f.18v] The weather worsened quickly according to the testimony of Thomas Smyth, the [customs] waiter, who could not appear in person. Lanthorn is ordered to pay the costs of making the award.

39. [*? 31 May 1613 x 20 June 1614*] *Parishioners of Stepney to Trinity House* [*See* **40.**]
At the request of their neighbour Benedicta, wife of William Cradle of Ratcliff, mariner, they certify that he lived among them in good reputation for 22 years. He spent £100 or more seeking help for his former wife, a lunatic, which also drove him into great misery. Afterwards he adventured his estate on 2 voyages to 'Guiana' [? Guinea], but lost his entire stock of £60 and his wages. His present wife then fell ill for a year which caused great expense. In an attempt to recover his losses he went as pilot of a ship to the East Countries, adventuring his whole estate and £100 more which he borrowed. The ship was cast away in a storm and he and a few others barely escaped with their lives. Finally, last Christmas, in a storm, 2 ships damaged his wharf and quay so that water threatened to wash away the fence and earth of his house; the repair cost £22. He cannot pay his debts and dare not show his head to provide a living for his wife and 4 children for fear of being arrested for debt. Trinity House are asked to petition the lord chancellor to issue letters patent authorising a collection in the churches of London, Middlesex, [blank] so that he can live again as an honest man.
Thomas Johnson, John Muffett, Robert Earle, Richard Beamont, Robert Goldinge, Roger Fryth, Henry Pickis, John Paull, Thomas Lane, John Mothe, Edmond Rolfe, Michael Austen, [? Alen ? Lullz], Joos Prastenborge, John Sitley, Richard Laws.
Ro. Kaile can say little from his own knowledge about these calamities,

but he can certify that Cradle and his wife are very honest and very poor.

40. [f.19. *31 May 1613 x 20 June 1614*][1] *Trinity House to lord Ellesmere, lord chancellor*
Commendation of the above petition [**39**].
William Ivie, master; Robert Kitchen, Robert Bradshaw, William Bigatt, Thomas Milton, Matthew Woodcott, Robert Rickman, Andrew Shilling, Roger Gunston, John Osborne, Thomas Malbie.

    1. Ivie was master from 31 May 1613 to 20 June 1614 (*THD*, 274).

41. *20 June 1613. Certificate by Trinity House*
The good services of the bearer, John Deane, mariner and gunner, in merchant voyages in queen Elizabeth's time is certified by masters under whom he served. Now, having been taken lame at sea, his disease has developed into a dumb palsy which surgeons say cannot be cured. Furthermore, he suffered heavy loss when the *Charytie* was captured by the Turks in the Straits 3 years ago. In view of his past service and utter inability to maintain himself, Trinity House cannot deny him a certificate to the good people of Norfolk where he was born.
William Ivie, master; Robert Kytchen, Robert Bradshawe, Thomas Malbye, Thomas Milton, Matthew Woodcott, Robert Ryckman, John Osborne, Roger Goonstone, Andrew Shilling.

42. [f.19v] *1 Sept. 1613. York House [London]. T. [lord] Ellesmore, lord chancellor, [to Trinity House. See* **43**.*]*
He has had sundry petitions from mariners who served in the *Mary Anne* complaining that their wages were unpaid. At the mariners' request, he referred the case to Trinity House but understands from renewed complaints that despite their pains the mariners are still unpaid. In accordance with his former request, they are to summon the mariners, merchants and owners to ensure payment of what is due.

43. [f.20] *4 Sept. 1613. Trinity House to lord Ellesmere, lord chancellor*
In accordance with his letters [see **42**] they have tried to secure the attendance of the owners and merchants of the *Marye Anne* to show why the mariners are unpaid. Of the 2 merchants, Mr Eldred is out of town and Mr Stapers is decayed in estate, in prison, and cannot attend or give satisfaction. William Squire, who was factor in the ship, came to represent the merchants and alleged that the master and crew failed in their duty, which resulted in the overthrow of the voyage; that he was not party to the charter party and cannot commit the merchants; and that the owners have brought an action against the merchants for freight in king's bench. At the request of Trinity House, the mariners agreed to accept 12 months wages for almost 16 months service. But the owners are unwilling to pay more than 8 months wages because they say that the negligence of the crew, if proved, may result in the loss of the entire freight. In addition to paying 8 months wages, they are prepared to covenant to make this up

to 12 months, on condition that they are able to recover the freight from the merchants, as they suppose they will, and provided that the mariners undertake to repay the wages if the whole freight is lost. Trinity House consider that since the mariners were hired on a monthly basis for a voyage to a country of which they did not dream, and which is forbidden by a treaty between princes, they deserve to have their wages. The merchants, having been abused by a 'Hispaniolized fellow' who frustrated their hopes of profit, have been induced by him to defraud the owners and the mariners. This happens frequently, and causes mariners to complain and to turn to piracy. The lord chancellor is requested to order payment of 12 months wages, subject to whatever conditions he sees fit.

44. [f.20v] *10 Feb. 1614. Trinity House to the same*
Request that the attached petition [**45**] be granted.
William Ivie, master; Robert Kitchen, Michael Geare, Richard Chester, wardens; Hugh Merrit, assistant; Robert Bradshawe, Matthew Woodcott, Robert Rickman, Rowland Coytmore.

45. [*Before 10 Feb. 1614*] *Mary Temple, widow of Limehouse, to Trinity House* [*See* **44**.]
John Temple, her late husband, was captured by pirates on several occasions during the last 3 years. In 1611, he lost goods worth £85 in the *Goodwill* of London on a voyage to Ireland and Calais. In 1612, Captain Easton and his consorts captured him in the *Marye and John* of Sandwich on a voyage to Faro, whereby he lost goods worth '50 and [MS. cropped] pounds'. Then in May 1613, when master of a small ship, the *Peter* of London, he was captured off the coast of Barbary by 3 ships of war manned by Turks and Moors, and 4 christians. He was taken to Sallee in Barbary and so misused that he died within 8 days. One of the crew was murdered, the rest tortured, and the boy forced to be circumcised and turn Turk. Temple lost £120 in the *Peter* and his widow and 4 small children are in great poverty.
William Monsones, Richard March, John Busfeild, Ralph Bradshawe, Edward Stevens, Michael Miryvall, Brian Tashe, Lewis Taites, James Benet, Jo. Graves, William Beck, Richard Harris, Robert Bence, Michael Johns [MS. cropped], at the request of their neighbour, certify the truth of this which is known to most of the addressees who are asked to petition the lord chancellor for letters patent for a collection in the parish churches of London, Middlesex, Kent, Sussex, Surrey, Berkshire, Buckinghamshire, Hertfordshire, Westminster, Canterbury and Chichester.

46. [f.21. *Before 12 March 1614*] *Parishioners of St Mary Matfellon alias Whitechapel to Trinity House* [*See* **47**.]
At the request of their neighbour, John Whithall of Wapping, formerly an owner of several ships, they certify that he has lived among them in good repute for 20 years. The *Blandina*, of which he was half-owner and John Keepus was master, was wrecked in a storm coming from Norway,

whereby he lost his share in the ship and goods amounting in value to
£600. Then the *John* of London, of which he was also half-owner and
John Stephens was master, by a similar misfortune was cast away with all
the crew on the coast of Barbary, whereby he lost £400. His creditors
have committed him to the Fleet Gaol and he is unable to provide for his
family. Trinity House are asked to request the lord chancellor for letters
patent authorising a collection for him in the city of London, Middlesex,
and elsewhere [blank] so that he can live as an honest man again.
Richard Wood, constable; Rowland Coytmor, churchwarden; James
March (his mark), Gregory Philpot, Timothy Pinder, William Mott, John
Bourne, Edward Jopkins, John Trotter, Robert Bornny, Ralph Suretis,
Robert Merrit.

47. *12 March 1614. Trinity House to the lord chancellor*
Commendation of the attached certificate [**46**].
William Ivye, master; Robert Kitchen, Thomas Norris, Robert Brad-
shaw, Hugh Meritt, John Kinge, Robert Rickman, Michael Geare,
Rowland Coytmor, Thomas Malbie, John Osborne, Roger Gunston.

48. [f.21v] *9 Apr. 1614. A certificate by Trinity House for Scarborough*
The owners and masters of ships trading to Newcastle and other northern
parts have certified to Trinity House that the piers at Scarborough in
Yorkshire have been damaged by storms, especially in a recent great
storm, which was also known to some of the present writers. It has been
said that if an old foundation formerly laid for an 'outermore' pier were to
be built up and heightened, and certain rocks between it and the
outermost pier removed, shipping would benefit greatly. At the request
of the bearers, William Thomson and John Lacye, burgesses of
Scarborough, Trinity House endorse that opinion. To meet the cost, a
levy on ships trading to Newcastle and other northern parts of England at
the rate of 4d on those under, and 8d on those over, 50 tons would be
reasonable. All shipowners and masters trading to the north are willing to
pay, as shown by a petition to Trinity House signed by over 400 of them.
Sealed in the presence of William Ivie, master, Robert Kitchen, Robert
Bradshaw, Michael Geare, Richard Chester, William Bigatt, Matthew
Woodcott, Robert Rickman, John Osborne, Rowland Coytmore.

49. [f.22] *13 May 1614. Award by Trinity House*
John Powle of Ratcliff, master of the *Hopewell* of London, and William
Thorne of London, part owner, have entered bonds of £30 each to accept
the award of Trinity House in their dispute over the accounts of a voyage
from 'Vyana' [? Viana do Castelo]. The findings are that Powell sold
'Akall' [a kind of cable] at Dartmouth for £11 10s which was not entered
in his account; charged 27s more than was right for victualling the crew at
his house before the ship's departure; and made no allowance to Thorne
for the wages of a youth who went on the voyage. The award is that
Powell add £11 10s to his account for cash received for the cable; that the
account be adjusted in view of the 27s overcharged; and that Powell
credit Thorne 40s for his youth's wages. When the freight is paid, each is

to discharge his part of the account and receive his due share of the freight. Both are to relinquish all claims upon each other in respect of the voyage.

William Ivye, master; Robert Kytchen, Michael Geare, deputy; Robert Bradshawe, Richard Chester, deputy; Hugh Merrett, Matthew Woodcot, Robert Ryckman, Rowland Coytmore.

50. [f.22v. *Before 22 June 1615*] *John Martyn, Richard Wasse, Marjorie Daynes, widow, and John Chaplyn to lord Ellesmere, lord chancellor* [*See* **51.**]

The petitioners have brought an action in chancery against Cuthbert Graye, hostman, concerning the loading of ships by part-owners with only their goods. If the practice continues, trade in coal and other goods between Newcastle and London will be disrupted, as will trade and navigation throughout the realm. For if a part-owner like the def. who has the smaller share in the ship can load her in proportion to that share, he will deprive the other owners of the greater part of the profit. In the attached certificate shipowners and mariners have affirmed that nobody will then be prepared to build ships. Graye is a coal hostman at Newcastle and is part-owner of the ship in which Martyn trades to Newcastle for coal. When Martyn refused to accept Graye's coal because of its poor quality, Graye had him arrested 12 times in frivolous actions in the court at Newcastle and at common law here. Graye intends to press the actions at the next assizes. Because of continuous employment at sea, the petitioners cannot attend the hearing. They ask the lord chancellor to refer the case to Trinity House and to stay proceedings at common law and in the court at Newcastle until Trinity House or chancery have decided the issue.

51. [f.23] *22 June 1615. York House* [*London*]. *T.* [*lord*] *Ellesmere, lord chancellor,* [*to Trinity House*]

Reference to them of the attached petition [**50**].

52. *5 Aug. 1615. Newcastle. Cuthbert Gray to Trinity House*

In their letter of 15 July they stated that on receipt of instructions from the lord chancellor, they intended to hear the cause pending against him in chancery brought by John Martyn and they directed him to appear at Trinity House in Ratcliff by 31 Aug. Since he is a merchant living at Newcastle, over 200 miles away, and his trade such that he cannot attend, he hopes that the lord chancellor will be informed of the equity of his cause now pending and the untrue surmises in the petition of Martyn. Since it is not a maritime cause, chancery is the proper place for it. Had he been sent a copy of Martyn's petition, he would have shown its idle surmises to be untrue so that they would not have meddled any further.

53. *27 Sept. 1615. Ratcliff. Trinity House to lord Ellesmere, lord chancellor*

Both parties were summoned to appear within 45 days; Martin came but

Graye did not for the reasons stated in the attached letter [**52**]. They await further instructions.

Richard Chester, master; Michael Geere, Andrew Shillinge, Roger Gunston, Rowland Coytmore, Thomas Best, Robert Kitchen, Thomas Mylton.

54. [f.23v] *14 Oct. 1615. Award by Trinity House*
Thomas Litchfield petitioned the lord chancellor against Humphrey Merrett, his co-executor, concerning the will of Job Palmer, deceased. In his letter of 25 Sept. last the lord chancellor referred the case to Trinity House, and both parties agreed to accept an award, provided that it was made by 14 Oct. The award is that Merrett shall pay £113 to Lytchfeild at the usual meeting place of Trinity House in Ratcliff by 18 Oct. 1615 of which £60 is for Litchfeild in settlement of his demands as co-executor upon the estate of Palmer and for his expenses; the remaining £53 is to pay the following bequests: £20 to Anne Palmer, mother of the testator; £10 to Esther Lytchfeild, wife of Thomas Litchfeild; £10 to Susan, wife of Robert Litchfield; £10 to Sara Tylley, wife of John Tilley: £2 to the poor of Claybrook in Leicester; £1 to 'the son [? of] Thomas Litchfeild'. Both parties are to give sureties to each other concerning the execution of the will.

Richard Chester, master; Andrew Shillinge, Roger Gunston, Ro. Coytmore, Robert Kitchen, Matthew Woodcott, John Moore, Michael Geere, Thomas Best, Nicholas Diggins, William Bygatt, Robert Ryckman. [f.24 is lacking.]

55. [f.25–25v] *17 Oct. 1614. Order of the privy council concerning herring exports from Yarmouth* [Printed in *APC 1613–14*, 594–5.]

56. [*After 17 Oct. 1614. Sir*] *H. Montagu and* [*Sir*] *Randolph Crewe* [*sergeants at law*] *to the privy council* [*Cf APC 1613–14*, 594–5.]
On perusal of the statutes, they find that no strangers ought by law to ship herrings but in English ships owned by the king's subjects.

57. [*Before 5 Nov. 1615*] *Trinity House to the privy council* [*Cf APC 1615–16*, 317–18.]
Upon the suit of Trinity House and the merchants of London last year, the privy council obtained counsel's opinion [**56**] and thereupon ordered that no herrings be transported in foreign bottoms, with a dispensation to the inhabitants of Yarmouth on that occasion because they had alleged that foreign ships with whom contracts had been made had already arrived at Yarmouth. Now 6 Dutch ships [cf **59**] have arrived at Yarmouth contrary to the order. Action to protect the navigation of the realm is requested.

58. [f.26–26v] *19 Nov. 1615. Order of the privy council concerning herring exports from Yarmouth* [Printed in *APC 1615–16*, 327–9. *See* **60**.]

59. [f.27. *Before 5 Nov. 1615*] *Shipowners and poor mariners of Yarmouth to the privy council* [*Cf APC 1615–16, 317–18.*]
They used to transport herrings to Harwich, Tilbury Hope, Gravesend, and other places in their barks for loading aboard English ships of greater burden bound for the Straits. They are now much decayed because of the use of strangers' bottoms. Six great Flemish ships [see **57**] have recently arrived to take all the herrings of the town. The petitioners will be undone, and shipping engaged in the transport of herrings to English ports and to the Straits will be unemployed, to enrich a few Dutch merchants, contrary to law. The prohibition of strangers' ships in the trade is requested.

60. [*6 x 17 Nov. 1615*][1] *The town of Yarmouth to the privy council*
On 5 Nov., the privy council appointed 'committees' [sic] to settle the dispute between Trinity House and the town. The privy council is asked to set a date for the hearing. Despite the fact that they live far away, they will then attend and accept whatever order is thought fit. Meanwhile, they ask that a licence be granted again this year for the export of 600 lasts* of herrings in strangers' ships. The herrings are already packed in Ligorne casks and are salted and prepared in a manner fit for those parts, and not England.

 1. The report of the committee, dated 17 Nov., was considered by the privy council on 19 Nov. 1615 (*APC 1615–16*, 327–9; **58**).

61. [f.27v. *? 12 Oct. x 19 Nov. 1615*][1] *Statement by Trinity House*
The reasons against the inhabitants of Yarmouth transporting herrings in strangers' bottoms are as follows: (a) It is against the law, as appears in the report of Sir Henry Montague and Sir Randolph Crewe [**56**]. (b) Two recent proclamations confirm and command the execution of the law. (c) The archbishop of Canterbury and the lord chancellor have declared in the council that the law should be enforced and navigation advanced by all good means. (d) The export of herrings in strangers' bottoms coming to Yarmouth has resulted in the unemployment of great and small ships. Formerly small vessels transported the herrings to Orwell, Harwich, Queenborough and Tilbury Hope whither greater ships went for better security. Many hundreds of poor seamen were employed and now they are impoverished as is evident from their late petition [**59**]. (e) The Yarmouth men have said that prices would fall, that all the herrings would not be sold, that their trade would be hindered and that fishermen would be discouraged. But stranger merchants pay more than native merchants and can then undersell them because freight rates in strangers' ships are lower. Native merchants have been squeezed out of the trade and the king loses £6,000 or £8,000 in customs which he would have got on the proceeds of the sale of the herrings on the return of the ships. If exports in strangers' ships were to be banned, strangers would then have to pay the same freight rates as English merchants who would be encouraged to re-enter the trade. The number of buyers will thereby be increased, thus raising prices. (f) A merchant 'of good sort' has provided information that the merchants who export herrings in strangers' ships

are free denizens, and their names are Jaques Debest, Mr Curteene and
Mr Dehoame of London.

1. See **57–60**. The proclamations mentioned in (b) were probably those of 17 Apr. and
12 Oct. 1615 (*Proc.*, i.137–8). If **61** were later than 19 Nov. 1615, the privy council ban on
exports (*APC 1615–16*, 327–9; **58**) would presumably have been mentioned.

62. [f.28] *24 Feb. 1616. Bonds* [partly in Latin.]
John Davis of Ratcliff and William Ball of Wapping, mariners, enter
bonds of £200 to accept the award of Richard Chester, Thomas Best,
Michael Geere and John Moore, or any 3 of them, in their dispute,
provided that the award is made at Trinity House at Ratcliff not later than
9 March 1616. [See **63**].

63. *9 March 1616. Award* [*by Trinity House. See* **62**.]
The award is that since Davis failed, as Ball alleges, to perform his promise
to keep company with him in their late voyage from Spain, he is to take no
action for the alleged wrong done to him by Ball. Likewise Ball is to take
no action. Both are to lodge at the usual meeting place of the writers at
Ratcliff, commonly called Trinity House, before 12 March 1616,
acquittances made before 2 or more witnesses in respect of all wrongs
done to each other up to 23 Feb. 1616.
Richard Chester, Thomas Best, Michael Geere, John Moore.

64. [f.28v] *3 Apr. 1616. Privy council to the master of the rolls and Sir
Daniel Dun* [*admiralty court judge*] *concerning exports in alien ships and
freight charges* [Printed in *APC 1615–16*, 468. Lord Knollis appears as a
signatory in **64** but not in *APC*.]

65. [ff.28v–29] *16 June 1616. Order of the privy council concerning freight
rates* [Printed in *APC 1615–16*, 611–14. At the end of **65** it is stated that
'the publishing of this order is entered in the next leaf', i.e. **68**.]

66. [f.29v] *26 June 1616. Certificate by Trinity House*
At the request of the bearer, Nicholas Rawledge, mariner of London,
they certify from the knowledge of some of them and of other seamen
that he was taken by the Spaniards at the latter end of the late queen's
reign, lost his estate and was held in their galleys for about 4 years. He
then engaged himself industriously in merchants' affairs but last Nov.,
when master of the *Feather* of London bound for the 'port of Portingale'
[Oporto], he was captured by 2 French men-of-war and lost his entire
estate. Later he lost his sight and is now utterly impoverished.
Thomas Best, Roger Gunston, Rowland Coytmore, Thomas Malbye,
John Moore, William Bygat, Thomas Milton, Matthew Woodcot,
Nicholas Diggins, Robert Ryckman, William Ivey, Robert Kytchen,
Michael Geere.

67. *31 Aug. 1616. Certificate by inhabitants of Wapping*
At the request of the bearer, Elizabeth, wife of Moses Mason, mariner,
they certify that her husband, who has lived among them for a long time,

is a man of honest life. On a voyage to the Straits as gunner's mate in the *Long Robert* of London, he was captured by the Turks and is still held prisoner. His wife and 3 small children are in such poverty that they cannot provide for themselves or for his release.

R. Gardener, rector of Whitechapel; Robert Bourne, constable; Robert Tyler, Tyman Warde, churchwardens; Edmond Jurden, John Beedom, William Mott, John Bourne, Jo. Dearsley, Thomas Hard, R. Wheatley, part-owner of the ship, Richard Bix, part-owner of the ship.

68. [f.30] *16 Oct. 1616. Whitehall. Order of the privy council* [Repetition of the final paragraph of **65** with the additional requirement that the order be published.][1]

G. [archbishop of] Canterbury, T. [lord] Ellesmere, lord chancellor, T. [earl of] Suffolk, [bishop of] Ely, [earl of] Pembroke, T. [earl of] Arundel, [Sir] Ralph Winwood, [Sir] John Digbye, [Sir] Thomas Lake, [Sir] Julius Caesar, [Sir] Francis Bacon.

1. On receipt of the Trinity House petition (**72**), the privy council wrote to the lord treasurer (**69**) and sent to Trinity House a signed transcript of the order of 16 June (**65**) to be set up in the Exchange (*APC 1616–17*, 42–3).

69. *16 Oct. 1616. Privy council to the lord treasurer concerning freight charges* [Printed in *APC 1616–17*, 42–3 under 13 Oct. 1616.]

70. [f.30v] *31 Jan. 1614. Privy council to the mayor and aldermen of Newcastle about silting in the river Tyne* [Printed in *APC 1613–14*, 340–1. The signatories in **70** are the archbishop [of ?Canterbury], the lord chancellor, the earl of Exeter, Sir Julius Caesar, Sir Thomas Parrie, and the 'lord chief justice' [? Sir Edward Coke].]

71. *7 Oct. 1614. Privy council to the mayor, aldermen, and sheriffs of Newcastle about silting in the river Tyne* [Printed in *APC 1613–14*, 579–80.]

72. [f.31. *16 June x 16 Oct. 1616*][1] *Trinity House to the privy council*
They have long been suitors to the privy council about the decayed condition of ships and seamen. From time to time the privy council has heard their pleas and on 10 [*recte* 16] June last, on the report of the master of the rolls and the admiralty court judge, ordered a table of freight rates which was fair both to the merchants and the shipowners, and which had been agreed by both parties, to be entered in the register of council causes and to be published [65]. Nothing is yet done and a proclamation or other action is requested.

1. The requirement to publish was omitted from the order of 16 June, but apparently added on 16 Oct.(**68**).

73. *21 Jan. 1617. Certificate by R. Wheatley, late part-owner, and Richard Bix, part-owner of the Long Robert of London*
At the request of the bearer, Nicholas Rudes of Dunwich in Suffolk, mariner, they certify that his natural son, William Rudes, mariner, was

captured by the Turks on a voyage to the Straits in the *Long Robert* of London. A large ransom is required but his father, being aged and poor, and his friends cannot provide it.

74. *25 Jan. 1617. Certificate by Trinity House*
Commendation of the above petition [73]. Rudes is a very young man. Thomas Best, master; Roger Gunston, Robert Kytchen, Robert Bradsho, Hugh Merit, Richard Chester, Nicholas Diggins, Robert Rickman, Matthew Woodcot, William Ivey.

75. [f.31v. *Before 11 Oct. 1616.*] *David Michell, mariner of Ratcliff, to lord Ellesmere, lord chancellor* [*See* **76.**]
Thomas Whitney, esq., owner of the *Thomas and Francis* appointed Michell as attorney to go to Newcastle to recover the ship and her furniture. After doing so, Michell went on 3 voyages in her to Newcastle for coal. On the instructions of Whitney, he then supervised the new building of the ship and paid the weekly wages of the carpenters. Whitney then sent him on another voyage to Newcastle, promising to clear his account and pay him for his time. The ship has now been sold but Whitney refuses to come to account or to refer the matter to arbitration. Michell, in view of his poverty and that of his wife and child, asks that Whitney be ordered to abide by arbitration.

76. *11 Oct. 1616. York House* [*London*]. *T.* [*lord*] *Ellesmere, lord chancellor, to Thomas Best, Hugh Merit and William Bygat of Trinity House, or any 2 of them*
Order to arbitrate in **75**. Michell has said that he is due to go on a long voyage.

77. *2 Nov. 1616. Ratcliff.* [*Return to the lord chancellor. See* **76.**]
No settlement has been made because Whitney wants them to report their findings to the lord chancellor. He also objects in general terms to Michell's accounts, but neither he nor the present writers can disprove any part of them or charge Michell with dishonesty. The account shows that £35 8s 1d is due to him, besides allowance of £10 or £12 more for the 8 or 9 months which he spent attending to Whitney's ship.

78. [f.32] *31 Dec. 1616. York House* [*London. Viscount*] *Brackley, lord chancellor, to Thomas Best, Hugh Merit, and William Bigat of Trinity House*
After receipt of **77** he has heard Whitney, gentleman, alone and together with Michell, mariner, a native of Scotland and does not mislike their certificate, but since Whitney alleges that he has further material evidence, they, together with such other members of Trinity House as they see fit, are asked to review the case to avoid any exception. He has such confidence in their judgement that he will accept their certificate and cause it to be implemented. A speedy decision is requested because Michell has long been delayed in his employment abroad owing to this business.

79. *8 Jan. 1617.* [*Return to the lord chancellor. See* **78.**]
They have re-examined both parties and find the state of the case unaltered. Whitney has provided no new evidence. £47 8s remains due to Michell, besides £3 or £4 incurred since their last report, leaving aside whatever is due for his loss of time and labour which is for the lord chancellor to decide. Also Whitney should covenant to discharge Michell of a debt of £30 for coal loaded at Newcastle on Whitney's account. Michell should discharge Whitney for the items in his account by a similar bond.

Thomas Best, Roger Gunston, Thomas Milton, Nicholas Diggins, Michael Geere, William Bigat, Matthew Woodcot, Robert Rickman, Thomas Malby, Richard Chester, William Ivey, Henry Rawlyn, Robert Bradsha.

80. [f.32v] *15 Jan. 1617. Lawrence Washington* [*register of the chancery court*] *to Trinity House*
Mr Sergeant Richardson, counsel for William Clarke, pl., today informed the lord chancellor that Clarke, a poor mariner, had petitioned the lord chancellor concerning wrongs done and wages owed to him by William Isack, def.; that the lord chancellor had referred the case to Trinity House, and that 5 masters had certified that £8 5s wages were due; that thereupon the lord chancellor had ordered Isack to pay but that he had refused to do so, and had prayed a new reference to Trinity House, alleging that Clarke had turned roman catholic, and had left the ship 'for religion', whereas according to counsel Clarke detested that religion and had received holy communion since his return; that on which petition, the case had again been referred to Trinity House but that they saw no reason to alter their opinion. If the 5 masters will make a further certificate, the lord chancellor will order payment.

81. *18 Jan. 1617. Trinity House to viscount Brackley, lord chancellor*
In accordance with his letters of 23 Dec. they were hearing the dispute between William Isack, master of the *Elizabeth and Joseph*, and William Clarke, one of the crew; Clarke was represented by his solicitor, Mr Fenn, who produced a chancery order [**80**], in view of which they are taking no further action.

Thomas Best, master; Roger Gunston, Rowland Coytmore, Robert Kytchen, Robert Bradsha, Richard Chester, John Vassall, William Hare, Matthew Woodcot, Nicholas Diggins, Robert Salmon, William Ivey, John Skinner, John Osborne, Henry Rawlyn, Robert Adams, John Maynard.

82. [f.33. *Received on 29 Jan. 1617. Younger*] *brothers of Trinity House to the master, wardens and assistants of Trinity House*
They are concerned about the weal and reputation of the fellowship and of every member according to their duties and oaths 'taken with all due respect to your worships as from inferiors to their superiors, or youngers to their elders', and crave assistance 'for the further manifestation of truth and justice' in a case already judged by the master, wardens and

assistants. They ask that a certificate be sent to the lord chancellor in the case of Isacke and Clarke [80–1, 83], so that he may be better informed. If the master, wardens and assistants rule that Isack must pay Clarke for time not served in the ship, 'he may be satisfied and the cause ended'; if not, Isack can be released from prison. The petitioners are concerned for their own sake and for that of a wronged brother. They prefer to seek justice from the master, wardens and assistants, who understand the cause, rather than to pursue other courses and prevent the inconveniences which might otherwise follow this example.

Thomas Johnson, John Bennet, Thomas Pye, Thomas Smyth, Henry Beale, Thomas Hunt, Daniel Bannister, Matthew Kevell, Thomas Needes, William Stevens, Robert Mott, Richard Bromfild, William Hayles, Richard Goodlard, John Goodlard, John Lyngwood, Gervais Hocket, William Shawe, William Care, Nathaniel Salmon, William Rickes, John Dennys, Robert Grant, Roger Sherman, Robert Tockeley, Peter Kenton, Richard Harris, Seth Hudson, Tristram Wise, John Bredcake, William Knight, Walter Whyting, Anthony Tutchen, William Cocke, Walter Cooke, John Bredcake.

83. *30 Jan. 1617. Ratcliff. Trinity House to viscount Brackley, lord chancellor*

His order of 23 Dec. directed them to examine the case of Isacke and Clarke. Many of the company being out of town, there was not a competent number so the master wrote to those away requiring their appearance on 18 Jan. On that day [81] Henry Fenn had produced a chancery order [80] and had said that they were to proceed no further because the lord chancellor intended to hear the case, whereupon their proceedings ceased. On 29 Jan. they received the enclosed petition [82]. They declare that they had considered the case and had delivered their verdict to Clarke before receiving the lord chancellor's letter of 23 Dec. and before Clarke's petition to the lord chancellor. Their opinion was that Clarke deserved no wages but rather punishment for reasons which can be explained if desired. Furthermore [f.33v] Clarke or Fenne has misrepresented them to the lord chancellor. The chancery order [80] states that they saw no reason to alter the certificate of the 5 masters whereas Trinity House had not examined the cause since receipt of the lord chancellor's letter of 23 Dec., much less confirmed the certificate, 'but directly contrary'.

[Signed] T. Best, Roger Gunston, Robert Kitchen, Nicholas Diggins, Ro. Salmon, John Vassall (his mark), Richard Chester, Matthew Woodcott, William Ivey, Robert Bradsho, John Osborne.

84. [f.34. *? Before 11 Feb. 1617*] *Owners and seamen of Ipswich, Aldeburgh, Harwich and Woodbridge trading in coal to Trinity House* [*Cf APC 1616–17, 138–9.*]

The king has granted letters patent to Andrew Boyd and others for the survey of coal at Newcastle, Sunderland and Blyth, and 4d per chaldron there laden, the burden of which is intolerable and will result in the decay of trade and shipping. The 4d per chaldron may not seem much but will yield about £4,000 a year, which is a large part of the profit of the trade, obtained with great labour and desperate adventure. The facts are as well known to Trinity House as to the petitioners, and in one respect concern Trinity House more because the king has given them trust for the increase and preservation of shipping. They are asked to petition the privy council to secure the removal of the imposition.

Ipswich:[1] Robert Bull, Richard Barnes, John Affield, Robert Longe, Thomas Lawsonne, John Warde, Thomas Colbye, James Peacocke, John Barnes, Edward Ellmint, Edward Maye, Edward Prat, Edward Laverick, Robert Hunt, Richard Barton, Richard Birlingham, Edmond Morgan, Richard Sadlington, John Evans, Thomas Bernard.

[? Aldeburgh]: Thomas Juell, John Steward, John Revet, James Talbot, senior, John Warner, Thomas Wright, Susan Lowe, Elizabeth Searles, William Searles, Samuel James, Thomas Galant, Nicholas Freeman, John Carnabye, Richard Fisher, William Hamand, Jeremy Cornelis, Thomas Cocke, William Lowe, Thomas Geslyn.

[? Harwich]: Jeremy Tye, Anthony Payne, Richard Tye, Henry Ford, Thomas Wilkinson, Robert Braye, Richard Wasse, Richard Boulle, George Haildocke, Robert Coates, Edmond Tye, James Talbot, Stephen Dykes, Thomas Balye.

Woodbridge: Thomas Bolton, Thomas Cole, William Carye, Jonas James, Robert Holgrave, John Redgrave, Nicholas Ellenger, William Herbert, George Burwood, Richard Oteley, John Whale, Richard Davye, Thomas Base, William Battelle.

1. Names in the MS are in 4 columns. Examination of wills suggests that not all names are in the correct column.

85. [f.34v] *12 Feb. 1617. Ratcliff. Trinity House to Sir Daniel Dun, admiralty court judge*

Dun wishes to be satisfied about the need for lights at or near Winterton. A motion has been made to them by masters trading that way and contradicted by others who would have to contribute towards the charges. Trinity House, from their experience, considered that there was at present no need since there are already lights and buoys not far away at Caister; and also in view of the small profit in the trade to Newcastle, additional charges should be avoided. Nevertheless, after the present foul weather, they are sending 3 or 4 of their most experienced men to sound the channels and to provide lights and seamarks as necessary. They have already conferred with some of Yarmouth about materials and workmen if needed.

Thomas Best, Roger Gunston, Robert Kitchen, Michael Geere, Robert Bradsho, Richard Chester, Matthew Woodcot, Nicholas Diggins, Robert Ryckman, William Ivey.

86. [? *Before 14 Feb. 1617*] *Trinity House to the king*[1]

A statute [8 Elizabeth, c. 13] gave them the right to provide all buoys, beacons, marks and signs for the sea throughout the realm. In 36 Elizabeth, the lord high admiral resigned all his rights in this respect to the queen because Trinity House were the most experienced and fittest for this responsibility, and thereupon the queen by letters patent granted the rights to them [C 66/1410, mm.11–12]. The king is asked not to grant rights in respect of the provision of lights or marks to any but the petitioners, who are responsible for the conduct and pilotage of his 'navy royal' and the greatest part of the shipping of the realm. They make this petition because they understand that the king has been asked to confer rights upon some who are not seamen and have no knowledge or experience. Since channels and sands alter with every great tempestuous wind, experience is essential. Otherwise ships, goods and men will be imperilled. [f.35 is lacking.]

1. Probably the petition considered by the privy council on 14 Feb. 1617 (*APC 1616–17*, 142–3). A virtually identical copy (**103**) states at the end that it was referred by the king to the privy council.

87. [f.36. *? Before 11 Feb. 1617.*[1] *Notes about Boyd's patent*]
Reasons against the 4d per chaldron of coal: (a) Owners will be soon impoverished and shipping decay. (b) The motive of trade is profit, and if removed, trade and shipping will decline; seamen will be forced to seek employment in Holland, France, Spain or Turkey, there to be pirates, and their wives and children forced to beg. (c) The best nursery for seamen will be lost; the king's navy will then either not have sufficient seamen or be forced to employ landsmen who for want of knowledge will imperil his ships or those of merchants. (d) The office of survey will be tedious and will hinder the 300 ships engaged in the trade of a quarter of their time; profits will be reduced, owners impoverished and seamen undone; exports of 40,000 or 50,000 chaldrons of coal will be lost and the city and other places will lack supplies; prices will rise and thereby 'the poor of all trades impoverished'. (e) The 4d per chaldron is more than the profit cleared by many ships at the end of the year.

1. Probably precedes a Trinity House complaint mentioned on 11 Feb. 1617 about Boyd's patent (*APC 1616–17*, 138–9).

88. [f.36v] *14 Feb. 1617. Order of the privy council concerning seamarks* [Printed in *APC 1616–17*, 142–3.]

89. *14 Feb. 1617. Order of the privy council concerning Winterton lighthouse* [Printed in *APC 1616–17*, 141–2.]

90. [ff.37–8] *14 Feb. 1617. Order of the privy council concerning the conservation of the river Tyne* [Printed in *APC 1616–17*, 147–50.]

91. [f.38v] *16 Feb. 1617. Order of the privy council concerning the conservation of the river Tyne* [Printed in *APC 1616–17*, 150–1.]

92. [*18 Feb. 1617*] *Privy council to the mayor of Newcastle concerning the conservation of the river Tyne* [Printed in *APC 1616–17*, 146–7.]

93. [f.39] *18 Feb. 1617. Privy council to the bishop of Durham and the sheriff of Northumberland about the conservation of the river Tyne*

[Printed in *APC 1616–17*, 145–6. The signatories, not listed in *APC*, were the archbishop of Canterbury, the lord high admiral, the lord chamberlain, the earl of Arundel, the bishop of Ely, lord Zouch, Mr comptroller, Mr vice chamberlain, Mr secretary Winwoode, Mr secretary Lake, the chancellor of the exchequer, the master of the rolls, and the attorney general.]

94. [f.39v. *21 Feb. 1617. Mayor and aldermen of London to the privy council about the survey of coals.* Printed in *APC 1616–17*, 165–7.]

95. [f.40] *28 Feb. 1617.* [*Sir*] *Ralph Winwoode* [*secretary of state*] *to Sir Francis Bacon, attorney general*
The king has ordered that Bacon and others of the king's counsel should consider what rights Trinity House have to provide seamarks under the statute of 8 Elizabeth [c. 13] and by letters patent, and report to the council.

96. *15 March 1617. The lord keeper to the privy council about the right of Trinity House to provide lighthouses* [The report of Bacon, who had become lord keeper on 7 March 1617, in reply to **95** is in the privy council order of 26 March 1617 (*APC 1616–17*, 204).]

97. *1 March 1617. Certificate by Trinity House*
The bearer, Mary Cooke, widow, is very poor. Her late husband, Henry Cooke, part owner of the *Mary Constant* of London, was taken with the ship by Turkish pirates and sustained great loss to his utter undoing. Her son, Martin Cooke, was also lately taken by the Turks and held in slavery. She cannot redeem him without help.
Thomas Best, Roger Gunston, Michael Geere, Robert Bradsho, Robert Kytchen, Hugh Merit, William Hare, Richard Chester, Robert Rickman, Thomas Mylton, Matthew Woodcot, William Ivey.
[Note at end] A true copy of the certificate given to Mary Cooke by Trinity House on the date stated; copied from the register today, 9 Jan. 1619. Thomas Best, Thomas Love, Roger Gunston, Matthew Woodcot, Walter Whyting.

98. *5 March 1617.* [*Trinity House*] *to Mr Norreys and Mr Geere*
They are to go without delay to Winterton and select a suitable site near Winterton Ness for a turret or watchhouse in which to maintain a light of sea coals for guiding ships from the sea into the roads, and sites for 2 other lighthouses for leading marks. They are then to arrange for the supply of materials and make contracts with workmen for building the lighthouses, so far as the £60 allocated to them for that purpose permits. If more money is needed, any which is taken up in the country will be repaid in London. They are to pay Mr Amys of Yarmouth for candles or wages delivered by him to Wilson, keeper of the lights at Caister. Accounts are to be rendered on their return. The keeping of lights at Caister and Stamport is to be inspected and they are to employ men and boats as needed to help in sounding the channels and sands.

Thomas Best, Hugh Merit, Robert Bradsho, Robert Kytchen, Roger Gunston, Nicholas Diggins, Richard Chester, John Osborne.

99. [ff.40v–41] *26 March 1617. Order of the privy council concerning seamarks* [Printed in *APC 1616–17*, 204–5.]

100. [f.41v] *29 March 1617. Certificate by Trinity House*
The *Seaflower* of London was cast away with all her goods and crew of 16 in foul weather in the Bay of Lisbon. They cannot say what adventure Nicholas Russell had in her.
Thomas Best, master, Roger Gunstone, Robert Salmone, Matthew Woodcott, Thomas Milton, Robert Rickman, William Ivie, Roger [*recte* ? Richard*] Chester, John Kinge.

101. [f.42–42v] *25 Feb. 1617. Order of the privy council concerning the office of surveyor of sea coal* [Printed in *APC 1616–17*, 165–7. f.43 is blank.]

102. [f.44 As in **85**.]

103. [As in **86** (see note).]

104. [f.44v As in **88**.]

105. [As in **89**.]

106. [f.45 As in **95**.]

107. [As in **96**.]

108. [f.45–45v As in **99**.]

109. [f.46] *4 June 1617. [Sir] H. Yelverton, attorney general [to the privy council]*
Mr Secretary Lake instructed him in April to consult other counsel about the king's power in erecting lighthouses and whether the statute of 8 Elizabeth [c. 13] so incorporates the power and sets the trust in such erecting in Trinity House that the king without straining the prerogative may not perform the same or delegate his power. The present lord keeper, as attorney general, has already partly resolved the question in his report [**96**]. Having heard the counsel of Trinity House and also Sir William Erskine, who has petitioned the king about erecting a lighthouse at Winterton Ness, opinion is given that (a) lighthouses are seamarks within the meaning of the statute; (b) by the statute Trinity House possess authority and trust to provide lighthouses if they will; (c) Trinity House cannot transfer this authority. But the grant to Trinity House does not inhibit the crown under common law because its provisions are in the affirmative, allowing Trinity House to erect lighthouses but not excluding the king from doing so; since the passing of the statute both he and the

late queen have authorised the erection of some lighthouses. So although authority is vested in Trinity House as persons of skill, if they fail to do so, the king is not restrained from providing lighthouses in all necessary places. The question of convenience as opposed to law is for [the privy council] to judge.

[Note at end] A petition about this business delivered to the [privy council] on 18 Feb. 1618 with 'inconveniences' are entered below [**115–16**].

110. [f.46v] *16 June 1617. Privy council to Trinity House and others concerning a levy to finance an expedition against the Turkish pirates* [Printed in *APC 1616–17*, 262–4 and dated 1 June 1617. The signatories, not listed in *APC*, were the archbishop of Canterbury, the earl of Worcester, lords Zouche, Stanhope and Carew, and Sir Ralph Winwoode.]

111. [*After 16 June 1617*] Trinity House [*to the privy council. Cf* SP 14/116/10; *CSPD 1619–23*, 161, ascribed to 7 July 1620]
In reply to their letter of 16 June [**110**], they summoned a meeting of all masters and owners of ships who are seamen and outlined the plan. All applauded it, and agreed that ships trading to the Straits east of Cape Gata will pay 1s 6d per ton; that those trading to the Straits west of Cape Gata and Spain from the Straits' mouth to the North Cape (viz. Cape Finisterre), the Islands, Barbary, Guinea, Benin, etc. will pay 8d per ton; and those trading to Biscay, France, Flanders, Holland, Friesland, Hamburg, Danzig, Melvin, Norway, Russia, Greenland and all northern parts overseas will pay 3d per ton. These impositions are to be paid every voyage, half at the entry* of the ship outward bound, the other half at her entry on her return home. A letter to the Customs House is requested so that they may have their deputy for collection there. Judging from the number and tonnage of ships employed in 1616, the following sums will be levied:

Imposition of 1s 6d per ton	£329
Of 8d per ton	£386
Of 3d per ton	£353
	£1,068

112. [f.47. *After 16 June 1617. Memorandum by Trinity House*]
After receipt of **110**, these masters and owners of ships being summoned agreed in writing to the proposed impositions:
John Davis, John Bigat, John Bourne, John Flud, William Case, Willam Rand, John Bennet, Reynold Hoxton, Robert Mott, John Hone, John Blake, Richard Plumpton, Peter Whyte, William Shaw, Robert Tyler, William Mathew, John Grant, Roger Sherman, William Becke, Edmond Gardner, junior, Walter Cooke, Robert Stevens, George Hatch, William Mallet, John Wootten, William Isacke, Robert Myller, Robert Bence, junior, Thomas Johnson, John Startup, William Cocke, William Dowglas, Thomas Hart, Simon Nickoles, John Rickes, John Patteson,

John Sayer, Anthony Tutchen, Peter Kenton, Lawrence Nixe, John Felton, Edward Nicholles, Richard Malym, George Lyssant, John Franckton, John Lyngwood, Thomas Needes, John Chester, William Startout, Josiah Church, William Bushell, Peter Blake, Stephen Church, Samuel Each.

113. [*Before 3 July 1617. Trinity House*] *to the lord keeper* [*See* **114.**]
In accordance with his reference to them of the cause of Isacke and Clarke, they have summoned Clarke to appear several times by letters left at his house and by their officer but he refuses to come. They know no more of the case than they did in the late lord chancellor's time when he referred it to them [**80–3**] which they can certify if desired.
Robert Salmon, Thomas Best, Robert Kytchen, Roger Gunston, William Hare, Richard Chester, Matthew Woodcot, Nicholas Diggins, William Ivey.

114. [f.47v] *19 July 1617. Ratcliff. Trinity House to the lord keeper*
In accordance with his reference to them of 3 July of the cause of Isacke and Clarke, they have tried to summon Clarke to appear but cannot find him. They therefore certify what they ascertained from earlier examinations [**80–3**, **113**]. Isacke was master of a ship on a voyage into the Straits for some of the Turkey company, and hired Clarke as cook. At Messina in Sicily Clarke quarrelled with a fellow seaman and being reprimanded by the master shortly afterwards went ashore with other members of the crew and 'insinuating himself to the Jesuits and others of the Inquisition there abiding' secured an order for the payment of all wages due to him to date contrary to his contract with the master under which wages would be paid on the return of the ship to London. Having also been persuaded to become a roman catholic, Clarke 'obtained so much from thence as that the master Isacke was fain to enter into bond in the sum of 2,000 ducats not to receive him into the ship again'. Clarke was sent by the Jesuits with letters to Rome and, he and others meeting Isack at Naples on the way, would have had him apprehended had he not escaped in great danger. On the evidence no money is due to Clarke for time not served in the ship, but rather the contrary because he did what might have turned to the overthrow of the whole voyage, the ship and the master.
Robert Salmon, master; Robert Kytchen, Thomas Best, Roger Gunston, wardens; Nicholas Diggins, Matthew Woodcot, William Ivey, Henry Rawlyn, Richard Chester, assistants.

115. [f.48. *Before 18 Feb. 1618*] *Trinity House to the privy council* [*See* **109.**]
The king referred their petition about lighthouses to the privy council, who concluded that Trinity House as persons trusted by the statute should have the sole right of providing all seamarks. But when Sir William Erskine pressed his suit, the king referred the case to Sir Francis Bacon, then attorney general, who certified that there was authority 'mixed with a trust' settled in Trinity House to provide lighthouses and other marks, and that this authority could not be transferred from them

by law [**96**]. When this opinion was read on 26 March 1617, the privy council confirmed their former opinion, saving the king's pleasure. Nevertheless Erskine has pressed his suit and obtained the king's hand and the grant is ready for the seal. The ensuing inconveniences [see **116**] are for the privy council to consider.

116. [*Before 18 Feb. 1618. Statement by Trinity House. See* **109**.]
The inconveniences of the king's grant if Erskine erects lights: (a) The grantees are unskilled and those whom they employ are less qualified than the masters of Trinity House to place lighthouses. (b) There are sufficient lighthouses already erected at or near Winterton Ness. (c) Multiplicity of lighthouses and seamarks confounds pilots, thereby endangering ships, goods and lives. (d) The contribution offered by traders to Trinity House to erect and maintain lights at Winterton Ness is only 6d per 20 chaldrons and no collections have yet been made. But the imposition approved by the king is believed to be 3s 4d on 20 chaldrons. (e) The discontent caused by so great a levy on so poor a trade is left for consideration. (f) Many ships will cease trading, thereby diminishing coal supplies and raising prices in the city and the country.

117. [*Early 1618. Trinity House*] *to the lord high chamberlain of England* [*See* **118**.]
They seek his assistance in the matter of lights which concerns not only them but also the navigation and all the seamen of the kingdom.

118. [*After 7 Jan 1618.*[1] *Trinity House*] *to the lord chancellor*
He has been a father to the country and to their house in love and in his opinion to the privy council when the king referred the cause to him [**96**]. They seek his continued support in the matter of lights both in their own interest and in that of the seamen of the kingdom.

1. **96** shows that the addressee was Bacon, who became lord chancellor on 7 Jan. 1618.

119. [f.48v] *20 Feb. 1618.* [*Sir*] *C. Edmondes* [*clerk of the privy council, to Trinity House*]
Their petition [**115**] was read this afternoon in full council. They, together with Sir W. Erskine and counsel, are to be heard on Sunday morning next.

120. [f.49. *Before 25 May 1618*] *Merchant adventurers of Newcastle to the privy council* [*See* **121**.]
By reason of the king's proclamation [on 17 Apr. 1615] against the use of strangers' ships, the petitioners have been forced, sundry times within these 2 years, after the sale of goods exported from Newcastle to the Seventeen Provinces, to make over money from thence to France and to other countries, causing losses to themselves and to the king's customs, because there were no English ships to transport back such goods as they could buy. Also by reason of the proclamation they are unable to export as much coarse cloth as formerly because they dare not venture loading a

whole ship in case of miscarriage for then they would be undone. The king loses customs both ways, the petitioners lose their trade, coarse cloth is unsold, and the return on such sales is lost. They do not believe that this was the meaning of the proclamation, and hope that Trinity House will confess as much. They seek permission to export in strangers' ships to the United Provinces and to Germany up to 6 small fardels of cloth in any one stranger's ship, as they used to do, and to bring back up to 20 tons of commodities, the master bringing a certificate under the seal of the port where the cargo was laden stating that no English ship was available. They hope that Trinity House will agree that this will not prejudice navigation but will advance customs and help the poor town of Newcastle.

121. *25 May 1618. [Sir] George Calvert [clerk of the privy council] to the merchant adventurers of London and Trinity House*
Request for an opinion on the petition [**120**].

122. *3 June 1618. Ratcliff. Trinity House [to the privy council. Cf SP 14/97/93; CSPD 1611–18, 543.]*
Their opinion and that of the merchant adventurers [of London] was sought on the petition [**120–1**]. They do not know the extent of the trade and the inconveniences which might be caused to the merchant adventurers [of London]. The Newcastle merchant adventurers might however load small ships of their own town without wrong to themselves by filling the rest of the cargo space with coal, the profit from which will pay for the freight and employ their ships and poor seamen. Besides there is at Newcastle a Trinity House whose care it is to maintain their own navigation and who pretend to have in that river as much privilege as Trinity House [of Deptford] in this but no certificate of toleration seems to have been made by them.
John Osborne, Thomas Best, Hugh Merit, Robert Salmon, Roger Gunston, William Wye, Thomas Malbye, William Hare.

123. [*f.49v. Before 8 July 1618*] *Peter Frobisher, heir to, and executor of, Sir Martin Frobisher, to the king* [See **124**.]
Because of the dangerous entrance to the river Humber, where there is continual loss of ships, men and merchandise, the Trinity House of Hull asked Sir Martin Frobisher to obtain from the late queen a grant for the erection of a watchhouse at Ravenspur or Kilnsea. Sir Martin died before it was fully effected. The petitioner, being asked to do so, is willing to forward so charitable a work which will benefit the king's subjects and strangers trading to northern parts, who are now cast away for want of a light. Subject to a certificate from the principal masters and owners trading to those parts concerning the need for a light, and the approval of the lord high admiral, he seeks letters patent for a watchlight at Ravenspur or Kilnsea. He would pay an annual rent of £6 13s 4d to the exchequer and seeks an imposition on shipping which is similar to that for the lights at Dungeness and Winterton.

124. *8 July 1618. Court at Windsor. [Sir] Sidney Montagu [master of requests] to Trinity House*
Order to consider the petition [**123**].
[Marginal note] The answer to this is at folio 53 [sic, see **135**].

125. *1 Aug. 1618. Ratcliff. Trinity House of Deptford to the Trinity House of Hull*
The king has asked for their opinion on the petition [**123–4**]. Since Frobisher alleges that the Trinity House of Hull proposed and approve the project, the opinion of that House is requested.

126. [f.50. *? Aug. 1618*] *Trinity House to the king* [*See* **127.**]
In 36 Elizabeth letters patent were granted to Trinity House conferring upon them, among other things, the office of lastage* and ballastage of all ships entering or leaving the Thames or elsewhere between London Bridge and the main sea [C 66/1410, mm.11–12]. The king is asked to confirm the grant. They use the revenue to support 200 poor, aged and distressed seamen, their wives and children.

127. *Aug. 1618. Statement [by Trinity House]*
The poor, aged, impotent, lame and distressed men, women and children supported monthly by Trinity House are as follows:

	Pensioners	£	s	d
London, St Katherine's, etc.	25	1	10	6
Wapping	16		16	0
Rotherhithe	15		15	0
Ratcliff	33	3	1	6
Limehouse	24	2	0	0
Poplar	15		15	0
Deptford	7	3	10	6
Rochester	12	1	4	0
Leigh	13	2	10	0
	160	16	2	6

This amounts to £209 12s 6d a year [i.e. 13 four week periods]. In addition, between £50 and £70 is given annually to English, French, and Dutchmen who have suffered shipwreck and to many more poor, lame and impotent men, women and fatherless children.

128. [f.50v. *After 19 Aug. 1618*] *Trinity House to the king*
In reply to **124**, they have consulted the Trinity House of Hull whose answer they have received [**135**]. Both Houses consider the proposal for a light at Ravenspur is impossible, while a light at Kilnsea, 3 or 4 miles away, would be dangerous for shipping, the reasons for which can be given if desired. If nevertheless the king decides that a light shall be erected, the allowances for the 2 earlier lights [at Dungeness and Winterton] would suffice for it and for many more lights, if needed.

129. [*Before 22 Sept. 1618*] *Trinity House to the king* [*See* **130.**]
Since doubts have been expressed concerning the wording of the letters
patent of 36 Elizabeth [C 66/1410, mm.11–12], and others may thereby be
enabled to provide beacons, buoys and landmarks, thus imperilling
navigation, the king is asked to confirm the letters patent and, subject to
the advice of counsel, to add a prohibition against others exercising these
rights.

130. *22 Sept. 1618. Court at Whitehall.* [*Sir*] *Lionel Cranfield* [*master of
the great wardrobe*] *to the lords commissioners of the treasury*
Order to consider the petition [**129**]. If they find it fitting for the grant to
be made, the king's solicitor is to prepare a grant for the king's signature.

131. [f.51] *10 Oct. 1618. Trinity House* [*to chancery*]
In accordance with the chancery order of 12 June last, they summoned
both parties and are of opinion that £23 10s is due to the widow Lawson.
They are informed that John Kinge, half-owner of the ship, has already
paid half, and John Harvye, a quarter-owner, should pay a quarter. The
other quarter-owner died in the time of the voyage, leaving as executor a
brother who is also dead. A third brother then became owner 'by
executorship' long after the end of the voyage. Whether he is liable for a
quarter is for the court to decide.
Thomas Best, master; Roger Gunston, Walter Whyting, Thomas Love,
wardens; Richard Chester, Thomas Mylton, Matthew Woodcot, Robert
Rickman, Robert Bradsho, William Ivey, assistants.

132. [f.51v] *11 Nov. 1618. Certificate by Trinity House*
At the request of the bearers, the bailiffs, burgesses and citizens of
Dunwich, Southwold and Walberswick in Suffolk, they certify that the
haven belonging to those towns is much decayed and unless action is
taken will be 'darved up' and become irrecoverable to the ruin of the
inhabitants and to the prejudice of the shipping and seamen of the
kingdom.
Thomas Best, Thomas Love, Roger Gunston, Walter Whyting, Thomas
Milton, Matthew Woodcot, William Hare, Nicholas Diggins, Robert
Rickman, Richard Chester, Robert Salmon, Robert Bradsho.

133. [f.52] *16 Oct. 1618. Order of the privy council concerning the
surveyor of coals* [Printed in *APC 1617–19*, 276.]

134. *16 Oct. 1618. Order of the privy council concerning Winterton
lighthouses* [Printed in *APC 1617–19*, 275–6.]

135. [f.52v. *19 x 31 Aug. 1618*] *Trinity House of Hull to Trinity House of
Deptford*
Their letter of 1 Aug. [**125**] was received on the 18th. It is true that 26 or
27 years ago their predecessors (none of whom is now alive) petitioned
Sir Martin Frobisher to secure the queen's permission to build a
lighthouse at Ravenspur. 'Kelsey' by 'which we rather suppose is meant

. . . Kilnsey' [Kilnsea] was not, however, mentioned in the petition, nor is it, or any other place near the river Humber, fitting for a lighthouse, apart from Ravenspur. At the time of the petition, Ravenspur was on very firm ground and was a good site, containing as it did at least 300 acres of dry ground. But, contrary to the expectations of their predecessors and of themselves, it is now utterly worn away and surrounded [by water]. Although their predecessors meant well in trying to provide a lighthouse, the imposition would have been an intolerable burden; 6d per 20 chaldrons would have been quite enough. Year by year, they have seen the ruin of Ravenspur and have not moved the petitioner, Mr Frobisher. Although he has shown them today proposals for a light which are signed by a number of neighbours and younger brethren of the guild among others, those who have put their hands to it were ill advised to do so and the reasons quoted were insufficient and tend more to the procuring of shipwreck than preventing it.

John Preston, mayor; Thomas Ferres, John Woodmansey, wardens; William Smorthwaite, Cuthbert Thompson, John Brighouse, Andrew Rakes, George Carlill, elder brethren; Thomas Woodmansey, Martin Jefferson, John Helmster, Robert Raykes, assistants.

P.S. Six days before receipt of the letter they sent to Ravenspur and places nearby, intending to set up a beacon, but could not find a site where one would have stood for 2 months.

136. [f.53. As in **21**, with slight variations.]

137. *1 Feb. 1619. Ratcliff. Letter from Trinity House [to an unidentified addressee. See **159**, **165**.]*
In reply to his letter, they have considered whether the wines of Malaga are the growth of Spain or of the Levant, and have concluded that they are of the growth of Spain for the following reasons: (a) Malmsey, muscadel and other sweet wines mentioned in the statute or letters patent [see **21**], whence the question arises, used to be brought to this kingdom in shipping of Ragusa and Venice, and came from Candy and from nowhere else. The Isle of Candy and the many islands thereabouts are said to be in the Levant (that is, in the east) because this is the furthermost part of the Mediterranean. (b) Ships of Ragusa and Venice were never known to bring wines of Malaga or of Spain to this land. (c) Spanish wines were never understood to be of the Levant but of the Ponent, which is of the west comparatively.

[Signed] T. Best, Michael Geere, Roger Gunston, Walter Whiting, Thomas Love, R. C. [? Richard Chester], Robert Rickman, Hugh Meret, Robert Bradsho, Matthew Woodcott, William Ivey, John Moore.

[Note] Mr Munsey had a copy of this certificate on 8 July 1628, with the seal of the House affixed. [Marginal note] Sr [? Signor] Fogrivell.

138. [f.53v] *24 March 1619. [? Trinity House] to Sir Henry Marten, admiralty court judge*
According to his direction they have inspected the wharf recently built by

ships at the Customs House, either on departure or return, whichever seems best to the privy council, would yield £2,000 a year:

Destination	Rate per ton	Yield £
East Indies:	4s	200
Within the Straits from Cape Gata eastwards:	2s	400
Within the Straits from Cape Gata westwards, the Straits mouth southwards (vizt. Barbary, Guinea, Benin, the Canaries, Madeira, and the Azores); the Straits mouth northwards to Cape Finisterre:	1s	500
Biscay, France, Flanders, Holland, Friesland, Hamburg, Danzig, Melvin, Norway, Russia, Greenland, and other northerly parts:	6d	700
Ships trading to Newcastle discharging at London will be rated at 1s per 20 chaldrons of coal:		250
		2,050

These estimates are based on trade in 1616.

141. [f.55] *14 Apr. 1619. Certificate by Trinity House*
At the request of Matthew Angell of Wapping and his neighbours, they certify that he was always reputed honest and of good estate. He was part-owner of a number of ships but within 7 or 8 years he has lost over £1,300 owing to losses caused by foul weather and the depredations of pirates and sea rovers. He is now aged, sick and impotent in his limbs, and unable to support himself or repay his debts without charitable relief.
Thomas Best, Thomas Love, Michael Geere, Roger Gunston, Walter Whiting, Richard Chester, Thomas Milton, William Hare, Robert Bradsho, Matthew Woodcot, John Moore.

142. [*? Before 1624*][1] *Report*
Reasons against the office for the survey of cordage: (a) If the cordage is made overseas, the surveyor will be able to judge only by outward appearances, but the quality of rope can no more be judged by the appearance of the cordage ends than cloth can be by the muster [i.e. by a specimen]. (b) Men of judgement can tell by sight the quality of workmanship but they cannot assess the kind of hemp. Consequently the seal will only delude and abuse, and will not profit, much less better, the commodity. (c) If the cordage is made here at home, every man can have whatever quality he likes and avoid abuse, provided he acts as his own surveyor. (d) Shipowners and masters who buy cordage have most concern to prevent abuse because their credit, their goods, and indeed their lives and those of their crews will depend upon it. Each must be his own surveyor, not relying on the judgement of others, and freed from unnecessary charge for the seal. (e) That shipowners and masters and the

workmen whom they employ are the best judges cannot be denied. (f) If an owner or master is deceived once, he gains advantage because he will be armed against similar abuses; according to a sea proverb, 'no man knows that sand so well as he that hath lost his ship upon it'.

These reasons satisfied the council, and it was their decree [untraced] and not the death of Mr Knowles which in those days ended the ridiculous suit. [f.55v] If these reasons are not accepted, the writers will prove their case on being shown the arguments used in the petition. The same reasons can be used against similar offices for apparel, meat and drink.

> 1. In 1594 Henry Bellingham had been granted an office for the survey of cordage for 15 years (*CSPD 1591–4*, 557). **142** probably relates to an attempt to revive the office, prior to the statute of 1624 against monopolies.

143. [*? Early 1619*] *A report on 'the greater ship of 6 or 700 tons'*[1]
Mr Burrell is to build 2 new ships for the king, one being 103 ft long and 34 ft broad within planks; the other being 93 ft long and 31 ft broad within planks. In the case of the greater ship, those whose names are underwritten [not entered] consider that the middle orlop* should be laid 5 ft from the lower orlop; that the distance from plank to plank between the second and third orlop should be 7 ft and that the sills of the lower ports should be 5 ft above water when the ship is laden. In the case of the lesser ship with 3 orlops, the distance between the 2 lower orlops should be $4\frac{1}{2}$ ft from plank to plank; the upper orlop should be $6\frac{1}{2}$ ft from the middle orlop; and the sills of the lower ports should be $4\frac{1}{2}$ ft above water when the ship is laden.

> 1. Burrell built 10 ships between 1619 and 1623. Probably this relates to the first 2—the *Happy Entrance* and *Constant Reformation*. The dimensions are not those given in Anderson (p. 18), but the measurements of ships as given in official documents at this period vary.

144. [f.56. *15 x 22 May 1619*][1] *Sir John Killigrewe to the king*
A light at the Lizard in Cornwall has often been sought because it is the most dangerous point for ships in the kingdom, and shipwrecks occur there 'upon the least distemper of weather'. His dwelling and estate are near the Lizard, and he could conveniently erect and maintain a light there which he is most willing to do, not so much from hope of gain, but because he has daily experience of the dangers to men there. He seeks letters patent for a term of 30 years, with powers to erect and maintain a tower to give direction and light, at his own expense. He will not ask any 'passenger' to contribute more than he is willing to pay, provided that there is a ban on other lights and seamarks nearby during the term of the patent and he will pay an annual rent of 20 nobles to the exchequer.

> 1. In draft on 15 May 1619 (SP 14/109/42); earlier than **145**.

145. *22 May 1619. Court at Greenwich. 'Char'* [? *Sir Christopher*] *Parkins to Trinity House*
Request for an opinion on the petition [**144**] by 3 or more of them. They are to certify the area within which other seamarks should be banned during the term of 21 or 31 years.

146. [*After 22 May 1619*] *Trinity House to the king*
In answer to **144–5**, the sea there is about 100 miles wide from coast to coast. The channel is fair, the depth good, and the coast bold. From this it is concluded that no light is necessary. Indeed it would be dangerous because it would pilot pirates and foreign enemies to safe landing places.

147. [f.56v. *? After 11 March 1619*][1] *Owners and masters of ships trading to Newcastle for coal, and all other ships trading to the north, to Trinity House*
For long they have employed Mr Dalton and Mr Cocke with others to find a remedy for the imposition of 1d a ton for the lights at Winterton Ness. They hoped to persuade either the privy council to make the patent void, or the patentees to end it in return for paying the imposition only for about a year or 2. Otherwise they must be forced to cease trading. Dalton and Cocke have concluded nothing with the privy council or the patentees. In view of the concern of Trinity House for navigation, the petitioners ask them to settle the business, either by composition with the patentees or otherwise. Any agreement will be accepted, and payments agreed or charges incurred by Trinity House will be met by continuing the levy of 1d a ton on every voyage at Customs House, either at Newcastle or London, until the money is raised. Thereafter they are willing to pay to Trinity House 6d per 20 chaldrons of coal, and on other ships trading to the north according to the first agreement, for so long as the lights are maintained.

1. On 11 March 1619 'the 2 coastmen, Edward Dalton and William Cock' were given 10 days to conclude a composition for the coastmen (BL, Lansdowne MS 162, f.247).

148. [f.56 *bis*] *23 June 1619. Ratcliff. Trinity House* [*to ? the admiralty court*]
According to an order of 7 May last they have considered the suit pending between William Appleby and Jeremy Swanley, late master of the *Elsabeth Consort* of London. They have interviewed men who served in the ship, and all affirm that Appleby left the ship at Algiers voluntarily, without being given cause to do so by Swanley. Thomas Symons, merchant, who travelled from England to Algiers in the ship deposed likewise and that (a) at the request of Swanley, first he tried to persuade Appleby to rejoin and then, with James Frissell, merchant, he induced the king's janissary to search the town for Appleby in order to bring him back by force, but Appleby 'kept himself private' and could not be found; (b) if Appleby had not intended to serve with Turkish pirates, as afterwards he did, but to return to England, he could have done so in the *Josua* of London, Joshua Downing master, which arrived at Algiers 2 days after Swanley's departure; (c) Symons remained at Algiers for 4 months after Swanley's departure, saw Appleby, and knew that he went to sea with Turkish pirates against christians. Thomas Nash, who also went on the voyage, has sworn that Appleby induced him to desert the ship, and that the janissary whom Swanley hired to search for him and others forced him to return; that otherwise Nash would have stayed like Appleby; and that he, Appleby, and 3 others who left the ship did so

wilfully without being given cause to do so. Thus it appears that Appleby forsook the ship without cause, and that he deserves no wages, but rather punishment for it is a custom of the sea that he who 'wilfully runneth from a ship in the time of his voyage runneth also from his wages'.
Thomas Best, Thomas Love, Walter Whiting, Roger Gunston, Nicholas Diggens.

149. [*f.56v bis*] *8 July 1619. From aboard the Bull in the Downs. Robert Adams [to an unidentified addressee]*
Since his departure from London, he fears that some ill office has been done to him at Trinity House: first because he did not take his leave but his business was more important than leave taking; and secondly because it is said that he revealed the business of the House to his son and daughter and to the scrivener who prepared his letter of attorney to Capt. Moore, which he denies. All this comes from Mr Kayles' procurement because he had left Kayles' bond with the addressee. The addressee is entreated to be his friend in this business. He sent from Gravesend 22s to the master of Trinity House so that the company could together drink a cup of wine to his farewell, but the money was refused. He prays the addressee to speak to Mr Samon [? Robert Salmon] for he is as innocent as an unborn child.

150. *12 Jan. 1620. Certificate by Trinity House*
Commendation of certificates [**151–2**] for Edward Crosse, mariner of Ratcliff in the parish of Stepney.

151. [*f.57*] *7 Dec. 1619. Certificate by Robert Bornne and others*
On or about 6 Jan. 1617, Edward Crosse, mariner of Stepney, lost at sea a hoy of about 50 tons, and on 22 Nov. last, one of about 55 tons with her cargo of timber. They are also informed that he lost £250 because of robberies at home. He can no longer support his wife and children.
Robert Bornne, John Greaves, Peter Pett, Andrew Small, John Dearsly, Edward Stevens, William Cob, Thomas Cob, John Lambert, Peter Marsh, Richard West, Edward Chandler.

152. [*Before 12 Jan. 1620*] *Certificate by the inhabitants of the parish of St James in the Isle of Grain, Kent [See* **150**.]
On 6 Jan. 1617, in a great storm with the wind at northeast, a hoy of Crosse, mariner of Wapping, was cast away at the Isle of Grain. Part of the hoy can still be seen.
James Thurston, Matthew Sparke, Thomas Godfrey, Thomas Haines, Henry Paine, John Yeomans, Robert Alyne, Edward Godfrey.

153. [*f.57v*] *16 Dec. 1619. Certificate by William Monson, Thomas Howard, and James Chester*
Capt. Reynold Whitfield, gentleman, now a prisoner in the hole of the Poultry Counter, has asked them to certify his services in the wars of the late queen and also the misery into which he has fallen owing to losses at sea since 'his majesty's happy reign' so that he is unable to bear himself as

a gentleman and satisfy his creditors. In 1589, he served in the queen's *Victory*, and in 1591, in the queen's *Garland* under the command of the earl of Cumberland. On the *Garland's* voyage, being sent home in a prize taken from the enemy, he was surprised by a fleet of galleys and taken to Spain where he remained prisoner for 2 years. In 1595, he served with Sir Francis Drake in the West Indies, and in 1596, was in the action of Cadiz. He served in the queen's *Lyon* in 1597, and was engaged in other actions. In 1598, after some casual losses, his ship the *Milkenap* (200 tons), valued with her freight at £1,200, was stolen by one Norice of Wapping and others and never recovered, although Norice and others were apprehended and some were executed. By which loss he was unable to satisfy his creditors, especially John Man and others, at whose suit he is held prisoner for a debt of £500 incurred for the stolen ship.

154. *19 Jan. 1620. Certificate by Trinity House*
Confirmation of the certificate [**153**] except for the valuation.
Thomas Best, John Moore, Thomas Love, Roger Gounston, Walter Whiting.

155. [f.58] *12 Feb. 1620. Trinity House to the justices of assizes of Kent*
On 10 July 1617 and 5 July 1619, the great inquest of the assizes at Maidstone in Kent presented that divers persons had been drowned because of defects in the common way over a creek between the parish of Stoke and the Isle of Grain. Trinity House certify that the bridge and way, when finished, will be very beneficial and will save lives, especially those of poor fishermen who, because of the bridge, will have a nearer way and will thereby escape many dangers.
Henry Rawline, Thomas Best, Walter Whiting, Hugh Merret, Michael Geere, John Moore, Robert Salmon, Nicholas Diggens, Thomas Milton, Roger Gunston, Matthew Woodcot, John Skinner, Rowland Coitmore, Robert Rickman.

156. *12 Feb. 1620. Report [by Trinity House]*
Their opinion was sought concerning the erection of dwelling houses for seamen at Blackwall, west of the landing place on the ground of Mr Burrell next to the Thames, and whether it would be prejudicial to the river. They consider that the site is suitable in view of the nearness of the east India works and the number of ships lying there. The river will not be prejudiced and the inhabitants will be a safeguard in the event of fires, storms, etc.
Thomas Best, Michael Geere, John Moore, Thomas Milton, Roger Gounston, Walter Whiting, Robert Rickman, William Bower, Rowland Coytmore, Nicholas Diggens, Hugh Merrit.

157. [f.58v] *11 March 1620. Ratcliff. Trinity House to the marquis of Buckingham, lord high admiral*
Robert Bourne, shipwright of Wapping, wishes to enlarge his wharf or building place for ships at Wapping by extending it 14 or 15 feet further into the Thames, as others of his profession have done, because ships are

now built of greater burden and length than formerly. To obtain a licence sooner he has asked for this certificate. Trinity House certify that the extension will not harm the Thames but will be useful for the building and enlarging of ships 'so as the said wharf be brought straight from Hedgors' wharf, being the wharf to the westwards, to the end of his own wharf to the eastwards'.

Henry Rawlin, master; Thomas Best, Thomas Love, Roger Gounston, Richard Chester, John Moore, Robert Bradsho, Michael Geere, Nicholas Diggens.

158. *19 March 1620. Certificate by Trinity House*
They have been asked by James Carter, mariner of Plymouth, and others to certify that he was master of the *John* of London (about 60 tons) bound from Kinsale in Ireland to Cadiz and Malaga in Spain when the ship was surprised by Turks and Moors on 17 Sept. last. He and all his crew, numbering 8, were taken to Arcila in Barbary, enslaved, sold 5 times, and cruelly misused. Carter lost his adventure of £140 in goods and merchandise. His release was secured by a Jew, and he was sent home to obtain ransom for himself and 5 others who are held in great misery at Tetuán in Barbary. The ransom of 800 rials a man, equivalent to a total of £420 for all of them, would make his total loss £560, which he will never be able to raise without help.

Thomas Best, Thomas Love, Nicholas Diggens, Michael Geere, Walter Whyting, Robert Rickman, Thomas Milton, Roger Gunston, Rowland Coytmore, Matthew Woodcot.

159. [f.59] *29 March 1620. [Trinity House] to Sir Fulke Gryvell of the privy council [See **137**, **165**.]*
They have summoned shipmasters who trade to the Straits to discuss his letter and after much debate conclude that the sea within the Strait of Morocco or Gibraltar is usually called the Levant Sea, and extends to the coast of Syria, viz. Scandarowne, Tripoli, etc. They received the same by tradition from their elders and from Italians and Frenchmen trading in those seas.

Henry Rawlin, Thomas Best, Thomas Love, John Moore, Nicholas Diggens, Robert Rickman, Matthew Woodcot, Rowland Coytmore, Roger Gunston, William Ivye, Robert Bradsho.
[The shipmasters] Daniel Banister, Edmond Gardner, Peter Kempton, Thomas Braadcoke, Abel Whyting, Walter Cooke, Richard Harris, William Knight, Anthony Titchen, Samuel Doves.

160. *28 March 1620. Certificate by Trinity House*
At the request of Clement White, mariner of Weymouth in Dorset, and others they certify that he was pilot of the *Hopewell* of Rye (about 35 tons) which last September sailed from thence to Bantry in Ireland where he loaded a cargo of pilchards. Sailing from thence to Alicante in Spain, the ship was surprised by a Turkish man-of-war near the Southern Cape. He was sold to the Moors in Arcila in Barbary who took him to Tetuán, where he was kept in cruel slavery for about 2 months. English merchants

then ransomed him for £30 which he now owes and cannot repay because he lost his estate of £40 when the ship was taken. He, his wife and 6 children are likely to perish.

Henry Rawlin, Thomas Best, John Moore, Nicholas Diggens, Thomas Love, William Ivie, Thomas Milton, Robert Rickman, Rowland Coytmore, Robert Bradsho.

161. [f.59v. *? Before 5 Apr. 1620*] *Owners and masters of ships to the king* [*See* **162, 164.**]

Whereas foreign shipping is daily employed to ports of this kingdom to transport coal and to import many goods of the king's subjects, whereby English shipping and mariners are unemployed and foreigners enriched, the king is asked to order that (a) no coal of Newcastle, Sunderland or Blyth be exported in strangers' ships except from the Thames or from western parts of England and Wales except from Plymouth; (b) the king's subjects are not to import or export in foreign ships if English ships are present; (c) if no English ships are present, those who use strangers' ships must pay to the king 10s a ton on goods loaded on this side of the North Cape, £1 a ton if loaded on the south side of the North Cape, and so much more according to distance. In return the petitioners will pay to the king 4d per chaldron of coal unladen in any English port or transported in English ships, and 6d per ton on goods loaded on this side of the North Cape and unladen in any English port.

[Marginal note] Earl of Oxford.

162. [*? Before 5 Apr. 1620*] *Trinity House* [*to the earl of Oxford*]

His letter is fair and honourable but they crave pardon for not subscribing [to **161**] albeit they will not oppose the staple. They prefer not to be suitors to the king, not because English ships engaged in the coal trade will be prejudiced—rather the contrary—but because the staple will cause inconvenience to the city and the large suburbs of London; moreover Newcastle will strongly oppose it. They therefore prefer to leave the furtherance of the petition to others. If the 6d per ton mentioned in the petition were to be dropped and the levy on strangers' ships increased, the project would meet more favour and much less opposition.

[Marginal note] Earl of Oxford.

163. [f.60] *7 March 1620. Hull. Trinity House of Hull to the Trinity House of Deptford*

The merchants of this port 'take freight of Scotchmen here for wine for [sic] Bordeaux, and likewise carry goods thither outwards'. The merchants and their deputies in the East Country also freight Hollanders there with flax and iron for this port although ships of the port or other English ships are available. Unless some remedy is found, the navy of this port will be ruined. They seek advice and have asked the bearer, William Clarke, a brother of the Hull House, to obtain their answer.

William Smorthwait, Henry Chambers, wardens; John Preston, Cuthbert Thompson, Andrew Barker, Andrew Rakes, William Dobsonn,

Joel Gaskein, George Carlill, Robert Rake, Christopher Frisby, John Helmester, John Johnson.

164. *5 Apr. 1620. Ratcliff. Trinity House of Deptford to the Trinity House of Hull*
In reply to **163**, the best redress is to petition the council, which is what they themselves do on all occasions. Moreover there is a project in hand [**161–2**] which may provide relief without further trouble about which they will write if there be cause.

165. [f.60v] *13 May 1620. Ratcliff. Trinity House [to an unidentified addressee. Cf SP 14/115/29: CSPD 1619–23, 145; **137**, **159**.]*
In accordance with his command, they have considered his letter. The Mediterranean Sea begins at the Strait of Gibraltar or Morocco and extends to Malaga, Alicante, the Isles of Majorca, Minorca, Zante, Candy, Cyprus, Scandarowne, Tripoli and Alexandria, and is called the Levant Sea, and has ever been so known to navigators of those countries. Malaga lies 20 leagues within the Levant Sea, with no land between, for the Levant Sea washes the coast of Malaga, even to the walls of the town, and wines of Malaga are rolled in casks into the Levant Sea and so are embarked in English ships. This they know by experience.
Henry Rawlin, Thomas Best, Thomas Love, Walter Whiting, Hugh Merrit, John Moore, Robert Salmon, Roger Gounston, William Hare, Robert Rickman, Matthew Woodcot, John King, Rowland Coytmore.
[Marginal note] Mr Munsey had a copy of this certificate on 8 July 1628 with the seal of the House affixed.

166. *27 May 1620. Certificate by Trinity House*
At the request of Sara, wife of Matthew Clarke, mariner of Limehouse, they certify their knowledge that he was master of the *Susan* of London (about 80 tons) on a voyage to Alicante in the Straits when on 5 Jan. last he met 2 great Turkish men-of-war, each of about 300 tons and full of men and ordnance, and fought for 9 hours in the night. Some of his principal men were killed and others sore hurt before the ship was captured and taken to Algiers. Clarke lost his adventure of £50 and he and the rest of the crew were sold in the market as slaves. They were given only bread and water and lay on the ground with chains on their legs. After 4 or 5 weeks Henry Warde, an English merchant lodging there, ransomed them for about £300. Clarke is to remain prisoner there until the money is raised, and neither he nor his friends can do so without help.
Henry Rawlin, Thomas Best, Walter Whiting, Hugh Merret, Michael Geere, Thomas Milton, William Ivye, Robert Bradsho, Rowland Coytmore, Robert Rickman, William Hare, Matthew Woodcot, John Osbourne, Robert Salmon, Richard Chester, Thomas Love.

167. [f.61] *7 July 1620. Privy council to the customs officers of London about the expedition against the pirates of Algiers and Tunis* [Printed in *APC 1619–21*, 240–1.]

168. [f.61v] *7 Oct. 1620. Certificate by Trinity House*
At the request of the bearer, William Leske, mariner of Ratcliff, they certify that he served in the *Mary Margaret* of London, Stephen Bennett of Tower Wharf master, on a voyage to Greenland, but she was cast away there in 1611. He then served in the *Elsabeth* of Dover, James Poole master, but she was also cast away at Greenland. Of late he went on a voyage into the Straits in the *Will and Raphe* of London, Richard Goodlard master, but homeward bound in May coming out of the Straits, the ship and her goods were captured by Turkish pirates. He lost his year's wages, his apparel and adventure. He has a wife and 4 children, the eldest of whom has been under the surgeon for 8 years, at great expense, to the utter undoing of himself and his family.
Thomas Best, Michael Geere, Roger Gunston, Rowland Coytmore, Robert Rickman, William Ivye, Thomas Milton, Nicholas Diggens, Robert Bradsho.

169. [f.62. *? Early 1621*][1] *Trinity House to the marquis of Buckingham, lord high admiral*
He leased to them the office of ballastage [in the Thames] and presented Mr Lanyer and Mr 'Alfonso' [Ferabosco] to them as tenants. After many discourtesies, they asked to be rid of these tenants, but since Buckingham spoke for them, it was agreed to keep them. Lanyer persisting in wrongs to Trinity House, they acquitted themselves of him at Salisbury; but Buckingham spoke again for 'Alfonso', and it was agreed that he should come to them to receive his lease and pay his rent. To this day, albeit 5 months since, he has not come to them to receive his lease and is three-quarters of a year in arrears. They are unused to such dealings, and wish to be free of him and to choose their own tenants as heretofore.

> 1. Dated 7 Oct. 1621 in *CD*, vii.446, but perhaps mistakenly. Buckingham, by then lord high admiral, was at Salisbury with James I in July–Aug. 1620 (*DNB*; J. Nichols, *The progresses of James I*, iv.614; *CSPD 1619–23*, 168, 170).

170. *4 Feb. 1621. Trinity House to the same*
Whereas by 8 Elizabeth [c. 13] Trinity House were empowered to provide all necessary beacons, buoys and seamarks, others have obtained the king's licence to provide certain seamarks contrary to the statute. On counsel's advice they have preferred a bill in parliament for redress and better to explain the statute. They seek his allowance and furtherance thereof.

171. *21 Feb. 1621. Trinity House to the same*
They refer to **170** but are informed that he is incensed both against the bill and against them because they purpose to derogate part of the prerogative pertaining to his office. They hope that he will think better of them, and if the statute was intended to entrust the provision of all seamarks to the corporation, that they will have his allowances and favour therein.

172. [f.62v] *9 Apr. 1621. Instructions of Trinity House to Mr Geere and Mr Cooke*
They are to go to Lowestoft, Caister and Winterton, inspect the keeping of the lights and buoys there, and reform all defects or abuses. If the number of candles in the lanterns is insufficient, one or 2 more may be added. The channels are to be sounded, and the siting of the buoys considered and changed if necessary. A gentleman living near the lighthouse is to be appointed to oversee the keeping of the lights. The channels at Stamport are to be sounded and a new buoy laid, if necessary, with the aid of 2 or 3 of the most sufficient seamen thereabouts. At Yarmouth Messrs Greenwood, Lucas and Lad are to be called to account for duties received, and new agreements made for future collections according to custom. Geere and Cooke are given full power to confirm or replace keepers of lights and buoys, and to increase charges for wages and candles, using the advice of others in the area, as necessary. They are given £20 to cover expenses, and if further money is needed Trinity House will honour their bills of consignment.
Thomas Best, John Wattes, Robert Bradsho, John Vassall, Rowland Coytmore, Richard Chester, Thomas Malbye, William Case.

173. *11 Apr. 1621. Certificate by Trinity House*
As requested they certify that the following portage, outward and homeward, free of custom, is appropriate: (a) Ships bound for Majorca or eastwards thereof in the Straits: the master, £100 in goods; the officers, £10 in goods; the seamen, £5 in goods. (b) Ships bound for Spain, Portugal, the Islands, Barbary, Guinea, France, etc.: the master, one ton in every 100 tons; the officers, 20 nobles in goods; the seamen, 5 marks in goods. (c) Ships bound for Zeeland, Holland, all the East Country, Hamburg, Muscovy, Russia, etc., according to former custom. The mercy and goodness of the king to poor seamen would be cause of much encouragement.
Thomas Best, Rowland Coytmore, Robert Bradsho, John Vassall, Nicholas Diggins, Robert Salmon, Richard Chester, William Hare, Thomas Malbye, William Case, William Bower.

174. [f.63] *28 Apr. 1621. Certificate by Trinity House*
On 17 Nov. last, the *Long and Costly* of Ipswich, Reuben Broad, master, on a voyage from Bordeaux, laden with wine, was overset by a gust of wind between Dover and the South Foreland. Four men and one boy were drowned and the ship was lost, to the undoing of Nicholas Paynter, fisherman of Woolverstone in Suffolk, the sole owner.
Thomas Best, John Vassall, Hugh Merit, William Ivey, Robert Bradsho, Nicholas Diggins, Richard Chester, William Bower, Henry Rawlyn.

175. *2 May 1621. Trinity House [to the house of commons]*
They were required by many knights and burgesses of parliament to consider the complaint of those men and their wives who petitioned parliament against the East India company for wages during the time that the men were captives of the Hollanders, the company having lost both

ships and goods. Both sides have been heard. With regard to the law, they submit to Sir Henry Marten, admiralty judge, who 'holding himself to the general maxims' concludes that where the owner loses his ship, and the merchant his goods, there the seaman loses his wages. But in conscience the case is different since the Hollanders offered the men wages to serve against the company, and when they refused, imprisoned them, kept them in irons and short of victuals, of which some died; 'more for their king they could not have done'. The consideration thereof has already moved the company to give the men one-third of their wages for the time in question, and to promise the other two-thirds when the company had received it from the Dutch. Meanwhile the men and women are in want and a little more would be 'as a fair sunshine day after a long and foul storm'.

Thomas Best, Ro. Salmon, Jo. Vassall, Richard Chester, Thomas Milton, Ro. Bradsho, William Ivey, Rowland Coytmore, William Case, Ro. Rickman.

176. [f.63v] *Apr. 1621. Business done by Mr Geere and Mr Cooke at Winterton, Caister and Lowestoft*

At Winterton the tower lighthouse and the lower house were repaired as appears in the account [not entered]. At Caister the houses were repaired, the annual salary advanced by £6 to £30 and 2 candles to burn in each. They have discussed with Mr Brightman, a principal gentleman of that place, his being overseer of the Caister light keeper, but no agreement was made and it is left to the company's pleasure. The channel at Caister was sounded and the buoys were found to lie well. The channel at Stamport was also sounded and a buoy was laid on the middle ground, but no agreement was made 'for the looking to it'. The houses there were also repaired.

[Signed] Robert Kitchen, T. Best, Ro. Salmon, Rowland Coytmor, Robert Bradsho, John Vassall, R.C. [? Richard Chester], N. Diggens.

177. *4 June 1621. Trinity House to Mr Cooke, collector of the duties for the lights and buoys of Caister and Stamport, in the port of Lynn*

A letter of the privy council dated 1 Apr. 1613 authorised them to collect 1s per 100 tons and 4d per ship on every vessel trading on the north coast for the maintenance of lighthouses and buoys at Caister and Stamport. It is pretended that ships of Hull and Lynn trading to Newcastle, Norway, the Sound, and Hamburg, and from those ports, take no benefit from the lights and buoys. He is therefore no longer to demand money of those ships, but for all other ships, including those of fishermen, he is to receive it as formerly.

Thomas Best, master; John Vassall, Robert Bradsho, Thomas Malby, Robert Kitchen, assistants; Michael Geere, Rowland Coytmore, William Case, Walter Cooke, wardens.

[Note at end] On the same day a similar letter was sent to Mr Andrew Barker, collector at Hull, and another to Mr Leonard Carr, collector at Newcastle, subscribed by William Ivey, Robert Salmon and Robert Kitchen [sic], besides those above.

178. [f.64] *26 May 1621. Doctors' Commons. [Sir] Henry Marten [admiralty court judge] to Trinity House*
By a clause in their charter, no seaman can be master or pilot of a ship entering or leaving the Thames, unless examined by Trinity House and having a sealed certificate listing the countries, coasts, and places for which he is qualified and also the approval of the lord admiral under the seal of the admiralty court upon pain of forfeiture of £20 for each offence. Nevertheless, he hears of many insufficient men but no man comes from Trinity House to perform the clause. Trinity House are to ensure that the provisions of the clause are observed and will otherwise be answerable.

179. [*? Apr. x Sept. 1621*][1] *Trinity House to the privy council*
Whereas Trinity House were authorised to collect £1,000 a year in the Customs House according to rates mentioned in a letter of 7 July 1620 from the privy council to the Customs House towards the cost of the ships against the Turkish pirates, the rates have been paid willingly, except by Mr Ralph Freeman, a merchant of London, who has farmed the killing of whales in Greenland and on those northern coasts. He has set forth 8 ships and owes £8 or £9, saying that he will answer to the privy council. The privy council are asked to enforce payment, lest others follow his example.

> 1. According to Purchas, Freeman despatched 7 ships in 1620, 8 in 1621, and 9 (but 8 according to Scott) in 1622 (one ship in 1621 and 1622 was for discovery). Whalers normally left in Apr. and returned in Aug. (S. Purchas, *His pilgrimes* (1905–7 ed.), xiii. 24–5; Scott, ii. 69).

180. *13 June 1621. [Trinity House] to Mr Leonard Carr at Newcastle*
In reply to his letter of 4 June, exemption has been granted to ships of Hull and Lynn trading as stated in the enclosed letter [**177**] and to all ports north of Winterton, since if no benefit is obtained, payment should not be enforced. The levy of 3s 4d stands because there is a special order for it. [Signed] Thomas Best, Rowland Coytmor, Michael Geere, William Case.

181. [f.64v. *? 18 x 24 Apr. 1621. Notes about Winterton Ness and Dungeness lighthouses*][1]
An act for explaining and enlarging the statute 8 Elizabeth [c. 13] concerning seamarks. The grant by patent to Mr [sic] Meldrum and others for the erection of a lighthouse at Winterton Ness, with power to put down a lighthouse formerly erected by Trinity House, with fees, condemned as a grievance. The grant by patent for a lighthouse at Dungeness, with fees, condemned as a grievance.

> 1. Parliament condemned both patents on 18 Apr. 1621 and a bill was delivered to the Commons on 24 Apr. (*CD*, iv. 233–5, 249).

182. [*Before 1 Aug. 1621*] *A note of the losses of John Linkes, mariner of Limehouse* [*See* **183**.]
(a) In 1593, coming from Newfoundland as purser of the *Thomas and John*, he was captured by French men-of-war and lost £175. (b) In the last

year of Elizabeth's reign, having been master of the *Guift* on a voyage to Barbary, he sold the ship there and was coming home as passenger in the *Unitie*, Arthur Pitt master, when she was captured by Dunkirkers at the South Sand Head, losing thereby 557 Barbary ducats in cash besides other commodities, apparel and sea instruments, valued in all at £315. (c) In 1610 he was master and part-owner of the *Mary Anne Blanch* on a voyage to Barbary where having landed linen cloth worth £60, he was hired to serve Mulie Zedan, a king in Barbary, at £28 a month; he served for 4 months, but the king violently retained the cloth and refused to pay him his wages, whereby he lost £100. (d) In 1613 he was master and sole owner of the *Felix* bound for Barbary when, in a storm, he lost 2 of his men and had to throw overboard some of the lading, cables, anchors, tackle, boat and the capstan: the masts were broken and most of the sails lost; he had to put back to Plymouth and was forced to sell the bark, whereby he lost over £120. (e) In November last he was pilot of the *Elizabeth* bound for Malaga when he was taken by a French man-of-war about 30 leagues off the rock of Lisbon, losing over £85 in goods, apparel and sea instruments, which was all he had.

183. *1 Aug. 1621. Certificate by Trinity House*
Commendation of Linkes [see **182**]. Some of the losses are known to all, the rest to many of the writers. His losses are valued at £795. He has an aged wife.
Thomas Best, Michael Geere, Rowland Coytmore, William Case, Walter Cooke, John Vassall, William Hare, Nicholas Diggins, William Ivey, Ro. Salmon, Robert Bradsho, Thomas Malby, John Osborne.

184. [f.65] *8 Sept. 1621. Ratcliff. Report by Trinity House*
At the request of Mr Bourne, they yesterday viewed his new but unfinished wharf at Wapping and found that he had exceeded the certificate [**157**] which they had given on his behalf to the lord admiral. The certificate was for only 14 or 15 ft, but he has carried it 25 or 26 ft further than his old wharf, so that it is some inconvenience to the river but in no way hurtful to the Bridge or the city.
Thomas Best, Robert Salmon, Rowland Coytmore, Walter Cooke, Walter Whyting, William Case, Michael Geere.

185. *12 Sept. 1621. Certificate by Trinity House*
By request they certify that Robert Ewens, mariner of Limehouse, deceased, was honest and of good estate, but sustained losses at sea. (a) About 4 years ago, he was part-owner of the *Thomas* of London, Edward Robertes master; he loaded her with 1,000 pipe-staves* in Ireland for Spain, for his own adventure, but the ship was chased by Turkish pirates and to escape the master had to run her aground, whereby Ewens lost over £30. (b) About 3 years ago, he was master and three-quarters part-owner of the *John* of London; he freighted her himself in Ireland with pilchards and other goods for Cadiz but, within 50 leagues of the North Cape, he was forced by foul weather to turn back to England but could not reach there; the ship was badly damaged, some of the goods

were thrown overboard, and the rest sold for very little, whereby he lost over £100. (c) About 2 years ago, having fitted out the ship again and being taken ill in Ireland, he appointed as master, James Carter, who loaded her with pilchards, pipe-staves, candles, tallow etc., but on a voyage to Cadiz and Malaga she was taken by Turks and Moors on 17 Sept. 1619 and carried to Arcila in Barbary where 2 of Ewens' servants are still in captivity; Ewens thereby lost over £250. These losses amounting to £380 and falling one after another nearly ruined him. He had £200 with him in Ireland when he died, which was the greatest part of what he had left. His brother, Roger Ewens, to whom the £200 was entrusted, died soon afterwards and the money was embezzled by strangers, leaving nothing for his widow, Grace, or his son, Thomas.

Thomas Best, Michael Geere, Rowland Coytmore, Walter Cooke, John Vassall, Ro. Salmon, William Ivey, Walter Whyting.

186. [f.65v] *15 Sept. 1621. Certificate by Trinity House*
At the request of Thomas Hammon, blacksmith, and William Hammon, tailor of Gravesend, Trinity House certify that their brother, Henry Hammon, mariner late of Gravesend, was on the *Long Robert* of London on a voyage to the Straits about 5 years ago when the ship was taken by Turkish pirates. He and others were carried to Tunis in Barbary where he is credibly reported to have been held ever since, in great misery. His ransom is set at £80 which the poor young man and his friends cannot raise.

Thomas Best, master; Michael Geere, Walter Cooke, Rowland Coytmore, William Case, John Vassall, Henry Rawlyn, Robert Rickman.

[Note] This certificate was granted upon the report of William Bigs, merchant of London, Peter Rowe of 'Milbrooke' [? Millbrook, Cornwall], and Thomas Griffen of Ratcliff that Henry Hammon was taken as stated and that he was known to be alive in captivity 3 months ago.

[Note] Mr Biges avowed before the company that about 3 months ago, he was credibly informed by Thomas Prator, who was taken with Hammon and who, when at Algiers, was released by Sir Robert Mansell [commander of the Algiers Expedition, 1620–1] that at the time of his release he was certainly informed that Hammon was alive and captive in Tunis. Peter Rowe and Thomas Griffen, who were recently captured by ships in which Hammon was forced to serve but lately ransomed, affirmed that he was alive at Tunis 4 or 5 months ago.

187. [f.66] *24 June 1619. The king to the privy council about illegal exports of ordnance*
Summary of **464** (order no. 11) with a certificate attested by George Hooker.

188. *June 1621. Propositions to the privy council concerning ordnance*
[*Cf* SP 14/121/139; *CSPD 1619–23*, 269.]
[Order no.] 13. Merchants who buy new ordnance for any new ship

shall obtain a certificate from Trinity House to the lord admiral of the burden of the ship, the number of her decks, and the ordnance requisite for her defence. The approval of the lord admiral shall be conveyed to the master of the ordnance who will cause it to be registered at the ordnance office. Bonds are to be taken there from the merchant, owner and master of the ship that the ordnance is only for her defence. The ordnance is to be entered at the Customs House and at the end of each voyage, or once a year, testimony is to be brought that the ordnance remains in the ship. Bonds are to be changed when the merchant, owner or master changes.

189. [f.66v] *16 Nov. 1621. Philpot Lane [London]. Navy commissioners to Trinity House*
The king has ordered the repair of the chain at Upnor or the devising of some other means to prevent all passages by night up the Medway, for the safety of the navy. Mr Burrell, who was required to consider the matter, has prepared a plan for a barricado which has been viewed by the 'lords' and others of experience. It is a matter of great consequence. They should confer with Mr Burrell about the proportions of the moorings, the distances of the passages in the barricado, and any other proposals to support or strengthen it. A written report is requested for the commissioners to consider at their next meeting.
[Sir] Thomas Smithe, [Sir] John Wolstenholme, J. Osborne, J. Cooke, W. Burrell.

190. *21 Nov. 1621. Ratcliff. Trinity House [to the navy commissioners]*
In reply to **189,** after much debate with Mr Burrell they conclude that his proposals for a barricado to protect the navy royal at Chatham in the Medway cannot be bettered, provided that he can do what he says, namely 'to pile and borne up both ends of the same barricado from the ends of it to the firm land on both sides' so that not even a wherry can pass. The barricado must be so fastened at both ends that no current, extraordinary tide, frost, or ice will displace it. Some 90 or 100 ft is sufficient for the passage. The channel in the barricado should be capable of being enlarged in case of need for the speedy passage of the king's ships. The cables underwater from ship to ship should be 15 inches. Of the 2 cables on the barricado, the ebb cable should be 12 inches and the flood cable 14 inches. Four of the 16 mooring cables should be 14 inches, and the rest 12 inches. Four of the anchors should be 20 cwt., and the remainder 14 cwt. The 2 ships at the sides of the channels should be cut down to 2 decks and have no masts, heads, or galleries. A crew of 6 or 8, 2 of whom should be gunners, will be needed in each ship. They should be changed monthly, and each ship will need a small boat 'to attend the business'. All strangers should be prevented from entering the Medway, at least from Rochester, to guard against treachery. Strangers' knowledge of the river will be forgotten within 7 years. At present it is as well known to them 'as to us'.
Thomas Best, Michael Geere, Rowland Coytmore, William Case, Walter Cooke, John Vassall, Robert Salmon, Nicholas Diggens, William Ivye, Thomas Malbey, William Becke.

191. [f.67] *28 Nov. 1621. London. [Navy commissioners] to Trinity House*

The lord admiral has informed them that John Dove of Leith in Scotland has recently built a ship called the *Mayflower* of Leith (300 tons). Dove has asked the king to buy the ship, affirming that she was built as a man-of-war and that her strength and goodness at sailing is inferior to no other ship in the kingdom. The king has ordered the writers to have her viewed and measured. Trinity House are asked to perform this task and to state in writing what ordnance she can carry, how much she is worth, and whether she should be bought for the king's service. The ship is now in the Thames, near Shadwell.

[Sir] Thomas Smithe, [Sir] John Wolstenholme, J. Osborne, Francis Goston, Richard Sutton, W. Burrell.

192. *28 Nov. 1621. Ratcliff. Trinity House [to the navy commissioners]*

In reply to **191**, they have been aboard and viewed the ship: length upon the orlop*, 91 ft; breadth upon the orlop from outside to outside, 25 ft; depth in hold, 9 ft 9 or 10 inches; her bow and quarter are not great and her side is flat. They conclude that she will be tendersided [heel too easily] and is insufficiently stiff or stout to be a man-of-war, much less a prince's ship. Her burden is some 220 tons. She is unfit for the king's service.

Thomas Best, Robert Salmon, Michael Geere, Rowland Coytmore, Walter Cooke, William Case.

193. [f.67v] *13 Dec. 1621. Trinity House to the privy council [Cf APC 1621–3, 110.]*

They report an abuse to the king, the state and navigation: within the last 3 or 4 months, 8 or 10 Dutch ships, each of about 200 tons [260 tons (in *APC*)], pretended to have been bought in Holland, have been brought into the Thames. The ships are fathered partly by free denizens, partly by natives, and are employed by them for Spain. Not one brings any ordnance, but as soon as a ship arrives a certificate is brought to Trinity House saying that the ship is in the Thames or some other port, and praying a certificate to the lord admiral for ordnance, some for 20 pieces, some for 16, more or less. Thus the ships are supplied with ordnance and are operated by strangers, directly or indirectly, whether by themselves or for others beyond the seas is unknown. Shipping is neglected and few mariners are employed because they require fewer men than English shipping. Ordnance is 'exposed to the pleasure of the stranger', whether denizen or not is unknown.

194. [c. Dec. 1621] *Trinity House to the privy council* [A repetition of **193** but with a request that Trinity House be instructed to issue no ordnance certificates for strangers' ships built abroad.]

195. [f.68] *29 Dec. 1621. Certificate by Trinity House*

At the request of the bearer, Richard Knott, mariner of St Katherine's near the Tower of London, they certify from the knowledge of some of them and by testimony of some shipmasters and seamen of the Thames that he is a well qualified seaman who has done good service. (a) He was master's mate of the *John and Fraunces* of London, Edmond Bostocke master, when on 13 May 1616 on a voyage from Bilbao she foundered 20 leagues off the coast of Biscay; he, with the rest of the crew, saved only his life, and spent 3 days in a boat before reaching shore; his loss was over £60. (b) He was master of the *Content* of London coming home from San Sebastian when on 4 Apr. last she foundered about 22 leagues from Belle Ile; he and the crew were saved by a small bark of Fowey but he lost over £70 in clothes, instruments and his adventure. (c) He was master of the *Faulcon* of London bound for Ayamonte when on 22 Oct. last he was taken, off the coast of Portugal, by 2 Turkish pirates who took all the means he then had in the ship worth over £130, and unmercifully beat him to make him confess what was in the ship; the ship being robbed even of tackle, apparel, and furniture was forced ashore by a storm and, striking the Manacle rocks near the Lizard, sank, he losing thereby his whole estate amounting to over £260, besides the loss of his time. Being disabled by the cruelty of the infidel and unfit to pursue his profession, he, his wife and 2 small children are exposed to perpetual misery without charitable relief.

Thomas Best, Michael Geere, Rowland Coytmore, Robert Salmon, Walter Cooke, Richard Chester, Henry Rawlin, William Becke.

196. [f.68v] *30 Jan. 1622. Certificate by Trinity House*
At the request of the bearer, Elizabeth Young of Poplar, they certify that her late husband, Henry Young, mariner of Poplar, was honest and of good estate, being master and part-owner of the *Delight* of London on a voyage into the Straits; on 23 Sept. last, he was surprised by 3 powerful Turkish pirates having in all over 120 pieces of ordnance. Knowing the cruelty of those pagans, Young and his crew resolved to die fighting rather than to submit. So fighting the ship was fired by the heathen and sank. Young and 17 of the crew prolonged their lives as long as they could on the masts. The hard hearted Turks let them perish and threatened to treat similarly an English ship which they had formerly taken if any of the crew offered to save their countrymen. Young's estate of over £300 consisted of his adventure in the ship, his part-ownership of her, his apparel and sea instruments. His widow and 2 small children are likely to perish without charitable relief.
[Note] Sealed and signed as the next entry [**197**].

197. *30 Jan. 1622. Certificate by Trinity House*
At the request of the bearers, Ursula Treago of Limehouse and Anne Bushnell of Ratcliff, widows of Roger Treago, master's mate, and John Bushnell, boatswain, of the *Delight*, Trinity House certify [the loss of the *Delight* as in **196**. Treago had been taken by sea robbers on 4 previous occasions with a total loss of over £200.] Their late husbands' estates, worth over £200, consisted of goods, apparel and sea instruments which were lost in the *Delight*. The widows and their children are likely to perish without relief.

Thomas Best, deputy master; Rowland Coytmor, William Case, Michael

Geere, Walter Cooke, Richard Chester, Robert Bradsho, Nicholas Diggins, William Ivey.

198. [f.69. *? May 1622*] *Trinity House to the marquis of Buckingham, lord high admiral*[1]
Some 2 years ago, Capt. Best and Capt. Love at Newmarket besought him on behalf of Trinity House to consider the heavy burden of a contribution towards the cost of the late voyage against the pirates of Algiers of £2,000 a year for 2 years, imposed by the council at the suit of the merchants. Trinity House were willing to pay £1,000 for 2 years and at their suit Buckingham had moved the king to signify to the council by the lord treasurer that they should be so charged. Called before the council, they were told to thank Buckingham and were then given a warrant under the hands of 10 members for collecting the money. The money has been paid in, although the collection was £600 less. Nevertheless the council are putting upon them £2,000 a year for 2 years, at the intemperate suit of the merchants, by whose errors the king suffers in honour and Buckingham is wronged. As their only patron, he is asked to take some order so that the council can be satisfied and they not further charged.

  1. Also in SP 14/130/27; *CSPD 1619–23*, 386, dated 6 May 1622; cf *APC 1621–3*, 212–13.

199. *8 June 1622. Certificate by Trinity House*
At the request of the bearer, Nicholas Rauledge, they certify the knowledge of some of them that in 1586 he was pressed to serve in the queen's ship, the *Makeshift*, for 12 months, and in 1588 in the queen's ship, the *Elizabeth Jonas*, on the voyage against the Spaniards and on other occasions later and gave good service. In 1596 he was master of the *Hope* under the lord admiral's licence when he was taken by the 'lanthatho' [? adelantado] of Spain off 'Cape St Maries' [? Cape Santa Maria, Portugal], and held captive to serve in the galleys for nearly 6 years, a ransom of 1,000 ducats having been placed upon him. His friends secured his release, and afterwards he had obtained a reasonably good estate when in 1615 as master of the *Feather* bound for Portugal he was taken by 2 French men-of-war, losing not only his whole estate but also was so misused that he lost his sight. He is now aged and destitute.
Robert Bradsho, master; Thomas Best, Walter Cook, Michael Geere, John Bennet, William Case, William Becke, Joshua Downinge.
[Note] Another certificate had been granted to him on 26 June 1616, as shown on f.29 [see **66**; for a further certificate, see **214**].

200. [f.69v] *17 June 1622. Robert Sparrow, gentleman, to John, bishop of Lincoln, lord keeper*
For 13 years he has been one-eighth part-owner of the *Lionell* of Harwich, Mr Maddison of Newcastle, Robert Hart of Harwich, and others unknown being the other owners. The ship has been used in transporting coal from Newcastle to London. Since 26 March 1618, Madison and others have freighted the ship with their goods, and Hart as master has transported the goods to London and elsewhere to the great

benefit of Madison, Hart and others but Hart has refused to render accounts to Sparrow for divers years and has paid him little money and nothing at all for $2\frac{1}{2}$ years, so that he cannot maintain himself. The lord keeper is asked to request Trinity House or others to summon Hart to render accounts for the period since 26 March 1618, and either to prepare the terms of a settlement with Madison and Hart in order to avoid law suits in the future or to certify their opinions to the lord keeper.

[Endorsed] A letter to be written to 5 or 6 of the masters of Trinity House to the effect of this petition.

[Initialled] J.L.C.

201. *13 July 1622. College of Westminster. John [bishop of] Lincoln, [lord keeper] to Messrs Best, Coytmer, Whitinge, Salmon, Davies and Bell, masters of Trinity House*
Reference to them of **200**.

202. [f.70] *30 Apr. 1623. Certificate by Trinity House*
At the request of the bearer, Elizabeth Haines, they certify that her husband Thomas, mariner of Bristol, was on a voyage to the Straits in the *Jacob* of Bristol when the ship was surprised by Turkish pirates on 'St Steven the Martyr's day last' [26 Dec.]. The ship was sunk in the fight, and all were killed or drowned except Haines and another who were saved by swimming and were taken up by the Turks. He was carried to Algiers and will remain there in miserable captivity unless charitable provision is made for his ransom, which is great and which he cannot pay because his adventure was lost. His wife and children are likely to starve in his absence.

Messrs Salmon, Case, Gunston, Vassall, Geere, Cooke, Downinge, Chester, Coytmore, Bennet.

203. *22 Feb. 1623. Privy council order for Sir Henry Martin, admiralty court judge, and Trinity House to consider a dispute about wages involving the East India company* [Printed in *APC 1621–3*, 429–30.]

204. [f.70v] *6 May 1623. [Sir] Henry Martyn [admiralty court judge], Robert Salmon, John Bennet, Walter Cooke, and Samuel Doves [of Trinity House to the privy council]*
In accordance with **203** they have considered the demands of the petitioners concerning goods taken from them by the Hollanders and wages for the time of their captivity. The petitioners have no 'colourable' claim on the East India company for the goods because the company apparently received no restitution for them. Indeed the agreement made with the Hollanders and confirmed by the king releases the Dutch from liability for goods taken from English seamen unless it appears that 'such goods came with effect to the use of the Dutch East India company', which the petitioners can hardly demonstrate. The writers were not prepared to examine whether the seamen should have wages as of right from the company for the time of captivity, but since the company had previously paid one-third by mediation of the admiralty court judge, they

did not rest until they had persuaded the company to pay the residue, subject only to the deduction of what the company could prove had been given to the petitioners by the Hollanders either in cash or in valuable goods during the period of captivity. Should there be any dispute, they reserved, with the company's assent, the right to impose their rule as to equity and hoped that they had done enough to ensure that the privy council need be troubled no further.

205. *14 May 1623. Certificate by Trinity House*
They certify at the request of the bearers, Audrey Noble of Wapping and Jane Micho of Battlebridge in Southwark, that their husbands, Richard Noble and Matthew Micho, were diligent seamen of good life and estate. They were in the *Hermitt* of London, William Sherwyn of Rotherhithe master, having all or most of their substance with them, when on coming out of Oporto on 18 Sept. last, Turkish pirates of great force surprised them. After a fight, the crew were taken to Algiers where they are kept in extreme captivity. The captives and their friends are unable to procure without charitable aid the ransoms of £50 for Noble and £60 for Micho. Their wives and small children are likely to starve and, not paying their rents, to be turned out of doors by their cruel landlords.
Messrs Salmon, Geer, Cooke, Bennet, Wattes, Gunston, Case, Beck, Doves, Vassall, Ivy, Coytmore, Davis.

206. [f.71] *23 June 1623. Chelsea. [Earl of] Middlesex [lord treasurer] to Trinity House*
They are to send a note of all iron ordnance for which they have given certificates during the last 6 months for supply to Dutch ships, signifying the names of the ships and of the masters or owners, details of the ordnance and the dates of the certificates.

207. *24 June 1623. [Trinity House to the earl of Middlesex] lord treasurer*
In reply to **206**, they have prepared a note of certificates [not entered] granted since 2 Sept. for Flemish ships upon affidavits according to the lord admiral's directions before the admiralty court judge that the ships belonged to the king's subjects. Yet they fear that indirect means may still be used on behalf of Flemish ships, for sundry Hollanders, shippers of Dutch ships, have of late secured letters of denization to free them, it is supposed, from the Dunkirkers and to procure English ordnance. Thus there is now in the river a great Holland ship of 400 dolls*. Her master, Nicholas Ryser, a Hollander and a 'batcheler', has got letters of denization, and he and John Triggs have made affidavit that the ship belongs wholly to Riser and to other denizens who are the king's subjects and he has asked Trinity House for a certificate for 26 pieces of ordnance, which they have not granted until they are further satisfied.
Ro. Salmon, Walter Cooke, Michael Gere, Jo. Bennet.

208. *25 June 1623. Chelsea. [Earl of] Middlesex [lord treasurer] to Trinity House*
In reply to **207**, the case of the great Holland ship will be considered at the

next meeting of the council and no certificate is to be granted until further order.

209. *25 June 1623. Privy council to Trinity House about the supply of iron ordnance to ships owned by denizens* [Printed in *APC 1623–5*, 27.]

210. [f.71v] *21 Nov. 1623. Privy council to Trinity House about the Lizard lighthouse* [Printed in *APC 1623–5*, 119.]

211. *[1] Dec. 1623. Ratcliff. Trinity House [to the privy council. Cf* SP 14/155/1; *CSPD 1623–5*, 122.]
In reply to **210**, they consider that the lighthouse lately erected at the Lizard is altogether unnecessary. Ships never seek the channel from the ocean at night. Besides, seamen seldom make their landfall at the Lizard but commonly at Plymouth or Dartmouth. The Lizard is very seldom seen outward or homeward bound, and the channel is there so broad that men may sail 'by course' at night or day without fear. As to the collection, they cannot justly certify, but conceive it may be about £400 a year, which is a great burden on seamen. Owners and masters here complain of paying 10, 15 and 20s every voyage in the port of London for such a needless light.
Robert Salmon, Walter Cooke, Michael Geere, Walter Whitinge, T. Best, William Case, John Bennet, [Richard Chester, Rowland Coytmor, John Davis, Joshua Downinge, William Ivey, John Osborne, John Vassall].[1]

    1. Omitted from Trinity House text.

212. [f.72] *17 Dec. 1623. Certificate by Trinity House*
At the request of John Duffe of 'St Maries', London, a Scotsman, they certify that he was master and owner of the *Angel* of London, which was cast away in foul weather at the Isles of Scilly coming from Ireland to La Rochelle, to his great loss.
Messrs Salmon, Cooke, Case, Davis, Whitinge, Downinge, Best, Coytmore, Bennett, Love, Dove, Geere.

213. *7 Jan. 1624. Certificate by Trinity House*
At the request of his brother Robert Mathew, the bearer, they certify their knowledge that Peter Mathew, merchant of London, was homeward bound from Aveiro in Portugal in the *Hope for Grace* of Preston [? Prestonpans] in Scotland (about 80 tons), Thomas Short of Preston master, which was laden with salt and oil, when on 6 June last, having sailed not above 15 leagues, the ship was surprised by a Turkish man-of-war. Mathew lost his whole estate, and was taken to Sallee in Barbary where the captain of the Turkish ship sold him for 350 Barbary ducats which at 8s a ducat amounts to £140. He lives in misery in iron chains, is forced to grind in the mill like a horse all day long, is fed on bread and water, and insufficient of that, and is tortured to make him turn Turk. A great ransom has been set on him which, because of his losses, he cannot procure without charitable aid.

Robert Salmon, master; Walter Cooke, John Davis, John Vassall, William Case, Thomas Best, Rowland Coytmore, Jo. Bennett, M. Geere, Samuel Doves.

214. [f.72v] *25 Feb. 1624. Certificate by Trinity House*
[Another certificate for Nicholas Rawleidge, Rauledge or Rawledge, similar to **199** except that (a) it is stated that in 1588, after being maimed by the Spaniards, he and others were carried ashore from the *Elizabeth Jonas* at Margate road and conducted by constables and officers from one tithing to another until they reached [Queen's House] Chatham Hill [residence of the dockyard officers] where they were paid their wages and where he remained a long time under the surgeon; (b) in 1596, the 'lanthatho' who captured him is described as the general of the Spanish galleys.]
Messrs Salmon, Best, Vassall, Bennet, Cooke, Whitinge, Downinge, Coytmore.

215. *6 March 1624. Certificate by Trinity House*
At the request of the bearer, Thomas Melvin, Scotsman, and on sight of a letter from George Hatch, master of the *Barbara* of London bound for Spain, presented to them by Captain Thomas Love and dated last November from Portland road near Weymouth, they certify that Melvin, being one of 9 christians, brought a small ship into Portland road. They had been taken by men-of-war of Algiers but had overcome 29 Turks who had held them captive and who had been using the ship as a man-of-war. Whether Melvin was master or pilot they cannot tell.
Messrs Salmon, Best, Geere, Bower, Cooke, Vassall, Whitinge, Bennet.

216. [f.73] *27 March 1624. Certificate by Trinity House*
At the request of the bearer Joan, wife of John Browne, mariner of Wapping, they certify that[1] about 12 years past her husband was master and three-quarters part-owner of the *Jonas* of Newcastle (about 100 dolls*) which was laden with salt and coal from Newcastle when she was cast away in foul weather in Yarmouth road to his great loss. About 9 years ago he was master's mate of the *Charity* of Portsmouth, William Jackis master, when she was taken in the West Indies by Spanish galleys. Browne remained captive in a galley for 19 months. About 6 years ago he was master's mate of the *God Keepe* of London, Richard Boyer master, when she was surprised by Turks on her return from 'Pharrow' [Faro] in Spain, and he lost all that he had in her. Finally he was master's mate of the *Mathew and Judeth*, Henry Taaton master, when the ship was taken by Turks on 17 Nov. last coming from Faro. He and the rest of the crew were carried to Algiers where they remain in great misery and cannot be released without charitable aid.
Messrs Cooke, Bennett, Davis, wardens; Salmon, Geere, Whitinge, Vassall.

1. 'that there is now in the river of Thames'; erased. Perhaps the beginning of an ordnance certificate.

217. *17 Apr. 1624. Certificate by Trinity House*
At the request of the bearer Ann, wife of John Dodson, mariner of
Ratcliff, they certify the knowledge of some of them that on about 29
Sept. 1622 her husband went as master's mate of the *Samuell* of London,
Richard Morris of Wapping master, on a voyage for Ayamonte in Spain
when returning homewards the ship was surprised by Turkish pirates.
Dodson and the rest of the crew were taken to Algiers and he was
afterwards sold into Tunis, where he remains captive. The Turks inflict
intolerable torments upon him. His wife cannot produce his ransom of
£160 without help.
Messrs Salmon, Best, Coitmore, Geere, Vassall, Case, Cooke, Bennet,
Davis.

218. [f.73v] *17 Apr. 1624. Certificate by Trinity House*
At the request of the bearer [blank] Morris, wife of Richard Morris,
mariner of Wapping, they certify that about 9 years ago her husband went
on a voyage in a small ship, the *Pearle* of London, and as is credibly
reported by the crew was taken by the Turks on 4 occasions, and
grievously beaten so that many small bones and splinters had to be taken
from his head, nearly costing him his life. He lost about £100 owing to the
loss of the ship and goods. About 2½ years ago, on a voyage in the *Dragon*
of London, the ship was cast away and he incurred a similar loss. He then
adventured the remainder of his estate in about Nov. 1622, and was
master of the *Samuell* of London when returning from Spain she was
surprised by the Turks. He and his crew were taken as slaves to Algiers
and from there he was sold into Tunis where he remains. His ransom of
£240 cannot be raised because of his former losses and that of £80 in his
last voyage and his wife and 4 small children are likely to perish for want
of relief.
Messrs Salmon, Cooke, Coytmore, Best, Davis, Bennet.

219. *17 Apr. 1624. Certificate by Trinity House*
At the request of the bearer Sara, wife of Henry Short, shipwright of
Limehouse, they certify the knowledge of some of them that he is honest.
About 13 [or 15] Dec. last, he was carpenter of the *Susan* of London,
John Taite of Limehouse master, returning from Lisbon [laden with salt][1]
when the ship was surprised by Turkish men-of-war. He lost his estate of
over £30 which he had with him and was sold in Algiers as a slave. He
cannot be released without payment of a large ransom which he and his
wife with 4 small children cannot procure without aid.
Messrs Salmon, Coitman [*recte* Coitmore], Bennet, Geere, Best, Case,
Vassall, Cooke, Davis.

    1. Stated in **220**.

220. [f.74] *4 May 1624. Trinity House to John, bishop of Lincoln, lord
keeper*
They certify further that in Dec. 1622 Short was carpenter of the
Assurance of London on a voyage for Spain and while at work on the ship
at Cadiz, certain malicious Spaniards inveighing against him, one of them

Mr Coytmore and find that it is no way prejudicial to the river or to the trade of Rogers, the anvil maker. Nor will it be prejudicial to the Thames if Rogers is licensed to build out his wharf only so far as the wharf of Coytmore, provided that he 'carry out his wharf only 50 ft adjoining to the wharf of Coytmore and then to fall off by a right line 15 ft and then again to go right out keeping equal distance from the wharf of Coytmore'. Thus finished, the wharf of Rogers will leave a way of 7 ft on it for the ferry place and for people to have free recourse to the waterside. The 'falling of' of 15 ft is to leave space for a ferry and boats to land, as hitherto.

139. [f.54. *? Late 1618*] *Report*[1] *by Trinity House*
Reasons for maintaining the cook's rooms amidships in the king's ships:
(a) Ordnance and men will not be hindered, which is of prime importance. (b) It is freer from enemy shot than in the forecastle. (c) Foul air created by the great number of men, stinking water, beer, beef and the closeness, lies between the 2 lower orlops* and in the hold. When the lower hatches are opened, it ascends and settles between the 2 orlops, endangering health and lives. The cook's fire, always burning at sea, purifies the air. (d) In their present place the cooks do not trouble others, nor are they troubled. (e) They have their provisions (beef, fish, fresh or salt water) close at hand. (f) If the cook's rooms were in the forecastle, the operation of 2 or 4 of the most serviceable pieces [of ordnance] would be hindered. The cook's provisions (trays, platters, kettles, pots, buckets, tallow, tubs, etc.) would inconvenience the men working in the forecastle where there are many ropes, namely fore-halyards [tackle to operate the lower yards], tacks, jeers, bowlines [rope to keep taut the weather edge of the sail] and other ropes belonging to the fore-mast and bowsprit. (g) The siting of the cook's rooms in the forecastle would spoil one of the best parts of the ship, for it would become noisome and offensive to the crew and gentlemen who come to see the ship. (h) In the forecastle, the cooks would be remote from their provisions.

Nevertheless, it would be convenient to raise the cook's rooms amidships as high and as near the orlops as possible, for that will 'advantage the hold and consequently the stowage'. Lastly, by adding weight amidships and in the floors of the ships, cambering will be prevented and the ships better preserved.
[Signed] T. Best, Hugh Merit, Michael Geere, Thomas Love, Walter Whiting, Henry Rawlyn, Robert Bradsho, Thomas Malby, John Vassall, Roger Gunston, Matthew Woodcott, Nicholas Diggins, Ro. Salmon, T.M.[? Thomas Milton], R.C.[? Richard Chester].

1. Probably concerning a proposal of the navy commissioners in about Sept. 1618 (Oppenheim, 206).

140. [f.54v. *? Jan. 1619. Trinity House*] *to the privy council* [*Cf* SP 14/105/47; *CSPD 1619–23*, 5.]
The rates detailed below, which should be collected at the entry* of the

struck him with a maul. A great part of his skull was 'drilled out of his head', and he was under the surgeon for above 12 months at a cost of at least £20, besides the loss of his time. [Then follows the gist of **219**.] Robert Salmon, master; Rowland Coytmore, John Bennet, Walter Cooke, John Davis, wardens; Joshua Downinge, Thomas Best, John Vassall, M. Gere, William Case, Walter Whitinge.

221. [f.74v] *12 Apr. 1626. Certificate by Trinity House*
The decay and ruin of the piers and jetties at Whitby in Yorkshire for many years is known to most of them and is affirmed in certificates shown by Francis Wynn and Richard Hunter, agents for the burgesses and inhabitants of Whitby. At their request, Trinity House certify that if the jetties and piers were to be repaired and preserved, the harbour there would be most commodious for ships of burden, crayers [i.e. small trading ships] and other vessels sailing to Newcastle and other northern parts in the event of contrary winds or tempestuous weather and they wish that the suit of the abovesaid agents will prosper.
Thomas Best, Robert Salmon, John Davis, Robert Bell, William Bushell, James Mowyer, Samuel Doves, Michael Geere, Walter Cooke, John Bennett, John Totten, Anthony Tutchen, Edward Maplesden.

222. *8 Apr. 1626. Certificate by Trinity House*
Richard Hooper, mariner of Deal in Kent, the bearer of this certificate, and others were granted letters patent [on 30 Nov. 1615 (C 66/2061, no. 18)] for clearing anchors and cables lost by ships in roads and harbours in the Narrow Seas between the Isle of Wight and Yarmouth in Norfolk. At the request of Hooper, Trinity House certifies that it is of the greatest necessity to clear these roads and harbours of anchors and cables if the king's and merchants' shipping is to be free of danger.
Thomas Best, Robert Salmon, Robert Adhams, Robert Bell, John Davis, Richard Chester, Walter Cooke, William Case, Edward Maplesden, William Steevens, William Ewins.

223. [f.75] *16 Sept. 1624. Order of the privy council concerning fees charged by customs officers* [only part of the order is entered. The whole is printed in *APC 1623–5*, 314–15. f.75v is blank.]

224. [f.76. *18 Feb. 1618 x 27 March 1625] Petition to the king*
A statute [8 Eliz., c. 13] empowered Trinity House to provide beacons, marks and signs for the sea. At the request of seamen sailing on the Norfolk coast, Trinity House, at their own expense, erected a stone lighthouse at Winterton Ness, and agreed to take, and did only take, 6d for every 20 chaldrons of seacoal carried by ships passing by. But Sir John Meldrom, on the suggestion that there was want of lighthouses there, obtained letters patent [on 18 Feb. 1618] to erect a lighthouse, which are void in law because about half a year before their issue a lighthouse had been erected. If it was true, as Meldrome pretends, that he had petitioned before the erection of the lighthouse, the letters patent are still void because Trinity House by authority of the statute had erected a

lighthouse before letters patent were issued. Meldrome takes 3s 4d for every 20 chaldrons, whereas Trinity House took only 6d, and he will not suffer shippers to have entries* made or cockets taken until duty is paid, which causes intolerable damage to seamen and is enforced on those who derive no benefit. The king is asked to revoke the patent.

225. [f.76v] *8 Sept. 1624. Trinity House [? to the privy council]*
As ordered they have considered what reparation to the fortifications of Scilly is necessary for the safety of the king's ships and the inhabitants of the island, and to deny any succour to enemies. (a) The Woolman blockhouse [? at Woolpacker Point] and the 2 other blockhouses nearby should be fortified to command the entrance to St Mary's Sound. (b) The castle of St Mary's should be well fortified to command the road so that no ship can ride there but at the courtesy of the castle, the castle and the blockhouse nearby being the chief security for St Mary's road. (c) The old castle at 'Fisher-towne' [? Old Town] should be repaired and fortified to annoy any who try to land there, and to provide relief for the inhabitants in case of an assault. (d) The bulwark at the entrance to Crow Sound should be repaired and fortified to prevent ships lying there, for with all westerly winds any ship, pirate or other, may [now] ride there notwithstanding the force of all the island. (e) Although ships may come through a third sound, Smith's Sound, to St Mary's road (where they would be under the command of St Mary's castle and the bulwark), the sound is known only to islanders and no fortification is necessary. (f) The dangers of Broad Sound are such that it is of no use; it is known only to the islanders who are fishermen. (g) In the north of the island, 'Grimbsbyes Sound' is a good port, the entrance being between Tresco and Bryher. Fortifications which used to command the port have decayed and should be repaired for otherwise ships could lie there despite the other fortifications of the island. Other petty roads are of no consequence. This report has been prepared in consultation with others.
Messrs Geere, Best, Davis, Whitinge, Bell, Osborne.

226. [f.77] *1 Feb. 1625. Trinity House to John, bishop of Lincoln, lord keeper [See also 251.]*
At the request of the bearer, William Bunn, mariner of Ratcliff, they certify that he was master and part-owner of the *William* of London (about 140 tons) on a voyage to Newcastle when in Nov. 1616 the ship was forced ashore on the head of 'Tilmoth' haven [? Tynemouth] owing to tempestuous weather, and he was in great danger. Afterwards he was master and half-owner of the *William* of London (about 260 tons) when, returning from the north, laden with coal, wheat, butter and other provisions, she was cast away in a storm on 16 Sept. 1622 at Stamport near Lowestoft. Finally, he was master and half-owner of the *Patience* of London (about 160 tons) on a voyage to the northern parts of the realm when on 29 Nov. [24 Nov. in **251**] last she was driven into the river Humber by an extraordinary storm, and both ship and goods were lost. His losses amounted to £1,120. He was a man of good reputation who paid customs and subsidies to the king and gave alms to the poor to the

best of his ability. Now he can no longer support his wife and family or satisfy his merciless creditors without some charitable relief.

Michael Geere, master; John Davis, John Bennett, Samuel Doves, Rowland Coytmore, wardens; Robert Adames, Thomas Best, Robert Salmon, Walter Whitinge, Walter Cooke, William Case.

227. [f.77v. *? c. Nov. 1624. Proposals referred to and considered by Trinity House*]

'1. A proposition': (a) How many mariners and gunners are required for a merchant ship of about 300 tons with 20 or 25 pieces of ordnance, and how many land soldiers may she carry in addition to the crew and victuals for 8 months? (b) What is the comparable information for a Newcastle ship of about 220 tons with 10 pieces of ordnance?

'The answer': The 300 tons ship would need at least 60 seamen and gunners and could carry 150 soldiers. The 220 tons Newcastle ship would need at least 30 seamen and gunners and could carry 100 soldiers. Both ships could carry enough victuals for 8 months provided that there is cider, vinegar,[1] or wine to drink. Many Newcastle ships are undersailed and would need to have their yards and sails enlarged at the discretion of surveyors appointed for the purpose.

[f.78] '2. Questions propounded to the masters of the Trinity House', and their answers [cf SP 14/175/86; *CSPD 1623–5*, 396].

(a) How many mariners and gunners are required for a ship of 300 tons with 20 or 25 pieces of ordnance, and how many soldiers could she transport for a month or 6 weeks? Sixty seamen and gunners at least, and 240 soldiers.

(b) For how long could such a ship be victualled, after the usual rations allowed by the king, how much longer if cider or wine is substituted for part of the beer, and how long if the soldiers are allowed one half proportion of beer? Two [3 (in SP)] months, but if provision is made [? as proposed] for drink, 4 months, seamen and soldiers being allowed the same.

(c) How many mariners and gunners are required for a Newcastle ship of about 220 tons with 10 pieces of ordnance, and how many soldiers could she transport for a month or 6 weeks? Thirty seamen and gunners at least, and 150 soldiers.

(d) [Question (b) is propounded for the Newcastle ship, with the same answer.]

(e) Newcastle ships are slow because they are undersailed. What is the cost for each ship of enlarging the sails to enable them to keep company with the other ships? £10 a ship.

1. An early 18th century physician advocated its use to combat scurvy (J. J. Keevil, *Medicine and the navy*, ii (1963), 266) but it was not a drink.

228. [f.78v. *? Before 15 March 1625*] *Shipmasters and owners to Trinity House* [*See* **229–30**.]

In 1617, the writers agreed to an imposition of £1,000 a year for 2 years to suppress Turkish pirates and to ensure more safety in trade and southern navigation. Trinity House promised that it would be levied for only 2 years. It has now continued for 4 years and double the agreed sum has been paid (namely £4,000), but they are still liable. Trinity House are requested to petition the duke of Buckingham to end the imposition. Bernard Motam, Thomas Browne, William Reickes, John Tomson, William Goodlard, John Hide, George Lissant, William Ball, Thomas Breadcake, James Ireland, Robert Tockly, Thomas Tomson, Humphrey Sallowes, William Craiford, John Wetherly, Edward Robertes, Thomas Davis, James Damarell, Tristram Wise, John Badiley, John Miller, John Goodwyn, William Peirson, Thomas Nicholles, John Mote, John Lingwood, Robert Bence, Robert Swyer, John Wharey, Thomas Martin, Thomas Gibbes, Roger Twiddy, Anthony Tichen, William Knight, John Ewers, Daniel Cadman, Henry Tawton, Anthony Wood, James Moyer, John Dennis, George Bodham, John Jenken, Edmond Grove, Richard Cooper, William Bushell, John Gibbs, Richard Hooper, Edward Acworth, John Hemmens, Richard Rassell, Squier Bence, William Grove, Jeremy Cornellis, Thomas Nelmes, John Gibbens, George Browne, John Bence, John Mason, Matthew Barret, Richard Broomfeild, Peter Milborn, Roger Sherman, George Clarckson, John Swanton, Robert Bowers, Edward Gardener, William Eeles, Matthew Wood, Richard Chamlet, William Mellowe, Thomas Addison, Thomas Sherwyn, John Andrewes, Thomas Foarde, William West, William Hill, John Ellman, William Low, Christopher Dunn, Henry West, John Stafford, William Smith, John Lowe, Robert Williams, John Arnold, William Goose, Richard Cole, John Johnson, William Smith, Henry West, Thomas Battell, Henry Page, John Bundocke, John Graunt, Martin Errington, John Sayer, John Doves, John Norwood, James Peterson, John Arnold, John Low, William Greene, Thomas Chall, Robert Rypinge, Nicholas Bradshow, Jonas Pereman, Thomas Montinge.

229. [f.79. *? Before 15 March 1625*][1] *Trinity House to the duke of Buckingham, lord high admiral*
About 4 years since, Capt. Best and Capt. Love attended him at Newmarket and he granted their request that they should be charged no more than £1,000 a year for 2 years only towards the cost of the Algiers voyage, which was the voluntary offer of Trinity House and of shipmasters and owners in general. The merchants were pressing for £2,000 a year for 2 years. Buckingham also persuaded the king to order the privy council, by Sir Lionel Cranfeild, then master of requests, that Trinity House should pay only £1,000 a year. Presently they were summoned to the privy council where lord chancellor Bacon signified the king's pleasure, and he and the 'bishop' of Canterbury bade them to thank the lord admiral [cf **198**]. They maintained the collection for 4 years and have paid £4,000, despite the first order for £2,000, but the merchants press the privy council for £2,000 or £3,000 more. Buckingham is their only defence on all occasions and they ask him to ensure that the collection should now cease, to free shipping of a grievous burden.

1. ? Earlier than **230**. But **230** refers to a petition to the king.

230. *15 March 1625. [Sir Edward Conway, secretary of state, to the privy council. Cf SP 14/185/53; CSPD 1623–5, 498; 228–9.]*
The enclosed petition to the king by shipowners and masters seeks the cessation of an imposition which was first levied with their consent for suppressing Turkish pirates, but which has continued for longer and for a greater amount than was agreed. The king has signified that if upon examination the information be true, the levy is to cease.

231. *[f.79v. ? After 15 March 1625. Unfinished and erased note by Trinity House]*
They petitioned Buckingham [**229**] and he procured the king's letters to the council, upon receipt whereof the council ordered them and the merchants. . . .

232. *12 March 1624. George [duke of] Buckingham, lord high admiral [to Trinity House]*
At Salisbury he ordered that from the lease of ballastage which he had made to them they should make a lease to Innocent Laniere or his partners for cleansing the Thames. Some of them, on behalf of their House, agreed. He is now informed that the lease has been granted to another to the prejudice of those to whom he intended good, and to that of the river. He is sensible of a 'cross carriage' towards himself which he may construe as an injury and he requires an explanation. They are to send their explanation by the bearer or take speedy action to honour their undertaking that he may remain their 'loving friend'.

233. *15 March 1624. Trinity House [to the duke of Buckingham, lord high admiral]*
In reply to **232**, Buckingham had said at Salisbury that, for reasons certified by Sir John Sucklinge, they need not deal with Laniere but that they should make a grant to Mr Alfonso [Ferabosco]. They were prepared to do so, but such unreasonable conditions were proposed, 'Mr Laniere steering the ship', that they could not agree. After further complaint to Buckingham [**169**], the settlement of the differences was referred by him to Sir John Sucklinge and Sir Ralph Freeman. Sucklinge negotiated a 3 year agreement between Laniere, Alfonso, and Trinity House, under which Trinity House were to pay 8d for every ton of ballast taken out of the Thames. Trinity House by their officers honoured this agreement, but during the 3 years Alfonso has sold his rights under the agreement and the patent from the king for ballastage in, and cleansing of, the Thames. Since Alfonso is satisfied, Trinity House have made a lease to William Burrell, the navy commissioner, to whom Alfonso has sold his rights. In view of what Buckingham agreed at Salisbury, they are under no obligation to Laniere, [f.80] and he should not be imposed upon them because they would then have no peace.

234. *[May 1623 x Aug. 1628] Trinity House to the same*
They ask him to consider the grievances of seamen and shipowners which arise from the heavy impositions for lights at Winterton and Dungeness.

235. [f.80v. *Before 25 Feb. 1626*] *Bailiffs and portmen of Ipswich to the king* [*See* **236.**]
Henry Rowndkettle, mariner of Ipswich, was part-owner and master of the *Christian Mary* when, on a voyage to the East Country, she was lost on 21 March last in foul weather on the coast of Norway near Wariburrow [? Waersbergen, now Varberg in Sweden] with his adventure of £170. He, his wife and family will perish unless the king extends his favour. All which was proved in open session, and this petition made at Rowndkettle's request.
Richard Cooke, Matthew Browninge, Tobias Blosse, Christopher Aldgate, Ro. Snellinge, William Cage, George Acton, Robert Sparrow.

236. *25 Feb. 1626. Trinity House to Sir Thomas Coventry, lord keeper*
Upon the certificate [**235**] and at the request of the bearer, Henry Rowndekettle, they commend him.
Thomas Best, Joshua Downinge, Samuel Doves, Walter Cook, William Rainburrow, Thomas Trenchfeild, Robert Salmon, Robert Bell, John Davis, Edward Maplesden, Christopher Browne.

237. [f.81] *14 Apr. 1626. Ratcliff. Trinity House* [? *to the navy commissioners. Cf* SP 16/24/77; *CSPD 1625–6*, 309.]
The navy commissioners required their opinion as to how fishing boats of the north coast from Harwich to Boston might benefit from the waftage* or convoy appointed for them. Their opinion is that boats from petty places to the south of Yarmouth, viz. Harwich, Aldeburgh, Southwold, Dunwich, etc., should repair to Yarmouth on a certain day, wind and weather permitting, and, in the road there, meet the ships which are to provide waftage. Meanwhile, the day should be notified to all places from Yarmouth, viz. Lynn, Wells, Boston, so that all can be at or near Cromer to meet the fleet coming from the south. One convoy should leave Yarmouth a tide or 2 before the rest and sail for Cromer´so that all can meet at the appointed time.
Thomas Best, Robert Salmon, Walter Cooke, John Davis, William Steevens.

238. [f.81v] *7 Jan. 1626. Trinity House to Sir Thomas Coventry, lord keeper*
At the request of the bearer, Elizabeth Ensome, they certify the knowledge of some of them that her husband Robert, mariner of Ratcliff, is honest. He was master of the *Unicorne* of London on a voyage to the Canary Islands, but returning homewards the ship was surprised by Sallee men-of-war on about 29 Apr. last, within 10 or 12 leagues of Scilly. Ensome lost his whole estate of at least £250, was taken to Sallee and sold as a slave. He is cruelly misused to make him forsake Christ and serve Mahomet. His ransom is set at 500 Barbary ducats which, at 10s a ducat, amounts to £250. Neither he nor his wife can procure this amount and she cannot maintain their 3 small children without charitable relief.
Thomas Best, master; Walter Cooke, Samuel Doves, John Bennett, wardens; Gervais Hockett, William Goodlard, Robert Salmon, John Davis, William Case, Anthony Tutchin.

239. [f.82] *14 [sic] Jan. 1626. Ratcliff. Trinity House [to an unidentified addressee. See* **240.***]*
According to his order of the 14th inst. they have interviewed the men listed below and have set out each man's monthly wages according to his own report.
St Andrew of Calais: Peter Lucas, master's mate, 36 guilder; John Martinn, gunner, 20 guilder; Bengebin Binher, gunner's mate, 21s; William Smith, 20s.
St George of Calais: Edward Dickinson, 23s; Nelles Alberson, boatswain, 27 guilder.
St Claude of Calais: Peter Dulsnea, master gunner, 25 guilder; Jacob Johnson, boatswain, 26 guilder; Peter Barnes, cook, 22 guilder; Jerricke Myer, carpenter, 25 guilder; Nicholas Tise, carpenter, 25 guilder; Symon Rych, sailor, 14 guilder.
If the king pays full freight to the owners of these ships as if the ships had arrived at their home ports, the wages up to the date of the arrival of the ships at Plymouth should be paid by the owners. If the king does not pay freight, then he should pay these wages which the enemy should have done in the previous case. From Plymouth they should be paid at the same rate as 'our own seamen' for the period that they were in the king's service.
Thomas Best, Robert Salmon, John Bennet, William Case.

240. *18 Jan. 1626. Ratcliff. Trinity House [to an unidentified addressee]*
Having received from Mr Cason the certificate which they sent 2 days ago to the addressee concerning the wages of Dutch seamen who were in the prizes [**239**], for his full satisfaction they sent to the *Nightingall* of Schiedam for the steersman, Bowen Johnson, the boatswain, Cornellis Clayson, and the cook, Clayse Janson, the chief officers in the Holland ships, who have certified that the monthly wages in their country are: steersman from Holland, 36 guilder; gunner, boatswain and cook, 23 guilder each; carpenter, 32 guilder; ordinary man, 12 and 13 guilder. While these men were before them, John Clayson, shipper of the *White Dove* of Medemblik, came and confirmed these figures.
Thomas Best, Robert Salmon, Walter Cooke, William Rainborow, Samuel Doves.

241. [f.82v] *11 Jan. 1626. Trinity House [? to the navy commissioners. Cf APC 1625–6, 294–5, 333–4;* **242**]
The ill service of seamen in the king's ships is due to the smallness of their pay and an increase is the only remedy. The pay should be such that they can live fairly on it, which they could do for 20s a month. This may be given without any increase in charges or harm to the service by a reduction of one-sixth in crews and by paying the men 20s a month, 12 months to the year. The common seamen in a ship allowed 200 men is about 167. A one-sixth reduction would leave 167, of whom 40 would be officers, leaving 127 sailors. Only men able to do all service, that is, for top yards, helm, 'leedes' [? taking soundings with the lead] shall have 20s. A small advance for the officers will give content: 20s a month for the

master, 25s for the pilot, 20s for the two master's mates, 6s or 7s for the quartermasters, and so according to that rate for the other petty officers, surgeons, trumpeters, drummers, etc. Trinity House will not meddle with [the rates for] officers resident in the ships. These rates given, the king will be well served, abuses of late years reformed, and the ships in more security. Provided always that 'it be death to every man that shall receive the king's money and not perform the service'. The difference in pay is:

	£	s	d
A ship with 200 men now paid 14s costs £140 a month for wages and for 13 months:	1,820	0	0
Victuals for 200 men at 8d a man per day:	2,433	6	8
	4,253	6	8

[Continued at the foot of f.83]

	£	s	d
The same ship with 167 men paid 20s a month will cost £167 and for 12 months:	2,004	0	0
The advance for officers for a year:	150	0	0
Victuals for 167 men at 8d a man per day:	2,031	16	8
	4,185	16	8

The saving is £67 10s a year. Towards the pay of the captain not accounted for above, there is 20s a month and the £67 10s a year.

242. [f.83. *? 29 Dec. 1625 x 14 Jan. 1626] A proposition for the Newcastle trade [Trinity House to the navy commissioners. Cf* SP 16/18/59; *CSPD 1625–6*, 221; *APC 1625–6*, 295; **241**.]

	£
Ten Newcastle ships of 350 or 400 tons each carrying 14, 15 or 16 pieces of ordnance with 60 men a ship at 40s a man per month:	1,200
Hire and freight of the ships per month:	460
Cost of 10 ships with 600 men:	1,660
Thirty barrels of powder, shot, muskets, swords and other necessaries for each ship for a voyage of 8 months:	2,000
Cost of wages, victuals [hire and freight] at £1,660 a month for 8 months:	13,280
	15,280

The business of raising the money is too weighty a matter for them, and they leave it to the state to whom it belongs. Each great ship trading for coal from 150 tons upwards should carry 4 pieces of ordnance. The new light pieces of about 3 cwt. with minion* bore [? drakes*], 3 pound shot and 2 pound powder to carry as far and as true as a minion would be very suitable for all ships, especially those trading to Newcastle.

243. [f.83v. *? 29 Jan. 1626*] *Trinity House to the duke of Buckingham, lord high admiral, about seamen's pay* [*Cf* SP 16/19/78; *CSPD 1625–6*, 239. The SP text is annotated '39' Jan. 1629.]

244. [f.84. *? 8 Feb. x 24 Apr. 1626*][1] *Trinity House to the house of commons*
The defence of the kingdom much depends on its shipping and navy, for which able and sufficient men are essential. Of late, whenever seamen have been required for any service for defence, however important, a sufficient number has been found only with difficulty, and being found, many have evaded the service of the state in favour of that of the merchants. Worse, some have fled to serve foreign princes and even enemies, and have been the instruments of great loss to 'our' merchants. The sole cause thereof is the smallness of the pay in the king's service which is based on an ancient rate when victuals and other provisions were much cheaper. The pay is not above 4d a day for ordinary seamen and according to the same mean proportion for officers. Since most have wives and children to support, it is far too little and not more than half the amount usually allowed '(and the same well paid) both by our merchants and by foreign states'. Furthermore merchant ships are vital for defence and 'a navy royal' cannot set forth without them. Only 2s a ton per month for merchant ships is allowed by the king, which, considering the wear and spoil of ships in war service, is no way proportionate to the loss, whereby shipowners are discouraged from building new ships or repairing old.

1. A proclamation of 24 Apr. 1626 provided higher pay and freight rates (*Proc.*, i. 173). Parliament had assembled on 8 Feb.

245. [ff.84v–86. *? Early 1626*] *Statement of wages for the king's navy on the basis of 20s a month* [*See* **241**, **243**.]
1st rank, 400 men; 2nd, 250; 3rd, 200; 4th, 160; 5th, 120; 6th, 70 or 'for 60 or 80 proportioned from the medium of 20s per man a month'.
Captain: 1st–6th rank, 1 apiece.
Master: 1st rank, £5 10s; 2nd, £5; 3rd, £4; 4th, £4; 5th, £3 10s; 6th, £3.
Pilot: 1st rank, £3; 2nd, £2 10s; 3rd, £2 5s; 4th–5th, £2; 6th, £1 15s.
Master's mates: 1st rank, 3, £6 15s; 2nd–3rd, 2, £4; 4th, 2, £3 10s; 5th, 1, £1 16s 8d; 6th, 1, £1 10s.
Boatswain: 1st rank, £2; 2nd, £1 16s; 3rd–4th, £1 10s; 5th, £1 5s [sic]; 6th, £1 6s 8d.
Boatswain's mates: 1st rank, 2, £2 10s; 2nd, 2, £2 5s; 3rd–4th, 1, £1 2s 6d; 5th–6th, 1, £1.
Quartermasters: 1st rank, 4, £5; 2nd–4th, 4, £4 10s; 5th–6th, 4, £4.
Quartermasters' mates: 1st–4th rank, 4, £4.
Yeoman: 1st–2nd rank, 4, £4; 3rd, 2, £2.
Master carpenter: 1st–2nd rank, £1 16s; 3rd–4th, £1 10s; 5th–6th, £1 6s 8d.
Carpenter's mates: 1st rank, 2, £2 13s 4d; 2nd–4th, 1, £1 5s; 5th–6th, 1, £1.
Carpenters: 1st rank, 9, £10 2s 6d; 2nd, 6, £6; 3rd, 4, £4.

Purser: 1st–2nd rank, £1 16s; 3rd–4th, £1 10s; 5th–6th, £1 6s 8d.
Steward: 1st–4th rank, £1 2s 6d; 5th–6th, £1.
Cook: As for the steward.
Steward's mates: 1st rank, 2, £2; 2nd, 1, 18s 6d; 3rd, 1, 18s.
Cook's mates: As for the steward's mates.
Surgeon: 1st rank, £1 16s; 2nd–4th, £1 10s; 5th–6th, £1 6s 8d.
Surgeon's mates: 1st rank, 2, £2 10s; 2nd–3rd, 1, £1.
Master trumpeter: 1st rank, £1 6s 8d; 2nd, £1 5s.
Trumpeters: 1st rank, 4, £4 10s; 2nd, 2, £2 5s; 3rd–6th, 1, £1 5s.
Drum and fife: 1st rank, 2, £2 5s; 2nd–4th, 2, £2.
Coxswain: 1st–4th rank, £1 2s 6d; 5th–6th, £1.
Coxswain's mate: 1st–3rd rank, £1.
'Skiffon' [skiff man]: 1st rank, £1 2s 6d.
'Skiffon's mate': 1st rank, £1.
Swabbers: 1st rank, 2, £2; 2nd, 1, 18s 6d; 3rd–4th, 1, 18s.
Swabber's mates: 1st rank, 2, £1 16s.
Armourer: 1st–3rd rank, £1 2s 6d; 4th–5th, £1.
Gunmaker: 1st–2nd rank, £1 2s 6d.
Master gunner: 1st rank, £1 16s; 2nd–4th, £1 10s; 5th–6th, £1 6s 8d.
Gunner's mates: 1st rank, 2, £2 5s; 2nd, 2, £2; 3rd–6th, 1, £1.
Quarter gunners: 1st–4th rank, 4, £4; 5th–6th, 2, £2.
Quarter gunner's mates: 1st rank, 4, £4.
Yeoman of the powder room: 1st–5th rank, £1.
Officers: 1st rank, 72, £91 2s 6d; 2nd, 53, £64 16s; 3rd, 42 [*recte* 44], £53 1s 6d; 4th, 34, £42 8s; 5th, 24, £29 3s 4d; 6th, 22, £26 3s 4d.
Able mariners at 18s each a month: 1st rank, 248, £223 4s; 2nd 147, £132 6s; 3rd, 118, £106 4s; 4th, 92, £82 16s; 5th, 72, £64 16s; 6th, 34, £30 12s.
Gromets [youths ranking between seamen and boys] and fresh men at 12s each a month: 1st rank, 74, £44 8s; 2nd, 46, £27 12s; 3rd, 36, £21 12s; 4th, 30, £18; 5th, 20, £12; 6th, 11, £6 12s.
Boys at 8s each a month: 1st rank, 6, £2 8s; 2nd–5th, 4, £1 12s; 6th, 3, £1 4s.
Total: 1st rank, 400, £361 2s 6d; 2nd, 250, £226 6s; 3rd, 200, £182 9s 6d; 4th, 160, £144 16s; 5th, 120, £107 11s 4d; 6th, 70, £64 11s 4d.
Remaining for the captain's pay each month: 1st rank, £38 17s 6d; 2nd, £23 14s; 3rd, £17 10s 6d; 4th, £15 4s; 5th, £12 8s 8d; 6th, £5 8s 8d.
Grand total: 1st rank, £400; 2nd, £250; 3rd, £200; 4th, £160; 5th, £120; 6th, £70.

246. [f.86v] *3 Jan. 1626. Certificate by the parson of Rotherhithe and others*
Michael Fletcher, mariner of Rotherhithe and husband of the bearer, was master of the *Litle James* of London on a voyage to a plantation in New England in America. Over a year ago, homeward bound and fully freighted, the ship was surprised by a Sallee man-of-war on the west coast, not many leagues from Plymouth. He and the ship were taken to Sallee and it appears from his letters that he is in miserable captivity there, having lost all that he is worth which, they are credibly informed, is

about £80. Neither he nor his wife can raise his £300 ransom. They have lived honestly and it would be charitable to help to redeem him.

Thomas Gataker, parson of Rotherhithe, Aaron Woodcocke, William Case, Gervais Hockett, David Edwardes, Henry Jesson, Thomas Wood, John Blake, Austin Smith.

[Marginal note] Certificate for Thomasin [Elizabeth erased] Fletcher.

247. [f.87] *15 March 1626. Trinity House to Sir Thomas Coventry, lord keeper*
Certificate [as in **246** with minor differences].
Thomas Best, Walter Cooke, Samuel Doves, Robert Salmon, John Bennett, Robert Bell, Thomas Trenchfeild.

248. [f.87v. *After 13 May 1626*] *Thomas Askew of Faversham to the same*
A petition seeking letters patent for a collection in Kent, Essex, Suffolk, Norfolk, Middlesex and the cities of London and Norwich for his relief, the need for which appears in the annexed certificates [**249–50**].

249. *27 Feb. 1626. Certificate by the mayor and jurats of Faversham*
At Askew's request they certify that he has lived honestly among them for many years, and is a mariner who was of good estate and who has employed and trained many young seamen, many of whom have served the king. On 2 July 1622, a small bark, the *Ann* of Faversham (23 tons), which was laden with coal, John Calliver [Cullyver in **250**] master, was taken by Hollanders between Gravelines and Dunkirk. He was sole owner of the bark and her cargo and he lost £60. On 14 Sept. 1623, another bark, the *Thomas* of Faversham (30 tons) was cast away in foul weather on the French coast on a voyage to load corn at 'St Valleries in Sun' [Saint-Valéry-sur-Somme] in Picardy. The master was Thomas Michell. Askew was half-owner and lost £45. On 12 March 1624, a new bark [the *Charles* of Faversham, of which Askew was master in **250**] (46 tons), was cast away in foul weather [in Yarmouth haven in **250**] when bound for Newcastle, laden with corn. The bark and most of the corn belonged to Askewe, and his loss amounted to £300, while that of other men came to £150. [f.88] On 2 July 1625, a bark, the *Hopewell* of Faversham (80 tons) worth £200, of which he was master and owner, was taken by a sloop or frigate of Blankenberge commanded by Capt. Cornelis Stone, when bound for Newcastle. The crew were taken to Blankenberge, cruelly handled and were kept in slavery for 5 months, despite the efforts of Mr Trumball, the king's agent at Brussels, to secure their release. They had to pay £155 14s 6d for ransom and charges, and the bark and her goods worth £660 were confiscated. In addition there was the loss of time and other damages. Askew's share of the loss was £360. His total losses amount to about £765 and he and his wife and 5 small children are undone.

John Castlock, Reynold Edmondes, John Woodds, John Lawrence, William Thurstone.

Certified by Edward Maplesden, John Totton and W. Bushill to be a true copy.

250. [f.88v] *13 May 1626. Trinity House to Sir Thomas Coventry, lord keeper*
A certificate [as **249** with the differences there noted].
Thomas Love, Thomas Best, Richard Chester, Samuel Doves, Edward Maplesden, Robert Salmon, William Case, Robert Bell, Robert Adhams, Walter Cooke, John Bennett, Gervais Hockett, William Bushell.

251. [f.89] *28 June 1626. Certificate by Trinity House for William Bunn, mariner of Ratcliff* [His misfortunes are recited as in **226** but (a) his losses are given as £100 in 1616, £700 in 1622 and £300 in 1624; (b) the third shipwreck is said to have occurred on 24 Nov. 1624; (c) in Nov. 1625 the *William and Thomas* of London (140 dolls*) of which he was master and part-owner, was cast away near Wells in Norfolk, whereby he lost over £100.]
Thomas Best, Robert Salmon, William Case, Robert Bell, William [? *recte* Edward] Maplesden, Michael Geer, Robert Kitchen, John Davis, William Ewens, John Totten, James Moyer.

252. [f.89v] *3 Oct. 1622. Hampton Court. G. [marquis of] Buckingham [lord high admiral] to Trinity House* [Cf APC 1621–3, 110.]
Upon complaints to the lords [? of the privy council] about the inconveniences which ensue from the supply of cast iron ordnance for the defence of ships bought overseas, their lordships asked him to consider and give guidance on the issue by Trinity House of certificates for ordnance. They may issue certificates as hitherto for ships which have been built in England or any other of the king's dominions, using care to avoid abuses because some masters and owners alienate their ordnance soon after having given bond not to do so. No certificate is to be granted to anyone who is not the king's subject and dwelling in the king's dominions or to anyone who is suspected of alienating ordnance. If they find plain dealing, certificates are to be issued without delay, neither hindered nor furthered by private respect. Trinity House must not be deceived by the owners or the alleged owners of ships built by strangers overseas. Owners' applications are to be supported by an affidavit made in the admiralty court (a certificate from the mayor of the port in which the ship lies will not suffice) and the affidavit must be mentioned in the certificate of Trinity House. Certificates should not only say that the ordnance is bought for the defence of the ship, but rather that Trinity House regard the request as reasonable. Many buy more than enough ordnance in order to be able to dispose of the surplus. Since other affairs prevent Buckingham from examining the certificates as closely as he would like, their care must be the greater, informing him of deceits and abuses.

253. [f.90. *1599 x 1603*] *Masters and owners of ships of London, Ipswich, Aldeburgh, Yarmouth, Lynn, Sandwich and other coast towns to Trinity House*
English merchants, who are the main employers of English ships and

seamen, transport most of their goods to and from France, Middelburg, Danzig, 'Quinssborough' and Melvin in strangers' ships, despite English ships being instantly to be had in those places and which lie idle in consequence, thereby forcing mariners to serve foreign princes. Examination of the ships and seamen of the coast towns fit to serve the queen now, and in 1588, shows the lamentable decay. Trinity House were petitioned previously and are now asked to approach lord Buckhurst, lord treasurer [1599–1603], for remedy or they will have to appeal to the queen, whom the premises most nearly touch.

For the port of Hull: Richard Pinperton, John Byrkhead. For the port of Newcastle: Thomas Nicholson. For the port of Melcombe Regis and Weymouth:[1] Henry Peet, John Platt, William Nuton, Griffen Floud, Henry Pasckowe, Robert Safan, Thomas Stevens, John Olyvers, John Holland, William Williams, Nicholas Carnabye, Richard Harris, Thomas Johnson, William Raddell, Jeffery [blank], Seryes Manderstian, Richard Stevens, Abraham Bonner, Thomas Carnabye the younger, John Tye, John Bynder, Barnabas Lowe, John Daniell, John Chaser, William Bardnell, Robert Kitchen, John Harris, Abraham Rawlins, Francis Olyver, Roger Hankyn, John Chiston, Richard Lawson, John Darns, Bartholomew Heggell, George Ireland, junior, John Lambard, Matthew Cuvell, Nicholas Hodson, Peter Olyver, T. Beste, Nicholas Isacke, John Bedome, Richard Done, Henry Maillim, John Badyley, James Lyell, Matthew Angell, Roger Gunston, John Johnson, Ninian Bowyer, Richard [blank], Thomas Whitt, Jonas Bonne, Robert Salmon, Michael Merrell, Thomas Carnabye, Peter Matham, Thomas Redwood, Francis Forman, William Dawson, John Cobbe, John Dofyld, Timothy Layerd, Robert Bence, Luke Barfoote, John Jacob, George Ireland, George Arell, Thomas Bailie, William Harvye, Richard Meller, Henry Rawlin, William Sayden, Benjamin Gonston, William Criske, Robert Coussens, Nicholas Richardson, Richard Chester, Edward Brian, Robert Freeman, Ralph Labon, William Bowe, Richard Danyell, Hugh Robynson, John Osborne, Robert Wheatlie, William Casse, George Hope, John Clarke, John Bedham, Robert Earlle, Thomas Marychurch, Richard Jenyns, John Gold, Henry Tonne, John Bowden, John Drake, William Rickes, Cobham Doves, Henry Churche, John Gollsound, Samuel Doves, Richard Ireland, John Franelton, John Swanton, Patrick Roche, Abraham Lambe, John Stead.

1. Clearly applying to only a few of the names which follow.

254. [f.90v. As in **57**]

255. [? *20 Oct. 1616 x 14 Feb. 1617*] *Trinity House to the privy council* [*Cf APC 1616–17, 141–2.*]
Almost all shipowners and masters trading to Newcastle for coal and other owners, masters and fishermen trading on the north coast requested Trinity House in writing to build lighthouses near Winterton in Norfolk for better security on that dangerous coast on dark and foul nights and have offered a voluntary allowance. The privy council are asked to permit the project and collections for it at the customs houses in all ports.

256. [f.91] *5 Jan. 1607. Whitehall.* [*Privy council*] *to the customs and other officers at Newcastle, Yarmouth, Hull, Boston and Lynn*
Suit has been made on behalf of seamen who trade to Newcastle and other northern parts of the realm for the placing of buoys and beacons between Lowestoft and Winterton Ness, because of the dangerous passage, where many have lately lost their lives and goods. Very many have signed an offer to pay 12d upon every 100 tons of ships, hoys and barks which pass that way, for every voyage. No doubt those who did not sign are also ready to pay, since the project is for their benefit and safety. A contribution cannot be collected except at the ports to which ships especially trade. The addressees are to collect the allowance from masters or owners and are to account for the money to Trinity House who have orders to use it for the said purpose. The names of any who refuse to pay are to be reported to the privy council.
[Archbishop of] Canterbury, [lords] Worcester, Ellesmere, lord chancellor, Northampton, Zouch, Dorset, Salisbury, Knollys, Nottingham, Mar, Wotton, Suffolk, Bruce.

257. [f.91v] *31 May 1607.* [*Privy council*] *to the same*
Further to **256**, Trinity House have provided the seamarks between Lowestoft and Winterton Ness. The levy of 12d per 100 tons was a voluntary offer but some seamen and others obstinately refuse to pay. Customs and other officers are to collect the imposition and pay it to Trinity House, who are to use it to pay for the continual and daily repair of the marks. Cockets of any who refuse to pay are to be withheld until they do so.
P.S. They are informed of a need for beacons and buoys in the harbours of the Tees, beyond Flamborough Head. A similar collection is to be made on ships of that harbour.
Lord treasurer, duke of Lennox, lord admiral, earls of Worcester, Northampton and Salisbury, lords Wootton, Stanhope.

258. [f.92] *31 May 1609. Whitehall.* [*Privy council*] *to the customs and other officers of ports between London and Newcastle*
They are credibly informed that a dangerous passage has grown at Stamport, not far from Lowestoft to the southward on the coast of Suffolk. Many have lost their lives and goods owing to want of marks, buoys, beacons and lighthouses. To meet the cost, the chief masters and shipowners trading to the north and the masters of Trinity House have agreed to pay 4d a ship, hoy, or bark for every voyage to or from Newcastle and the same amount for ships sailing from Hull, Boston and other northern parts, either from port to port or overseas, for they also benefit. It is reasonable that the contribution should be collected at the Customs House in London, and at other customs houses, on the arrival of each ship. The levy is additional to the 12d per 100 tons for buoys and beacons at Caister. The money must be paid to Trinity House (who are to provide the marks) or their assignees before the cocket or other discharge is given.
Lord chancellor, lord treasurer, lord privy seal, lord admiral, lord

chamberlain, earl of Worcester, lords Zouch, Knollys, and Wootten, Mr Secretary Herbert, Sir Julius Casar, chancellor of the exchequer.

259. [f.92v] *14 Jan. 1623. Order of the privy council concerning collections for the Algiers expedition* [Printed in *APC 1621–3*, 392–3. *APC* states that ships trading into the Straits east of Cape Gata are to pay 8d per ton, while those trading to the west and certain other places are to pay 18d. These amounts are transposed in the Trinity House text, which is probably correct in view of *APC 1619–21*, 240–1; also **111.**]

260. [f.93] *20 March 1626.* [*Trinity House*] *to collectors of dues*
The privy council letter of 1 April 1613 authorised [Trinity House] to collect 12d per 100 tons and 4d a ship on ships trading to the north coast towards maintaining lighthouses and buoys at Caister and Stamport. It is now pretended that ships and barks of Hull trading for Holland and from thence home to their own ports derive no benefit from these seamarks. From henceforth dues on such ships should no longer be levied unless it is known that they benefit. Collections are to continue on all other ships, including those of fishermen and others of Hull who trade to Zeeland because they benefit.
Thomas Best, Robert Bell, Walter Coke, Robert Salmon, John Davis, John Totton.
[Marginal note] Sommersfeild, Hull.

261. [f.93v] *20 March 1626.* [*? Trinity House to the privy council*]
According to the reference of 16 March, they have ascertained the number of English captives in Sallee, having interviewed 3 men lately come from there and having seen several letters written from there to some of the petitioners. Previously they had examined divers men come from Sallee who had sought help in paying their charges in travelling home. It is evident that there are some 1,200 or 1,400 English captives, all or mostly taken in the Channel, within 20 or 30 miles of Dartmouth, Plymouth and Falmouth. When the ships are full of the king's subjects, the pirates return to Sallee, sell the captives in the common market, and then return for more. They winter in Flushing and in Holland, and all their needs are furnished there. The coast is unguarded by ships, and friends are not restrained from helping the infidels.
Messrs Best, Davis, Cooke, Salmon, Bell, Bennett.

262. [f.94] *15 Oct. 1626. Trinity House to Mr John Wyldes*
In reply to his letter of '2th present', they thank him for his care in purchasing the house. He is asked to be advised on whether the surrender can be taken in the name of the corporation, viz. the master, wardens and assistants of Trinity House, without risk of forfeiture to the lord. Otherwise it should be taken in the names of Thomas Best, Walter Coke, Samuel Doves and William Goodladd and their assigns for ever. They appoint him assignee and deputy of Trinity House to take up the surrender. There is some error over £20 which he desires Trinity House to pay to Mr Batten, because the £8 due to him at midsummer was paid in

accordance with his letter of 5 June to Mr William Burgesse, ironmonger, and they have his receipt; they have paid Batten £12, and they have his receipt.

[Marginal note] Mr Wyldes to take up the surrender of the house for Caister lights.

263. [f.94v] *18 Nov. 1626. Trinity House [to the privy council. Cf APC 1626, 168–9.]*
According to the order of 22 Sept. they have perused the orders of the board, viz. those of 21 Dec. 1617 and 8 Aug. 1626, and the entries* of goods by English merchants in strangers' ships, as presented to Trinity House by masters of ships trading to France. Since 20 Apr., about 800 tons of goods have been shipped in 12 strangers' ships, and only one English ship has been employed. But last summer was extraordinary because for most of the time 'we had a stay here of our shipping, and in France'. For fear of the Dunkirkers and because of the stay in France, merchants were constrained to employ strangers' ships, and to consign their goods to Frenchmen under the name of Frenchmen's goods, and 'all to blind the time'. Merchants are found to be resolved not to freight strangers' ships, once an agreement is made with France. Given the times, the hindrance to English ships and men is not great. But for the future, the board is asked to order that merchants trading with France, Flushing, Middelburg, Holland, etc. should freight native ships.

264. [f.95. *13 Feb. x 22 March 1621*] *Trinity House to the house of commons* [Cf *CD* ii. 74; v. 64.]
They are grieved at the aspersion that they had allowed by certificate or otherwise the carrying away of 100 carriages [of ordnance] to Spain. They are not guilty and would stake their lives thereon. If a member of their corporation has allowed it, he should receive condign punishment.

265. [*Before 25 Dec. 1632*] *Certificate by Trinity House*
Certificate about William Kempster as **269** [with variations, but omitting the 1618 incident].

266. [f.95v] *24 Sept. 1631. Certificate [by Trinity House]*
They have been asked to certify concerning the condition of Capt. William Hockerage, a slave in Algiers, taken by 12 Turkish men-of-war. He has commanded several ships in the service of the East Indies company and otherwise. His ransom of £250 cannot be paid without charitable help. He lost £2,000 when the ship, of which he was sole owner, and her goods were captured.
Samuel Doves, master; Robert Salmon, T. Best, etc.

267. *June 1632. Certificate by Trinity House [See 268.]*
At the request of the bearer, Mary Croft, they certify the knowledge of some of them that her husband John, mariner of Ratcliff, is honest and maintained his wife and family by his industry. He was master of the *Flying Drake* of 'Lyme in . . . Devon' [? *recte* Lyme Regis, Dorset] on a

voyage to Viana do Castelo in Portugal. On the voyage homewards, the ship was surprised by Turkish pirates of Algiers. He and his crew lost all that they had on the voyage and were sold as slaves at Algiers. They have been cruelly misused to make them forsake Christ and serve Mahomet. They cannot be released without the payment of ransoms which they and their poor wives cannot procure. Together with their wives and children, they will perish without charitable relief.

Robert Bell, John Bennett, Gervais Hockett, John Totton, Thomas Best, Ro. Salmon, William Bushell, William Case, Anthony Tutchin, William Rainborrowe, William Stephens.

[Marginal note] Those taken with John Croft were John Croft [sic], John Robins, Thomas Batten, George Craford, Francis Webb, Henry [Nicholas erased] Browne, Nicholas [George erased] Darby, Thomas Archer, Richard [Edward erased] Hayward, Edward Holloway.

268. [f.96] *18 Apr. 1632. Certificate by Roger Corbett, George Griffith and Elizabeth Littleton*
Certificate about John Croft [similar to **267**], some of those certifying being adventurers in the ship.

269. [f.96v] *10 May 1633. Certificate by Trinity House [See **265**, **270**.]*
On information from the bailiffs of Aldeburgh, they certify that William Kempster, mariner of Aldeburgh in Suffolk, was master of the *Paule* of London (about 140 tons) bound for High Monten [? Ayamonte] in Spain, when on about 26 Dec. 1631 the ship was captured by Turks of Algiers. He and his crew of 15 were carried to Algiers where they live in miserable slavery. Kempster lost £200. Furthermore, in 1618, bound for 'Lynn in Norwood' [? Lynn in Norfolk] in the *Rose* (about 200 tons) he lost a quarter part amounting to £100; in 1627, he lost about £240 [£120 in **265**] when a Dunkirker took and sank his bark coming from 'Island' [? Iceland]: in 1628, a French man-of-war pillaged him when he was homeward bound from London, whereby he lost £100 in cloth, victuals and money. His total losses amount to about £640. He and his crew are unable to pay their ransom, and they are condemned to ruin without charitable relief.

Robert Bell, master; William Case, Gervais Hockett, John Benett, Christopher Browne, George Hatch.

270. [f.97] *19 March 1633. Statement of the losses of William Kempster of Aldeburgh in Suffolk, taken prisoner in 1630 and still a captive* [As in **269** with the following differences: the bark lost in 1627 was the *Speedwell*, valued with her cargo of fish at £1,000; as quarter-owner, he lost £240; the ship in 1628 had also been on an 'Island' voyage; the Frenchmen ran her ashore, and Kempster's loss was in goods; the incident of 26 Dec. 1631 in **269** is said to have occurred in 1630, and the ship's tonnage to have been 100 tons; he was a quarter-owner of the ship. See also **265**.]

271. [*An erased note*]
'Whereas Mr William Isaack, an ancient seaman, is through the hand of

God disabled. . . .' [? Beginning of a certificate to row on the Thames (cf. *THD*, 250–2).]

272. [f.97v] *6 May 1639. London. Depositions in the admiralty court* [? *relating to an application for ordnance*]
On 4 May 1639, Timothy Thornehill, merchant of St Magnus, Thames St. London, aged about 22, was sworn before William Sames, doctor of law and surrogate of Sir Henry Martin, the admiralty court judge. He deposed that about 4 or 5 months ago he was resident in Dunkirk when he received a letter from Mr Thomas Thornehill, merchant of London, asking him to buy a ship of 300 or 400 tons. On 8 Feb. last, he accordingly bought in Dunkirk a Flemish built ship of about 380 tons called the *Fortune*, a prize which had been taken from the Hollanders and which had been put up for public sale by authority of the admiralty of Dunkirk. He bought her for Thomas Thornhill, an Englishman resident in London. Afterwards he hired a crew to bring her to England, and she is now in the Thames and named the *Mary and Barbara* of London, belonging to Thomas Thornehill, Edward Thornehill and himself, all of whom are natural Englishmen and subjects of the king. No stranger has any interest in her. They are fitting her out for a voyage to the West Indies under his command.
On the same day, William Rensham, mariner of Ratcliff, aged about 30, deposed that the ship was bought in April [sic] in the circumstances described above. He and others were hired by Thornehill to view the ship before purchase, and he was one of those who brought her to London. Since her arrival he has had her measured, and she is 100 ft long by the keel, 21 ft broad by the beam, and 9½ ft above the mainmast [f.98] deep in the hold and 10½ ft abaft the mainmast. He is to go as master's mate on the voyage to the West Indies. Thomas Thornhill is reputed to be owner, but he has heard him say that his brother, Edward Thornhill, is quarter-owner. He has also heard Timothy Thornehill say that he is to be a part-owner. Thomas, Edward, and Timothy Thornehill are all natural Englishmen, and he has not heard that any stranger has an interest in her. Thomas Wyan, register. [f.98v is blank.]

TRANSACTIONS, VOL. II

273. [f.1] *10 March 1627. Memorandum*
Today Capt. Weddall left at Trinity House a box of writings concerning himself and Mr Tracey. It is not to be given to either without the consent of the other. The box is put in the trunk.
[Signed] T. Best, Robert Bell, Walter Coke, John Bennett.

274. *10 Apr. 1630. Memorandum*
Today Mr Walter Coke left at Trinity House a box of writings concerning himself and Esther Lunne, widow of Ratcliff. It is not to be given to either without the consent of the other.

[Signed] William Case, Christopher Browne, William Ewen, John Bennett. [f. lv is blank, apart from a rough calculation.]

275. [f.2. *25 May 1626*] *William Gunter, John Westhorrle, S. Wells, H. Lydiard and Edward Stevens* [*? to Sir John Coke, secretary of state*][1]
According to the warrant sent to them on 4 May they have measured divers colliers in the river. Those most in use have large bilges, long floors, and 'shoal decks' for the sake of ease and of profit, which makes them more inconvenient for service [of the king] when the need arises. They chose the *Adventure* of Ipswich, which is specified in the warrant and is one of the greatest 'bilged' ships amongst them, as a model upon which to base their calculations. A ship can be measured according to the old way as used by the king's shipwrights or the new one recently practised. The old way is nearer the truth but since the basis is unknown to them, the writers have discarded it. They reject the new way because it is based on the dead weight of coal 'which lades a ship fitter to sink than to swim in the sea'. They have therefore devised a middle way. The tons and tonnage* of a ship can be regarded in 3 ways: in casks, 2 butts or 4 hogsheads making a ton; in ft, 40 ft of timber making a ton; or in weight, making 20 cwt. a ton. The 'feet' way is the most convenient for measuring an empty ship; the 'weight' way is the most uncertain because the hold can be filled with 'dead lading of differing weights'; the 'cask' way is best because it both allows a convenient burden to the ship and ordnance for defence. Elsewhere, a ship's burden is based upon her capacity to carry casks. They define the hold as 'the cavity of the vessel contained between the lines of her greatest breadth and depth within board, not regarding the ill laying of their orlops*, which "streightneth" the hold, but supposing the lower edge of the beam to be pitched at the breadth, to the end that the ship being fitted in warlike manner and deep laden with her victuals and other necessaries, she may notwithstanding make use of her ordnance'. They next considered how many casks could be carried in the hold, first by drawing the bends* and the form of casks in each bend. This way being subject to error, they used an arithmetical approach, allowing $4\frac{1}{2}$ ft as the length of a butt, 2 ft 8 inches for the depth of the first tier, and 2 ft 4 inches for that of other tiers. They calculated it in ft and divided the whole by 60 because they found that a ton of casks stowed to the best advantage took up 60 solid ft of space. On that basis, the capacity of the hold of the *Adventure* was 207 tons. From that an easy rule can be deduced for the use of measurers, which is understandable by shipowners. The depth of the ship at her greatest breadth to the ceiling* should be taken; at half the depth, the breadth within board should be measured; this mean breadth should be multiplied by the depth, the product by the length of the keel, and the total divided by 65 to obtain the content of the ship in tons. So the mean breadth of the *Adventure* within board is 22 ft, her depth from the ceiling 9 ft 8 inches, and her length 63 ft 6 inches. These multiplied together, make 13,504, which divided by 65 is $207\frac{3}{4}$. [f.2v] If $69\frac{1}{4}$ is added to allow the third part for tonnage, the ship is 277 in tons and tonnage. A comparison was made with her coal carrying capacity. The [coal] meters office showed that she unloaded 187 and

181 chaldrons on 9 Aug. and 6 Sept. 1624, a 'medium' of 184. Allowing 1½ tons per chaldron (although others think 1⅓ tons), that is equivalent to 276 tons. With this cargo, 'her upper wale and breadth' are under water. According to measurements which they have taken, her midships port would be within a foot of the water, and she would be then unfit for service. Measurements of the *Amity* of Woodbridge show that her coal carrying capacity is 298 tons, and her burden in tons and tonnage is 295. The figures for the *Hermitt* of Woodbridge are 289 and 286.

> 1. Cf SP 16/27/67; *CSPD 1625–6*, 341. Gunter has been identified as Edmund Gunter the mathematician, and Lydiard as Hugh Lydiard, clerk of the check at Woolwich (Pett, xci, 226, 229). But Gunter's christian name is clearly William in the Trinity House and SP texts, and *CSPD* states that Lydiard is an incorrect copy of Hillyard (but cf Oppenheim, 267). Wells' christian name is given as 'John' in SP.

276. [f.3. *2 June 1626*] *Trinity House* [*to the special commissioners of the navy. Cf* SP 16/29/7; *CSPD 1625–6*, 346.]
According to the order they have considered the ways of measuring ships as presented in **275**. As to the first or 'cask' method, Gunter and Wells have made the utmost use of art to ascertain the cavity of the hold by ft but to find the content by art is impossible. Besides, no account was taken of the fact that ships carrying casks require ballast, which is called 'kentledge', without which ships will not 'sail-fast' or be fit for the sea in any way and for which seamen allow 12 or 13 tons per 100 in stowing casks. So from the first rule, the *Adventure* is 232 in tons and tonnage*. The second way is rejected because a ship's burden cannot be accurately measured by taking the measurements within board. The thickness of plank and timber varies, which makes a ship greater or smaller. It is also contrary to experience because when a ship's side is furred 6 or 8 inches, she will carry 10 or 12 tons more, and if 15 or 18 inches, 25 or 30 tons; yet in each case the measurements within board would be the same, which would be absurd. This also applies when measurements are taken of the depth, which should be taken not from the ceiling*, but from the outside of the plank next to the keel. Accordingly, the *Adventure* is 229 in tons and 305 in tons and tonnage, based on a length 63½ ft, a breadth of 26½ [26 ft 8 inches], a floor of 21½ $\frac{1}{12}$ [21 ft 7 inches], and a depth of 11¼ ft. The third or 'old' way, which Gunter and Wells think is more accurate, is not so in the case of ships lately built such as colliers which have great floors. It does hold good for old ships which have small floors. On the old rule, the *Adventure*, with a length of 63½ ft, a breadth of 26½ $\frac{1}{6}$ [26ft 8 inches] and a half breadth of 13⅓, would be 225 tons, to which must be added 75, making a total of 300 in tons and tonnage. Contrary to the view of Gunter and Wells, the dead weight method at 20 cwt. to the ton is a certain one if truly applied, 'for their reason that this way is uncertain, it is no reason; for let the severals of dead weight be of what nature it will, still the quantity, viz. 20 cwt. to a ton holds'. If a ship is laden until she is settled in the water to her breadth, which is the lading mark, then the weight in her is the certain burden in tons, at 20 cwt. a ton, to which must be added tonnage. This method is based on reason, experience, antiquity and art.[1]

[Marginal note] Trinity House's answer to Mr Gunter's rule for measuring ships.

1. Postscript in SP text: Unless owners are paid for the full burden, they will be discouraged from building ships, and in any case the rates paid by the king are only half those paid by merchants.

277. [f.3v] *3 Feb. 1627. Inhabitants of Colchester and Wapping to Trinity House*
John Wells of Colchester, the bearer, lost by shipwreck a hoy, the *Hopewell*, of which he was master and part-owner [owner in **279**], whereby he lost £110. Later [on 24 Aug. 1621, in **279**] he lost another hoy, the *Susan*, which was laden with fuller's earth and of which he was master and owner, whereby he lost £127. He is now in great poverty.
Philip Ewers (his mark), William Mace, John Kinge, Ralph Lellie, Robert Coborne, John Beale, Daniel Russell.

278. *3 Feb. 1627. Merchants of the city of London to Trinity House*
John Wells of Colchester, the poor bearer, was master of a hoy, the *John*, outward bound from London to Amsterdam laden with goods worth £1,300, when [on 14 Oct. last, in **279**] she was cast away in foul weather. His loss was £85, and because of this and other losses, he is in great poverty.
Christopher Elan, Nathaniel Wright, George Rookes.
[Endorsement] The loss of the *John* is certified by inhabitants of Wapping: Thomas Cobb, constable; John Dearsly, churchwarden; John Brady, William Greene, Edward Bartly, William Tristram, John Davies, John Houghton, John Caseby, James Ireland, George Humble, Francis Blizard, Peter Marshe, an overseer of the poor.

279. [f.4] *21 Feb. 1627. Trinity House to the lord keeper*
[Certificate on behalf of John Wells specifying the losses mentioned in **277–8**.] He lost a further £230 owing to bankruptcies and other bad debts. His total losses, following suddenly on each other, amount to about £552. He is utterly impoverished and, having fallen into debt as a result of his losses, cannot satisfy his creditors or maintain his wife and small children.
T. Best, W. Cooke, Ro. Bell, Jo. Totten, Ja. Mowyer, Ro. Salmon, Jo. Bennet, William Case, Samuel Doves, Jo. Weddall.

280. [f.4v. *27 Feb. 1627*] *Master shipwrights and Trinity House 'to the high commissioners'* [*Cf* SP 16/55/36; *CSPD 1627–8*, 70.]
A rule to find the burden of ships was requested. They have held a meeting of mariners and shipwrights, and their view is that the best method is that of dead weight in the interest both of the king and of subjects. This is how much 'massie' commodities will settle a ship in the water to her breadth, reckoning 20 cwt. to the ton. The rule is to take the length of the keel from the pitch of the forefoot [the foremost part of the keel] to aft of the post or posts; the breadth at the broadest point, measuring outside the planks; and the depth from the diameter of the breadth to the bottom of the keel. These figures multiplied together

according to the rule will produce the burden in tons according to dead weight. When that is put to the trial, there should be 3 or 4 to represent the king and the same number to represent subjects to avoid complaint. T. Best, [Walter] Cooke, W. Case, John Totten, James Mowyer, W. Ewins, Edward Maplesden, M. Geere, Ro. Salmon, John Bennet, Ro. Bell, S. Doves, John Weddall.

Master shipwrights: John Graves, John Dearsly, Edward Steevens, John Taylor, William Burch.[1]

1. Postscript in SP text: The rule is to multiply the length, breadth and depth together, and divide the product by 94 to obtain the tonnage.

281. [f.5. *27 Feb. 1627*] *Trinity House* [*to the lords commissioners of the navy. Cf SP 16/55/34; CSPD 1627–8, 70.*]

According to the order of 20 Feb. they have considered the number and burden of the ships required to intercept Lübeckers' ships in passage for Spain, for what time, and at what places. Two second rank ships of the king and 2 merchant ships of 300 tons should ride at the bar of Lübeck, which is a safe road for them. If the bar is thought to be unfit in view of the king of Denmark, they should ride at 'Lapsand' [? Lappegrund], which is 4 or 5 miles on this side of Elsinore. The great ships of Lübeck which come by Elsinore pass by that way. Smaller ships bound for Spain may come by the Belt, but 2 or 3 merchant ships riding in the Belt within the Skaw between the 'Holmes' [? Hjelm] and the Anholt would intercept these. In the Belt there are one or 2 places from which small ships can come and go to Spain, but the 2 or 3 ships stationed in the Belt shall command these. The time must be the whole summer from 15 March until 30 Sept., since ships come from all parts of the Sound to sea during this period.[1]

1. Signatures in SP text: Michael Geere, William Case, Robert Salmon, Samuel Doves, William Ewen, John Teemsome [? Tomson], James Moyer, T. Best, Robert Bell, Edward Maplesden, John Bennet, Jo. Weddell, Richard Chester.

282. [f.5v. *c. 1626–7*][1] *Report by John Goodwin and others*

'Having diligently sought out the proportion of corn and cask, we find near 60 foot cubic to be contained in a ton square of cask with the vacuities and of corn but 46 without any vacuities, and having made a medium between these 2 we find 53 square feet to be in a ton, too much in corn, too little in cask. And yet a ton contained in 2 butts allowed to be cylinders at the bigness they are at the bouge [belly] contain but 50 feet.' So the 53 feet seems indifferent. Mr Wells found the cubic content of the *Adventure* to be 12,420 solid feet, which divided by 53 produces 234 tons, and 312 in tons and tonnage*, which agrees with 'our' way because the depth of the *Adventure* at the waterline is 13 feet, her breadth without board 26⅔ feet, and her length 63½ feet. Multiplied all together, the product is 22,013, which divided by 94 is 234 tons, and 312 in tons and tonnage as before.

1. See **275–6, 280**. Perhaps after 3 Apr. 1627, when John Wells and John Goodwin had reported on the subject (SP 16/59/26).

283. [f.6] *2 May 1627. Trinity House of Deptford to the Trinity House of Dover*[1]

For many years, the pilots of the Cinque Ports, especially those of Deal, have wronged the corporation. Despite the benefit which these pilots obtain from buoys and beacons, and the agreement between the 2 Trinity Houses, they refuse to contribute for beaconage and buoyage. Only 1s in the pound is sought, which is what members of Trinity House Deptford have to pay, as compared with 2s which others pay. Only 1s is demanded because of the 1s which they pay to their own fellowship [of the Cinque Ports]. Trinity House Deptford have often conferred with some of these pilots, namely the Ranns, but they say that the 2s [sic] demanded is paid to 'your corporation'. There should not be 2 payments for the same thing but if there are, the Dover corporation is in debt to Trinity House Deptford. If no payments have been made, it is hoped that no ill will be taken if these refractory fellows who abuse both corporations are brought to account by imprisonment or some other course. To prevent further abuses, the addressees, especially Mr John Pringle, and the master and wardens are asked to accept this delegation for the collection of dues from pilots who take ships within their liberties or fellowship into or out of the Thames. Such good offices would be reciprocated.

1. The Dover fellowship of lodemanage was never incorporated as a Trinity House.

284. [f.6v] *9 June 1627. Ratcliff. Trinity House to Sir John Sackvill*

In reply to **285**, they have conferred with, and think that they have satisfied, Capt. Dupper about the waftage* of colliers and the defence of the north coast. Three of the ships which are to serve as men-of-war should be made ready with all expedition to attend the next fleet, and the other 3 should be ready shortly afterwards so that the colliers can have notice to meet their escorts. For frugality, the commanders should be able seamen with long experience of the trade and the coast. The 6 ships will accompany the fleet to and from the Shields with as much coal as they can carry (about 60 chaldrons) without prejudice to the operation of ordnance and function as men-of-war. They will discharge their coal at London with the rest, load ballast, and be ready to sail back again with the first colliers. Each should have a crew of 60, of whom one-third should be watermen and landsmen who can fire muskets, divided into 2 or 3 squadrons at the discretion of the commanders. This will be sufficient for the London trade. With able seamen as commanders, the profit from the coal sales will cover the cost of the freight of these ships. They should keep together so as to make the more voyages and profit from the 60 chaldrons. Each ship should make a profit of £50 a voyage, making a total of £2,100 in 9 months, leaving aside the 6d a chaldron payable by all coast ships which will maintain 2 other men-of-war. They should always be at sea to defend the north coast and will not go into harbour as the other 6 will do. Every ship of 150 tons and over should carry 4 pieces of ordnance, and those with more should retain them. The wafters will be at sea from 1 Feb. until 31 Oct., and in that time 7 voyages should be made, provided that the city [of London] undertakes to discharge the fleet expeditiously

83

at reasonable rates for each voyage. [f.7] One half of the colliers will not benefit from waftage because they must stay at London to sell their coal or else sell at a loss. The king's council should order the owners of coal at Newcastle not to raise prices or to abate measures.

285. *5 June 1627. Westminster. Sir John Sackvile [to Trinity House. See* **284**; **372–3**.]
In view of the losses imposed upon merchants and inhabitants of the northern parts by Dunkirkers, the king and the lord admiral have instructed him to arrange for the raising and maintenance of 6 men-of-war to waft* colliers to and fro, and to defend the north coast. Capt. James Duppa has been appointed commander of the fleet. No doubt they will wish well such a worthy work, and they are asked to meet Duppa to discuss the proposals which he will propound.

286. [f.7v] *29 June 1627. [Sir] Henry Martyn [admiralty court judge] to Trinity House*
'A', the half-owner of a ship 'B' with her apparel and tackle, freighted his share to 'C', the other half-owner, for £12 a month, as per charter party. 'C' took out letters of marque and fitted the ship with shot, munitions and ordnance. The ship returned with a prize. They should examine the charter party and consider whether 'A', as half-owner, is entitled to half the third part of the prize.
[Marginal note] About Mr Slany and Mr King.

287. *4 July 1627. Ratcliff. Trinity House [to Sir Henry Martyn, admiralty court judge]*
In reply to **286**, 'A' as owner is entitled to a share in the third part, but not a full half because 'C' furnished ordnance, powder and shot, whereby he had the greater adventure. They have received from Mr Kinge a charter party between him and Mr Slany, but it says nothing about prizes and relates only to a merchant voyage.
Messrs Cooke, Salmon, Bennett, Case, Raineborow, Ewins, Swann, Totten.

288. [f.8] *13 July 1627. [Sir] Henry Marten [admiralty court judge to Trinity House]*
He referred to them a case and a charter party between Humphrey Slaines, merchant of London, and Thomas King, mariner [**286**]. Their opinion [**287**] is not so plain as he would like. They should reconsider the matter and the charter party and report speedily whether Kinge should have a part of the prize and how much, not consulting anyone who is not of their company.

289. *26 July 1627. Ratcliff. Trinity House [to Sir Henry Marten, admiralty court judge]*
In reply to **288**, they had considered that **287** was a full answer to the general question, and it was compiled without consulting anyone not of their corporation. Now that the reference is made particular to the case of

Slany and Kinge according to the charter party, their view is that Kinge is entitled to such a part of the third share as is proportionate to his adventure in the ship.

Mr Cooke, deputy master; Sir H. Manneringe, Messrs Downinge, Kitchen, Rainsborow, Bennett, Case, Totten, Mowyer, Trenchfeild, Swanly, Swann.

290. [ff.8v–9] *13 July 1627. Order of the privy council concerning payment for the league with Algiers from money collected for the Algiers expedition* [Printed in *APC 1627*, 415–16.]

291. *18 July 1627. Order of the privy council concerning money collected by Trinity House for the Algiers expedition* [Printed in *APC 1627*, 423–4.]

292. *21 July 1627. Receipt by John Cordall, treasurer of the Levant company*
Received £550 from Trinity House, by virtue of the privy council order of 13 July 1627 [**290**], being part of the money remaining in their hands as a result of the levy on shipping for the Algiers expedition. The privy council ordered that this money be paid to the Turkey company.

293. [f.9v] *24 and 28 July 1627. Award by Trinity House*
A statement of the differences between the owners and victuallers of the *William and John* of London, which both sides referred on 24 July to the captains and masters of Trinity House, and the award of Trinity House dated 28 July 1627. Questions put to Trinity House:
(a) Should the owners pay for the muskets as well as the ordnance? Award: Yes.
(b) Should the owners provide all unexpendable munitions and instruments such as pikes, bandoliers, swords, pistols, latten cases, rammer heads [for cannon charges], sponge heads, ladles, wooden and latten budge barrels [i.e. small barrels of gunpowder], sheepskins, dark and light lanterns, and other small provisions for the gunner's store? Award: Yes.
(c) Since the cost of the victuals amount to more than half the value of the ship, what allowance should be made for setting her out as a man-of-war with 19 pieces of ordnance and a crew of 80 or 90 victualled for 6 or 8 months? What powder, shot and other munitions are requisite for the gunner's store? Award: 25 barrels of powder and 25 shot for each gun. The cost to be borne equally between both.
(d) Ought the fire works, namely 6 fire pikes, 6 trunks, 12 fire-balls and grenades and 3 or 4 dozen fire-pots be provided by the owners? Award: Equally borne.
(e) The shallop [a heavy sailing boat] is built for the benefit of the whole voyage. Should the owners provide 2 murderers*, sails, oars and a grapnel, or should the victuallers share the cost? Award: Equally borne.
(f) Should the owners provide 2 grapnels for the ship, foreign colours,

and the carpenter's store? Award: The owners, the grapnels and the carpenter's store; the victuallers, the foreign colours.

(g) Should the surgeon's chest be provided by the victuallers or partly by the owners or, if purchase [prize] is taken, by the company? Award: The victuallers.

(h) What shares belong to the captain and officers, and what pillage to the company, and what 'duties' [perquisites] belong to officers, prizes being taken? [**294** was probably attached to answer this question.]

(i) Should the captain pay for the 2 letters of marque, or should the owners or victuallers pay part? Award: Equally borne between 'both'.

Messrs Cooke, Bennett, Ewins, Case, Tutchen, Hockett, Totton, Swanly, Swanne.

294. [f.10] *1 Aug. 1627. Statement by Trinity House* [This entry is crossed out.]

The ancient custom in queen Elizabeth's time concerning shares and other 'duties' belonging to the officers of men-of-war was as follows: the captain has the best piece of ordnance; the master, the best anchor and cable; the gunner, the second piece of ordnance; the boatswain, the main-topsail; the boatswain's mate, the fore-topsail; the master's mates, the bonnets [canvas tied to the bottom of a sail to catch the wind] and spritsail; the quartermasters, the mizen [? sail]; the coxswain, the topgallantsail; the surgeon, the surgeon's chest and all 'chirurgery'; the carpenter, all carpenter's tools; the trumpeter, the trumpets, if any. The mariners' furniture, apparel, chests, etc. is pillage for sharing among the whole company as follows: captain, 9; master, 8; master's mates, 6; midshipmen, 5; gunner, boatswain, quartermasters, carpenter, cook, surgeon, trumpeter, 4 each; boatswain's mate, carpenter's mate, steward, coxswain, cooper and all under officers, 3 each. The master's mates, midshipmen, quartermasters, boatswain and gunner are always the sharemakers. After they have laid out each man's share, the master or captain usually 'meddle' to remedy defects. The sharemakers are to lay out such dead men's shares as seem meet to them. The captain and the master are to consider what single and deserving men on the voyage should have these. If an officer or a man is slain or dies when or after the prize is taken, he is to have the share appropriate to his place. Anyone chosen to replace dead men is to be paid from the dead shares.

Sir Michael Geer, Messrs Cooke, Salmon, Bennett, Rainborowe, Totton, Case, Doves, Tutchen, Hockett, Swann, Swanly, Tompson, Mowyer, Trenchfeild.

295. [f.10v] *14 Sept. 1627. Doctors' Commons* [*London. Sir*] *Henry Martyn* [*admiralty court judge to Trinity House*]

Mr Wilson, the bearer, said that they had furnished him with a clause from an ancient record of their House concerning shares under letters of marque [**294**], but without date or names. They should add the date and some of their names to certify its authenticity to enable him to settle a case concerning pillage.

296. *15 Sept. 1627. Ratcliff. Trinity House [to Sir Henry Martyn, admiralty court judge]*
In reply to **295**, they found **294** among some of their old papers, without date. It concurs with the experience of the ancients of the company who 'used these affairs' in the time of queen Elizabeth. A copy is attached.
Ro. Salmon, M. Geere, William Case, Ro. Bell, W. Coke, William Rainborow, John Bennett, John Totten.

297. [f.11] *19 Sept. 1627. Trinity House of Deptford to the Trinity House of Dover*
Their last letter [? **283**] was taken by Mr Samuel Doves, a brother of Trinity House Deptford, who on his return reported that Rannd had certified the Dover corporation before Sir John Hepsley that he had paid or given satisfaction for pilotage to some of the Deptford corporation. But they cannot find any record of his having paid since their agreement with lord Zouche, although payment was often demanded. About 4 or 5 years ago, Rannd offered £14 or £15 on condition that he was indemnified against the claims of the Dover corporation but they had refused his offer and had told him to pay what was due to both corporations since when they have heard of no payment made by him. They understand that he 'gives braving terms', but they hope that Sir John Hepsley and the Dover brethren will take some order with him.

298. [f.11v] *6 Oct. 1627. Trinity House of Dover to the Trinity House of Deptford*
They have been unable to reply previously to **283**. They summoned those of Deal who were sworn to their fellowship to appear at a court held on 29 Sept. before Sir John Hisperley, lieutenant of Dover castle, and themselves, the master, commissioners and wardens of the fellowship. **283** was read, but the Deal men affirmed that they had paid to the Deptford corporation 1s in the pound for every voyage, either in person or through their appointed brokers. The wrongs committed by the Deal men against the Dover fellowship are so heavy that satisfaction for them cannot be given. Seeing no remedy without much trouble, all past offences have been remitted on their promise to offend no more, but wrongs against the Deptford corporation are left to that corporation's discretion. For the future they have decreed that the Deal men are to be accountable to the fellowship for the 1s in the pound due to the Deptford corporation and a man has been appointed and sworn to keep a book of pilotage purchases and turns,[1] and to receive the payments due to the Deptford corporation. He will pay the money to the Dover fellowship every quarter day, and state what each man has paid, by which means all duties belonging to the Deptford corporation will come safely to hand.
Thomas Tiddeman, master; John Pringle, Edmond Woodgreene, John Varlye, John Chaser.

1. Pilots were arranged in a rota and undertook pilotage in turn.

299. [f.12] *11 Oct. 1627. [Sir] Sackville Crowe [treasurer of the navy] and [Sir] William Russell [to Trinity House. See 300.]*
Victuals are to be sent to the king's army on the Île de Ré, and each ship must carry seacoal instead of ballast in addition to victuals. Advice is sought on the appropriate quantities.
[Marginal note] Letter about the transport of coal to St Martins.

300. *11 Oct. 1627. Trinity House [to Sir Sackville Crowe, treasurer of the navy, and Sir William Russell]*
In reply to **299**, they called together their company. Ships that have broad and long floors and are not over pressed with much ordnance could carry 10 chaldrons of seacoal for every 100 tons burden in place of ballast. Those which have sharp* and narrow floors, which carry much ordnance and have 3 decks whereby the ordnance is carried high should not have coal in place of kentledge as ballast because coal is very bulky and is not solid enough. Their experience is that to carry coal in a ship which is laden with victuals risks 'spoiling of the whole bulk'.
Mr Cooke, master; Messrs Doves, Bell, Hocket, Mowyer, Trenchfeild, Rainborow, Bennet, Totten, Swanly, Thompson.

301. [f.12v] *14 Nov. 1627. Report by Trinity House*
Sir John Cooke, secretary of state, ordered them to provide a pilot to take the king's ship, the *Adventure*, to Goeree on the coast of Holland. They can only find Peter Hilles, who has been there once or twice but who dares not undertake the task, so they are unable to recommend him or anyone else. Flushing, being a safe and near port, may be fitter if the king is employing his ship on that coast; the master would then be as sufficient a pilot as any they know.
Messrs Coke, Case, Doves, Swann, Tompson.

302. [f.13] *28 Nov. 1627. [Sir] John Wostenholme, William Burrell [navy commissioners] and [Sir] William Russell [to Trinity House. See 303.]*
They enclose a letter from Mr Kitchen of Bristol stating that the roads of the port of Bristol are unsafe for any of the king's ships of charge, namely the *St Andrewe* and the *Antelopp*. The writers are required to give the lord admiral their opinion about ships riding there, and the suitability of the *Antelopp* for guarding the Irish coast. The advice of the addressees is sought, since opposition may be met. When the ships were at Bristol before they last went to sea, Mr Burrell had to order 'the "heelding" of their ports under water', and dared not careen the ships. Mr Burrell considers that since the *Antelop* is a ship without a floor,¹ and cannot be quickly examined and graved if she springs a leak, she is unfit for the Irish coast. A reply is requested today.

   1. ? The underside of the bottom was so narrow that she could not remain upright when grounded.

303. *28 Nov. 1627. [Trinity House to Sir John Wostenholme, William Burrell, navy commissioners, and Sir William Russell]*
In reply to **302** about the safe riding of the *St Andrewe* and the *Antelopp* in

the river of Bristol or adjoining ports during the winter, their view is that the river [Avon], Hung Road and King Road would not be safe. Because of the narrowness of the river and the swiftness of the tide, their keels would lie in the deepest water and there is no suitable place for careening or graving. Since the *Antelopp* is a very sharp* ship, it would be dangerous. The great draught and small floor of the *Antelop* makes her less fit than other ships of the king for service on the Irish coast. Ships with less draught and better floors would be safer for going in and coming out, and could be easily graved and cleansed.
Messrs Cooke, Chester, Totton, Best, Case, Bennet, Hockett.

304. [f.13v] *26 Nov. 1627.* [Sir] *William Russell, William Burrell, Edmund Sawyer and 'Den' Flemminge* [to Trinity House. See **305**.]
Enclosed are 2 references from James I and Charles I concerning a patent which Mistress Euphemia Murrey seeks for herself and her assignees for an office for 31 years to survey and seal all sackcloth, poldavis [i.e. coarse canvas] and hemp cloth made in England and Wales. The addressees should state whether the erection of such an office will enable the production of sufficient for the shipping of the realm, whether it will be made better and more lasting, and whether any benefit will accrue to the poor by keeping them in employment.
[Marginal note] The commissioners' letter about poldavis.

305. [f.14. *After 26 Nov. 1627.*] *Trinity House* [to Sir William Russell, William Burrell, Edmund Sawyer and 'Den' Flemminge]
In reply to **304**, the creation of an office as requested by Mistress Murrey will not result in greater production of mildernix [i.e. canvas] and poldavis than now, which is far from sufficient for the shipping of the realm. As much is made now as in former times. The creation of the office would not result in a more lasting and serviceable product. The true remedy is the execution of the statute made in 1 James I [c. 24] against the deceitful manufacture of mildernix and poldavis from which sail cloth for the ships of the navy and others is made. Those who are prepared to pay for good material can have it. Every man buys for the use which he has for it, obtaining both good and bad according to his need at various prices. The office would not benefit the poor by providing them with work.
Thomas Best, Robert Salmon, Samuel Doves, Gervais Hockett, Richard Swann, William Ewins, Walter Coke, William Case, Robert Bell, John Bennet, John Totton, John Tompson.

306. [f.14v] *29 Dec.* [1627] *Trinity House to the king* [Cf SP 16/87/59; *CSPD 1627–8*, 481.]
According to his command they assembled in the presence of Sir John Wostenholme and Mr Burrell all owners and masters of ships trading to Newcastle who live here near the city and have their shipping in the Thames. The king's question about the prices which they would want per chaldron of coal if the king provided them with a convoy was put. They requested and were given a respite and on their return sought freedom in

their trading, asking that no price be set. If it was fixed, they would be discouraged in their trade and from building ships because the profit must be small while the loss was uncertain and could be greater. If the gain was small when the adventure is great, they would never build ships to replace those lately lost. They prefer to take their fortune in the market. They were then asked what, if the king granted their request, they would be prepared to contribute per chaldron of coal in return for safe convoy. They answered that they now provided their own convoys and had at great expense furnished their ships with ordnance, small ones with 4 pieces, some with 6, the better sort with 8 or 9. They carry 3 or 4 men more in each ship than formerly, and they go in fleets of 40, 50, or 60 ships. Despite the wishes of the owners and masters to run their own convoys, Trinity House consider that the king should make provision for the sake of his honour and safety of his subjects.

[Marginal note] This answer was delivered to the king on 29 Dec. at the council by the master, Capt. Best, Mr Doves and Mr Totton.

[f.15. Note] Owners and masters trading to Newcastle who gave the above answers here in the House: William Case, Robert Bell, John Totton, Samuel Doves, William Ewins, Edward Dalton, Peter Leonard, William Cocke, Mr Pulman, Thomas Davis, William Joanes, Thomas Martyn, James Peterson, Mr Hudson, Robert Toackly, Jonas James, George Clarkson, Mr Holt, John Elmnor, John Hall, John Cordett, John Curtise, Mr Greene.

307. [f.15–15v] *20 Dec. 1627. Trinity House and shipowners to the commissioners of the navy about the payment of freight for ships employed by the king* [*Cf* SP 16/87/30(1); *CSPD 1627–8,* 476–7. SP states that the document emanated from the shipowners but a marginal note in the Trinity House text says that it was presented by the master of Trinity House. Both texts have the following names appended (not listed in *CSPD*): Richard Chester, William Case, Robert Bell, John Totton, Samuel Doves, William Ewins, Anthony Tutchin, Edm. Morgan, Miles White, John Lowe, Robert Toackly, John Hide, William Goodladd, John Bundocke, Edward Dalton, John Thompson, Robert Salmon, senior, Jonas James, Thomas Davis, William Joanes, Richard Beomounte, Emmanuel Finch, Thomas Hackwell, Henry Houlton, Robert Salmon, junior, John Pountis. The Trinity House text has the following additional names: Anthony Havelland, William Traddall, Peter Leonard, John Morris, William Pulman, Edward Crosse, William Cock. The SP text has the following additional names: John Heaman, Gervais Hockett, Brian Harrison, John Gibbon, John Briand, John Curtis, William Grene, John Webber, Thomas (? Peach), William (? Coppard), William (? Pulman).]

308. [f.16] *4 Jan. 1628. A proposal* [*Cf* SP 16/54/27 and *CSPD 1627–8,* 58, incorrectly dated 16 Feb. 1627.]
Ships of 3 decks are of greatest force and most useful as men-of-war if built as follows. The lower orlop* should be laid 2 ft under the water

[line]. The bread room and all other store rooms, coiled cables, the crew's chests and other luggage, and boarded cabins for officers should be on this orlop, as would be the lodging for most of the crew. The second orlop should be 6 ft or at least 5½ ft higher, and the sides made 'musket free' [immune to musket fire] fore and aft. A ship as long and as broad as the *Lyon* should have 9 ports a side, besides the 4 chase-ports*, fore and aft. These should be at least 2 ft 9 inches square, and above 2 ft from the deck to the sill of the port. Between every 2 ports, there should be hanging cabins [hammocks] to fold up to the decks, as lodging for the men. Loopholes should be cut for the firing of small shot in close fight. There should be 22 culverins* on this orlop. The third deck should be 6½ ft higher, between plank and plank 'but it shall not be whole through for her waist shall be only a grating' where there will be no ordnance, only 2 or 3 great murderers* or fowlers a side; this area will be used for stowing boats. There will be 8 demi-culverins* abaft the mast and 4 in the forecastle. There should be a little 'rising' [? screen] out of her forecastle and abaft her steerage, with loopholes for small shot and murderers placed there to clear the decks if the ship is boarded. There should be a 'snug round house' aft for the master, his mates, the lieutenant and the preacher. The bulkhead should be made musket free. Loopholes should be cut and murderers placed to clear the decks as aforesaid; abaft, a scuttle should be cut to enable retreat into the great cabin if they are beaten from [the round house]. On the upper deck, there should be stanchions in the waist upon which to hang chains to keep up the waist cloths [coloured cloths used to conceal men in action, or as an adornment]. No galleries should be built on her sides but only a cobbler's shop aft. The great cabin should be divided by a bulkhead: the aft part should be a lodging and a closet for the captain, and the fore part a dining room and a placing for 2 pieces of ordnance. Such a ship could hardly be captured, sunk, or set on fire, and she would be much better than those now in service. The hold will be kept sweet and the victuals preserved. She could not be surprised being always ready for fight, the cables, chests and other luggage which now hinder the use of ordnance being on the lower deck. There will be more lodging for the crew which is [f.16v] a principal thing for the conservation of their health, and the lodging would be snugger than now. Although less ordnance would be carried, the ship would be of greater force because she could be employed in all weathers, and the crew would be immune to small shot. If 500 men were to board her, they could be beaten off because of her ability for close fighting which none of the king's ships now built can do because they are 'all open and have no close fights'.

309. *[4 x 16 Jan. 1628. Duke of] Buckingham [lord high admiral] to the commissioners of the navy [See 308, 310.]*
They are to consult Mr Burrell, Trinity House, Capt. Pett and others of the king's shipwrights, and others as necessary about **308**, 'and particularly to consider whether it will not be best for service that the lower tier of ordnance lie not above five ft above the water'. A speedy reply is requested.

310. *16 Jan. 1628. Trinity House [? to the commissioners of the navy. See* **309.**]

They have considered **308**. The design is for the master shipwrights but it is not new as is pretended, but has been used for all good merchant ships. As to the proposition that 3-deck ships are of greatest force and use as men-of-war, the most important characteristic of the king's ships is that they should be 'good sailers'. Experience has shown that 3-deck ships require more timber, planks and iron, adding more weight and strength 'so is it in nature of a clog and much hinders her sailing'. Nothing is more prejudicial to a man-of-war. Ships of the *Lyon's* rank with 2½ decks, a fair forecastle, 2 tiers of ordnance fore and aft (the lower being 5 ft above water), having 4 months' victuals, are best for the king's service, both offensive and defensive, and are best for the crew. A third deck lying 2 or 3 ft under water is alleged to provide the crew with more commodious lodging and to be better for their [f.17] health. But it would be a dungeon and the air would not be so sweet and clean as on the second orlop*. The placing of storerooms on the third orlop is not worth answering because raising them from the hold will diminish the ship's stoutness and stiffness. A fair depth between decks is about 6 ft, 'one inch or 2 more or less breaks no square'. As for the sides of the ship being musket free, that is already so in all the king's ships; more timber plank would be prejudicial. The proposals about the number and sizes of ports are good instructions for carpenters who have never seen ports or built ships. 'And for galleries we allow not, neither those great cabins which is cause of the displacing of 4 pieces of ordnance, and of the weakening of the force of the ship's quarters.' A neat cabin for the captain with a little dining room 'that so all room be disposed for ordnance' and the contriving proposed for greater defence against being surprised, sunk or fired add no security. How a ship can carry less ordnance, yet be of greater force, is beyond their understanding. As for boarding a king's ship, the only case is that of the *Revenge* in the time of queen [Elizabeth]; the enemy lost then many 100 men and at last gained her, only 'by composition'. Seamen in merchant ships fear not boarding, even though the crew number only 40 or 50. The king's ships with 200 and 250 men and well furnished have much less cause for fear; 'neither want they close fights', having half decks, forecastles and ports to scour with ordnance fore and aft. Nothing can be bettered for close fights.

Walter Coke, Sir Michael Geere, Capt. Best, Messrs Case, Totton, Hockett, Tompson, Salmon, Bennett, Bushell, Tuchen, Swan, Bell.

311. [f.17v] *27 Jan. 1628. [Sir] Ro. Heath [attorney general] to Trinity House [See* **312.**]

He has been directed to ask whether they make a charge of 7d a ton on all strangers' ships entering the Thames, and 8d for every foot of water they draw, and if so, by what authority.

312. *[After 27 Jan. 1628] Trinity House [to Sir Robert Heath, attorney general]*

In reply to **311** they assign pilots to take all strangers' ships out of the

Thames clear of the sands for which they demand 7d a ton according to ancient custom, but not 6d a ton is received. Likewise at coming in they demand 8d for every foot of water drawn which is in the nature of 'loadmony' [cf **430**] or poundage. Their authority is their charter which empowers them to appoint pilots for all strangers' ships at such a reasonable rate as they think fit, according to the size of the ship. Strangers are not wronged because charges for ships of the king and merchants are no less. Pilotage charges abroad are much greater. Apart from a small charge of 2s 6d, 4s or 5s, as their duty to the corporation, fees are not levied on small pinks and hoys which draw little water and come over the sands at high water regardless of channels. The greatest part of the money is spent on the strangers' poor shipwrecked men who come daily for relief.

313. [f.18] *31 Jan. 1628. Whitehall.* [*Privy council to Trinity House. Cf APC 1627–8, 254.*]
Because of continual advertisement of preparations by foreign enemies, the king has ordered the writers to instruct the addressees to cause all shipowners to make ready their ships, in case they are required for the defence of the realm. Owners of ships taken up will receive such pay as will content them.
[Lords] Mandevill,[1] Pembroke, [Burly[2] erased], 'Bi Dearham' [? bishop of Durham], bishop of Bath and Wells, [Sir] T. Edmundes, [Sir] John Coke, [Sir] Richard Wiston, 'Francis' [? *recte* Sir Humphrey] May.

1. ? Earl of Manchester; his son, who bore the courtesy title, was not then a privy councillor.
2. ? William Cecil, lord Burghley, but 2nd earl of Exeter since 1623.

314. [ff.18v–19] *5 Feb. 1628. Survey by Trinity House* [*Cf* SP 16/92/45; *CSPD 1627–8*, 546.]
Ships now in the Thames which could be made fit for the king's service are as follows:
[(a) tons; (b) 'ordnance capable'; (c) ordnance aboard]
Ships appertaining to the East India company:
Greate James (a) 900, (b) 40, (c) nil, and *Charles* (a) 700, (b) 36, (c) nil, in Blackwall dock; *Jonas* (a) 700, (b) 36, (c) 36, and *Expedition*, (a) 200, (b) 10, (c) 10, prepared for sea; *London* (a) 800, (b) 38, (c) nil, and *Reformation* (a) 300, (b) 24, (c) nil, riding at Erith; *Greate Neptune* (a) 600, (b) 34, (c) 34, earl of Warwick.
Merchant ships:
London (a) 500, (b) 30, (c) 10, and *Unicorne* (a) 450, (b) 24, (c) nil, new ships; *Dragon* (a) 450, (b) 30, (c) 30; *Hector* (a) 350, (b) 28, (c) 28; *Assurance* (a) 300, (b) 22, (c) 22; *George* (a) 300, (b) 24, (c) 24, *Peter and Andrew* (a) 260, (b) 26, (c) 26, *Seahorse* (a) 260, (b) 18, (c) 18, *Paragon*, (a) 250, (b) 24, (c) 24, and *Merchant Bonaventure* (a) 220, (b) 20, (c) 20, newly come home from the king's service; *Neptune*, (a) 200, (b) 19, (c) 19, *Lyones* (a) 200, (b) 16, (c) 16, and *Merchant Bonaventure*, (a) 160, (b) 16, (c) 16, newly come from Cornwall with tin; *Ann* (a) 160, (b) 14, (c) 14; *Plaine John* (a) 180, (b) 14, (c) 14; *Speedwell* (a) 140, (b) 12, (c) nil, a

prize ship; *Increase* (a) 160, (b) 12, (c) 6; *Pilgrim* (a) 160, (b) 14, (c) 6; *John and Francis* (a) 120, (b) 12, (c) 12; *Litle Neptune* (a) 140, (b) 12, (c) 9; *Hopewell* (a) 200, (b) 16, (c) 16, newly come from Hamburg; *Neptune* of Chester (a) 140, (b) 12, (c) nil.

Ships ready and bound to sea:
Abigall (a) 300, (b) 26, (c) 26, *Faith* (a) 250, (b) 20, (c) 20, *Endeavor* (a) 180, (b) 16, (c) 16, *Blessinge*, (a) 200, (b) 16, (c) 16, *Elizabeth and Maudlyn* (a) 160, (b) 10, (c) 10, and *Charity* (a) 200, (b) 20, (c) 18, ships ready; *Exchange* (a) 200, (b) 18, (c) 16, *Lemmon* (a) 140, (b) 11, (c) 11, *Jonas* (a) 250, (b) 20, (c) 18, *Blew Dove* (a) 150, (b) 14, (c) 12, *Susan* (a) 180, (b) 16, (c) 16, and *St Peter* (a) 240, (b) 12, (c) 12, newly come from sea.

Newcastle ships:
Desire of Ipswich (a) 250, (b) 16, (c) 16, *Elizabeth* (a) 200, (b) 14, (c) 6, *Ann* (a) 250, (b) 18, (c) 18, *Susan and Ellyn* (a) 250, (b) 16, (c) 16, *Hopewell* (a) 150, (b) 10, (c) 10, *Ann Speedwell* (a) 240, (b) 14, (c) 5, *Mathew* (a) 240, (b) 14, (c) 14, *Recoverie* (a) 240, (b) 12, (c) 6, *Mary* (a) 240, (b) 14, (c) 7, *Resolution* (a) 240 (b) [14 in SP], (c) [nil in SP], *Josias* (a) 200, (b) [12 in SP], (c) [5 in SP], *Seaflower* (a) 240, (b) 12, (c) 9, *Constant Mary* (a) 240, (b) 14, (c) 6, *William* (a) 240, (b) 16, (c) 10, *Patient Adventure* (a) 240 [210 in SP], (b) 16, (c) 16, *William and Thomasin* (a) 240 (b) 14, (c) 5, *Camelion* (a) 250, (b) 16, (c) 16, *Abraham* (a) 240, (b) 16, (c) 10, *Francis* (a) 200, (b) 12, (c) 3, and *Convert* (a) 240, (b), 16, (c), 11, newly come home from the king's service; *Sara* of Newcastle (a) 150, (b) 10, (c) 4; *Hope*, a flyboat, (a) 200, (b) 10, (c) 6, come home from the king's service.

To further the service, they have given a warrant to each master or owner in accordance with **313**.

315. [f.19v] *13 Feb. 1628. Report by Trinity House*
Their opinion has been asked on whether the loss of the *Samuell* of London (John Gibbins master and part-owner), burnt during the 'briminge'[1] or drying of the breadroom, should be borne by the owners or by the hirers. They know of many such casualties but never that the hirers had to compensate the owners for the ship, because the master and not the hirers has charge of her. The master is trusted by the owners and the hirers, for his skill and diligence, to have the care of the ship, her furniture and goods. If casualty happens owing to fire, ill mooring, or a sailing error, 'the master will be found short in point of good discretion, of care, or of skill, but the indiscretion of the master hath ever passed for good discretion . . . because it was the master his best discretion'. The owners must bear the loss of their ship; the hirers the loss of their goods.
Messrs Best, Totton, Ewins, Bell, Goodlad, Coke, Salmon, Bennett, Swann, Doves, Hockett, Tutchin, Thompson.

1. Perhaps brimstone (sulphur) was used. It was later used for fumigation.

316. [f.20] *23 Apr. 1628. Memorandum [by Trinity House]*
John Goodladd has sundry times spoken very scandalously and to the detriment of the corporation, as appears by sworn testimony of Messrs

Doves, Tompson, Hart [**317**] and Steevens. Goodladd was called before the company, and it was agreed to commit him to the Marshalsea until he gave better satisfaction. A warrant dated 16 Apr. was sent to Solomon Smith and the keeper of the prison. On 18 Apr. he went to the Marshalsea and stayed there for 5 or 6 days. He was then sent for again by the House, confessed his fault, and asked forgiveness, promising not to offend again. [Marginal note] John Goodlades was released from the Marshalsea upon his submission.

317. *2 Apr. 1628. Concerning the abusive speech of John Goodladd, master of the Talbott of London*
On Shrove Tuesday 1626 [sic], they were on Tower Hill with inhabitants of that place. Goodladd told divers disorderly seamen there that they were a company of fools and that if they would be ruled by him, and did not get their wages that day, he would counsel them (some 400 or 500 of them) to come down to the Trinity House and pull it down unless those [of Trinity House] took action to secure wages for them. To prevent danger, Mr Bernard Mootam took him to the Rose tavern, and there Goodladd disparaged the corporation and particular members.
Samuel Doves, John Tompson, Timothy Hart.
[Note] Doves and Hart testified on oath to the truth of the above; Tompson swore that Goodladd came to him afterwards and told him that he had spoken thus on the Hill.

318. [f.20v. As in **294**.]

319. [f.21] *27 June 1628. Trinity House to Mr Walter Cooke and Mr William Ewins, members of the company*
According to an order of 25 June they are to repair to Yarmouth, Lowestoft, Caister and Winterton; inspect the keeping of the lights and buoys; sound the channels; consider whether the lighthouses and buoys are well placed as leading marks and repair any defects. They are to direct the erection of a new lighthouse as an upper light in Lowestoft (the other being in daily danger of being swept away by the sea). Mr Wylde and whoever they think fit should be asked to oversee the completion of the work once they have arranged the supply of material and workmen, who should be paid either on a daily basis or by great [i.e. by the piece]. They are empowered to act on behalf of the corporation, and whatever is spent will be repaid on submission on their accounts or those of their contractors, or by assignment.

320. [f.21v] *2 Aug. 1628. Agreement between Trinity House and John Eaglefeild of Stratford Bow and John Howland of London, gentlemen and customary tenants of Stepney*
Eaglefeild and Howland on behalf of themselves and of many other customary tenants of the manors of Stepney and Hackney obtained an exemplification under the great seal of a statute of 21 James I for the confirmation of the copyhold estate and customs of divers copyholders of those manors, according to an agreement and decree in chancery

concerning the lord of the manors and the copyholders. At a court held at Trinity House on 2 Aug., the exemplification was delivered to Trinity House for safe keeping so that it can be produced and used for the benefit of the tenants as necessary. Trinity House acknowledge receipt and agree to produce it for any tenants, on reasonable request. They also promise not to let it leave their possession unless the borrower deposits at least £5 so that [f.22] a new exemplification can be obtained if it is not returned within 2 months.

321. [f.22v] *1 Aug. 1628. Thomas Wyan, deputy register [of the admiralty court] to Trinity House*
The *William and John* of London (250 tons), with a crew of 80, and the *Willinge Minde* of Topsham (140 tons), with a crew of 92, took a French ship, the *Renee*, laden with merchandise, which was sold for £1,898 7s 6d. The sentence of the admiralty court is that this sum should be divided between the 2 captors, ton for ton, and man for man, according to the custom of the sea. Sir Henry Martyn, the judge, seeks the advice of Trinity House on how the money should be divided.

322. *9 Aug. 1628. [Trinity House to Sir Henry Martyn, admiralty court judge]*
In reply to **321**, £994 5s 6d should be awarded to the *William and John*, and £904 1s 9d to the *Willinge Minde*.
William Case, Robert Salmon, Walter Cooke, John Totton, Joshua Downinge, William Bushell.
[Marginal note]

	£	s	d		£	s	d
Great ship	405	12	8	Small ship	227	3	1
Her 80 men	294	6	5	Her 92 men	338	9	4
Their victuals	294	6	5	Their victuals	338	9	4
	994	6	5 [sic]		904	1	9

[Note] The figures in the margin were not delivered to the judge.

323. [f.23] *13 Aug. 1628. Order of the privy council about the convoy of Newcastle colliers* [Printed in *APC 1628–9*, 101.]

324. [f.23v] *18 Oct. 1628. [Trinity House] to Sir Ro. Mansfeld*
They have informed the company of Trinity House of his wishes in respect of Croxson. All of them regret Croxson is such an unworthy creature, but such is their respect for Mansfeld that they accept Croxson as their tenant for 3 years from last Michaelmas at an annual rent of £10, payable quarterly. If he fails to pay his rent, he will be dismissed. His arrears at Michaelmas last were £28 6s 8d, which he must pay before 1 Nov. Thereupon they will withdraw from the suit against him but otherwise will continue it and dismiss him from the office of ballastage. They will agree on the charges he must pay when he brings his rent.
[Signed] William Case, T. Best, Walter Coke, Gervais Hockett, Ro. Salmon, John Bennett, William Stevins, Robert Bell.

325. [f.24] *20 Oct. 1628. Yarmouth. Benjamin Couper [to Trinity House. See 326.]*
They asked him to nominate a man as keeper of Caister lighthouse and accepted his choice. However, the keeper has neglected the work himself, and employed a poor woman who has failed to maintain the lights properly. No doubt they have heard how prejudicial this has been. Since the keeper has not performed the work himself, but found other employment within Yarmouth, and has appointed an unfitting deputy, Couper suggests the appointment in his stead of the bearer, Robert Hill, an honest fisherman of Yarmouth, who knows the importance of keeping the lights, and is willing to perform the service himself, and to reside there.

326. [f.24v] *8 Nov. 1628. Trinity House to Benjamin Cooper, esquire, at Yarmouth*
They thank him for **325** and his care. Hill has been accepted on the same condition as his predecessor, namely £37 a year payable quarterly, beginning on Christmas day. Meantime Hill is to move his dwelling from Yarmouth to Caister, where he will reside as keeper. He is to burn 3 candles in 'either lighthouse . . . of 3 to the pound and not under', to be lit at sunset and maintained until it is fair day again. He will perform the business himself, and not employ a deputy. Cooper is asked to see that Hill moves to Caister, and to inform Alborow. Hill will take from Alborow any candles which he has left at the price that he paid for them. Mr Case, Sir Michael Geer, Capt. Best, Messrs Salmon, Coke, Benit, Benit [sic], Totten, Tutchen.
If Alborow fails to maintain the lights until Christmas, he should be dismissed forthwith and replaced by Hill, to avoid just complaint.

327. [f.25] *12 Nov. 1628. Report by Trinity House*
Several shipowners of Bristol and other western parts have asked whether the vails due to captains, masters and officers of men-of-war when a prize is taken [see **294**] are due out of each prize if several are taken on the same voyage. Trinity House answer that each officer is to have his due from each prize and that this has been anciently allowed to all men-of-war in queen Elizabeth's time and that the king allows it to his captains and masters.

328. *[1 Jan. 1629. Sir] Henry Martyn [admiralty court judge, ? to Trinity House. See 329.]*
The bearer, Terrick Reinerson, master of the *Fortune* of Stavoren, has demanded average* from William Felgate, merchant, for saving divers goods in the ship, of which he will give details in person. They are asked to resolve the difference if they can, or to certify the facts and their opinion.

329. [f.25v] *9 Jan. 1629. [? Trinity House to Sir Henry Martyn, admiralty court judge]*
In reply to his letter of 1 Jan. [**328**], they have been unable to resolve the

97

dispute. The merchant is not prepared to accept their arbitration because he considers that the insurers will not allow their award. Their opinion is as follows:

	£	s	d
Costs borne by Reynardson for damage to the ship and the expense of saving the merchant's goods, to be included in the average*:	100	0	0
Costs borne by Felgate for the loss of 2,460 hogshead staves which were thrown overboard and lost:	13	14	0
	113	14	0
The master's adventure in the ship, all provisions and munitions, and the freight for the pipes and hogshead staves:	300	0	0
The merchant's adventure in pipes and hogshead staves:	376	0	0

The shipper is to allow £50 9s for his damage, and the merchant £63 5s.

330. [f.26. *? c. March 1629*] *Miles Croxton to the king* [See **331.**]
He has a lease, with many years yet to run, under a great rent for a ballast wharf and land at Greenhithe in Kent. From there he has served ballast to the king's ships and other ships since time out of mind (his wharf being conveniently sited near to Chatham). He has always been subject to urgent warrants from the king's commissioners, and provides suitable ballast for the king's ships at low rates. But now the masters of Trinity House, usurping powers, have issued strange warrants in the king's name commanding that none shall buy his ballast, which oppresses the petitioner, is contrary to the laws and liberties of the kingdom, and hinders the supply of ballast to the navy. He has also been arrested and troubled with law suits which are not pursued, but which prevent him from carrying on his business and benefiting from his lease, which provides 30 men with work. He has been prevented from following his own suit in the star chamber against Edward and John Berry and others, who of late shot him with 2 poisoned bullets, from which he has languished for 4 months. His suit is that no new powers be granted to Trinity House until his grievance has been examined by those whom the king appoints, and that meantime he may proceed in his ballasting.

331. [f.26v. *11 x 16 March 1629*] *Miles Croxton, John Harden, Samuel Harden and the seamen of the kingdom whose names are annexed* [*not entered*] *to the house of commons*
Trinity House pretend that because of their patent, nobody can sell gravel or ballast without their permission. Croxton has leased from Thomas Swime, esquire, a wharf and ground at Greenhithe in Kent, from where the best ballast in the kingdom comes. He pays £90 annual rent to Swaine [sic], and spends about 20 marks a week on servants, horses, etc., besides other charges. Time out of mind, the owners and possessors of the ground have had full liberty to use it as they wished until in recent years they have been hindered by Trinity House. John Harden, owner in

fee simple, was so wronged that he was forced to sell the freehold, and is now aged 92 and lives on parish charity. After him, Samuel Harden had to pay the great rent of £20 a year to Trinity House, and finally had to leave. John Harden and his son Samuel lost about £400. Croxton then took a lease from the landlord, but Trinity House made him take one from them for £20 a year. He is at great charge in keeping 15 horses and 30 poor people at work ballasting ships. The corporation do not bear a penny in charges. Croxton has sustained other crosses and damages because Trinity House have forewarned by warrant many masters and mariners from coming to his wharf. His ballast is much desired by seamen for long voyages and by those trading to Newcastle, Ipswich, Harwich and other places, being firm and dry gravel able to sustain the rage and roughness of the sea. Many ships which would otherwise have been lost have thereby been saved. Woolwich ballast is sandy, causing the loss of ships. Owing to hindrances upon him, Croxton's rent is in arrears, and he has been forced into debt to pay his expenses. He has been damaged by the corporation to the value of about £100 in the past half year. [f.27] He has paid part of his rent to Trinity House but cannot find the great amount which they demand. They want him to take a new grant 'at yearly rent'. When he refused, they again warned ships by warrant in the king's name not to come to his wharf. They had him arrested in the sheriff's court of London, put him to great charge, and then nonsuited themselves. Later they had him arrested by a writ from the king's bench, and again put him to great charge, but they would not come to trial. The arrests are 'upon great actions', and he has been so disabled that his creditors have impleaded him to his utter undoing. The arrests happened shortly after he had been shot by pistols, and had 2 bullets in his body which caused him to bring a suit in the star chamber against Edward Bery and others. When he prosecuted his suit at the Old Bailey, London, he was arrested by presentment of Trinity House and their clerk. Seamen cannot buy the ballast which they want, and have to pay 12d a ton when they could get better for 5d or 6d. Many of the seamen petitioners have been arrested or 'threatened daily to be laid by the heels'. Since Trinity House are strong and rich, and Croxton is weak, he is likely to be undone unless parliament extend their favour. Owners and farmers of all chalk, coal and lead mines and stone quarries do not have to pay collateral rent as he is made to do for a ballast mine. Since he cannot keep a wharf and pay servants to ballast only the king's ships, parliament is asked to allow seamen to obtain ballast freely from him or others.

[Memorandum] Croxton desires Trinity House to accept the king's bills for the rent in arrears which they say is £28, and to accept £10 yearly in ballast in future, and to send ships as formerly to receive it. On Tuesday last, 10 March [1629 (see **324**)], 2 ships which came to receive ballast were arrested.

332. [f.27v] *9 May 1629. Agreement between Trinity House and John Ponnyett*
Ponnyett shall keep the buoy laid at the east end of the Gunfleet for the guidance of ships entering or leaving at Goldmer Gat. If the buoy is

displaced by a storm or a ship, he will restore it to its place. If the buoy and the chain are lost, he will provide and lay a replacement, and his account will receive favourable consideration. His annual salary is £15, payable quarterly, beginning at midsummer.

The mark of John Ponnett.

[Signed] T. Best, Robert Bell, Thomas Trenchfeild, James Moyer, W. Bushill, R. Swan, Robert Salmon, William Case, John Totton, William Ewen, Anthony Tutchen, Gervais Hockett, John Thomson, Walter Coke. Witnesses: Anthony Downes, etc.

333. [f.28] *30 Apr. 1629. Privy council order about the buoy at Goldmer Gat* [Printed in *APC 1628–9*, 421–2.]

334. [f.28v. *Before 15 Dec. 1628*] *Shipmasters and owners trading on the north coast, to eastern parts and to Newcastle for coal etc. to Trinity House* [*See* **336.**]

The channel of the Spitts is grown very dangerous, with not above 7 or 8 ft at low water. Trinity House are asked to lay a buoy at the east end of the Gunfleet so that ships can go in and out at Goldmer Gat, which is a fair channel with 4 or 5 fathoms at low water. Since the provision and maintenance of the buoy will be a great charge, the petitioners will pay 10d per 100 tons on ships, or 10d per 50 chaldrons of coal (Newcastle measure).

London: Jonas James, John Coborne, Edward Sheppard, Ellis Henderson, William Ewins, Robert Bell, Roger Harman, Christopher Newgate, John Ebbson, William Truddull, Anselm Humphry, John Totton, Anthony Tuchen, George Wattkins, John Eldred, Thomas Nelmes, Edmond Bostocke, John Sayer, William Hacker, Wolston Goslin, William Williams, John Atkins, Rowland Langram, Robert Swyer, Robert Salmon, junior, Thomas Tompson, Daniel Gattes, Thomas Mayde, Edmond Grove, Thomas Hall, John Cordall, Richard Williams, Samuel Doves, William Goodladd, Richard Swann, William Swanly, Thomas Doggett, John Gunner, Richard Dale, Peter Mayden, Daniel Russell, William Rivers, Anthony Coale, John Elmum, Thomas Martin, John Moore, John Corrall, Henry Rivers, George Clarke, Roger Cooper, Richard Fayre, William Wills, William Tompson, George Claxon, John Hudson, James Stonehouse, William Cooper, James Ricrast, Josias Joye, William Anderson, Thomas Baddyley, William Smith, John Morris, Timothy Bugbie, John Tompson, William Bushell, John Hyde.

Ipswich and Harwich: Zachary Bromwell, Roger Yaxly, Robert Hudson, James Talbott, James Peacock, William Hazlewood, John Whale, Anthony Paine, Peter Carfild, Ambrose Masters, William Baker, Thomas Peach, John Treadgould, William Peach, William Battle, Thomas Clarke, Richard Gilderser, Robert Ree, Giles Hubbert, William Lee, Edward Hanckin, Edward Clarke, Thomas Shrive, Thomas Coppin, John Barnes, Thomas Bayly, John Lowe, Edmond Morgan, John Sweetman, Edward Paine, Daniel Wilkinson, Robert Lowe, Saphony Parker, John Moulton, John Fassaker, John Kinge, Samuel

Tye, John Martyn, Richard Davie, Edward Peach, Edward Lavericke, Adam Browne, Thomas Barly, John Emmerson, Stephen Dunton, Thomas Silvester, Robert Jinkinge, John Dagnam, John Grimble, Richard Hanckin, Edmond Greene, William James, William Earnett, John Tillott, Humphrey Witah, John Masse, Robert Castone.

[f.29] Yarmouth: Thomas White, Titas Strudder, William Tracy, John Addames, Gilbert Walters, John Barton, Robert Draper.

Newcastle: Edward Bowmer, Gerard Huchinson, John Sommers, Humphrey Blunt, John Harrison, John Burrell, Joseph Bryant, Samuel Cocke.

Hull: Thomas Skynner, Thomas Collingwood [sic], William Tomlinson, Henry Johnson, Robert Ripley, Richard Preistwood.

Scotland: James Browne, Thomas White, Thomas Collingwood [sic].

335. [f.29v. *15 x 24 Dec. 1628*][1] *Trinity House to the privy council*
Owners and masters of ships trading to Newcastle for coal, and to Russia, Greenland, Norway, the Eastland and Hamburg have petitioned the corporation to set out a new channel to replace the Spitts which has grown dangerous. Trinity House have surveyed and buoyed a new channel called Goldmer Gat. The cost of buoys, chains, millstones and maintenance will be a great charge, and the masters and owners have offered to contribute 6d per 100 tons on shipping. It will be paid by the masters and owners on ships coming from the north to the Thames and Medway on every voyage inwards, and will not fall upon merchants or their goods. The privy council are asked to authorise Trinity House and their assignees to collect the dues at the Customs Houses of London, Rochester and elsewhere.

1. After **336,** when the offer was 10d, but before a privy council order of 24 Dec. 1628 (**349**) when the offer was 6d.

336. [f.30] *15 Dec. 1628.* [*Trinity House*] *to Mr Cooper at Yarmouth*
They inform him of **334** and their petition thereon to the privy council who all applauded save one; he said that the corporations of Ipswich, Yarmouth and Newcastle should be consulted. Instructions were issued for letters to be sent to those corporations, telling them to consult the owners and masters of ships trading for coal. The original petition contained 150 names, including some from his town, and a list of these is enclosed [see **334**]. He can answer any objections to the proposed charge from this letter. Coal brought from Newcastle and those parts to the Thames amounts not to 85,000 chaldrons a year (London measure), or 43,000 (Newcastle measure), according to the lord mayor's register kept for that purpose. The charge will yield only £35 a year less the cost of the collection (10%), but above £60 has already been spent, and Mr Ponnyett is paid £20 a year to look to the buoy, so that if but one buoy a year is lost, the collection would be insufficient. They do not wish to gain by it. If the petition to the privy council is approved, the buoy may be maintained; if not it will cease and they must bear the costs incurred.

337. [f.30v] *19 Dec. 1628. Benjamin Couper to Trinity House*
He received **336** late this night, and since the bearer wishes to depart early

in the morning, he cannot write as he desires. Nobody at Yarmouth, Ipswich, or Newcastle can speak against, much less oppose, such a worthy project. He will inform shipowners and masters as soon as is convenient, but no difficulties need be feared here. He wishes to be remembered to his friends, Messrs Best, Salmon, Cooke and Bennett, and to the rest of the worthy company.

338. [*24 x 31 Dec. 1628*] *Trinity House to Mr Cooper*
They thank him for **337**, dated 19th of this month. Some shipowners and masters trading to the north have petitioned the council that 10d per 100 tons is too much, asking the council to persuade Trinity House to accept 6d and they, not seeking gain, agree. A privy council letter is enclosed [**349**]. He is asked for a certificate for delivery to the council together with those of other corporations. The messenger will await his convenience.

339. [f.31] *15 Dec. 1628. Trinity House to Ipswich* [Similar in content to **336**.]

340. [f.31v] *21 Dec. 1628. Ipswich. Richard Fisher to Trinity House*
He received **339** by messenger. He has informed his neighbours and friends of the privy council's letter to the town's bailiffs. The need for the buoy is agreed, but some say that the charge seems great. He will report further when the letter has arrived and the meeting has been held.

341. *29 Dec. 1629* [*recte 1628*] *Trinity House to Ipswich* [Acknowledges **340**. Similar in content to **338**. Capt. Morgan and Mr Caston are said to be able to provide further information.]

342. [f.32] *15 Dec. 1629* [*recte 1628*] *Trinity House of Deptford to the Trinity Houses of Hull and Newcastle* [Similar in content to **336**.]

343. [f.32v. *? 29 Dec. 1628. Trinity House of Deptford to the Trinity House of Hull*. Similar in content to **338**. Mr Crome is said to have delivered the letter of 15 Dec. (**342**). For reply to **343**, see **356**.]

344. [f.33] *31 Dec. 1628. Trinity House of Hull* [*to the Trinity House of Deptford*]
The letter of 15 Dec. [**342**] arrived on 29 Dec. and was approved by them and by a meeting they called of masters and mariners of the port trading mostly to these northern parts.
Henry Chambers, mayor; John Preston, Thomas Ferres, Martin Jeffarson, William Smorthwaite, Cuthbert Tompson, Robert Raykes, Samson Sympson, Thomas Barnard.

345. *22 March 1629. Trinity House of Newcastle* [*to the Trinity House of Deptford*]
They have approached the mayor 2 or 3 times about the answer to **349** which they had delivered to him. All he said was that Mr Warmoth of the town had taken the answer of the mayor and aldermen to the privy

council [on 24 Jan 1629 (cf *CSPD 1628–9*, 457)]. They have certified to the mayor that those of Newcastle Trinity House who own ships approve the Gunfleet buoy and the charge of 10d [? *recte* 6d] per 50 chaldrons. Their certificate to this effect [346] can be shown to the privy council if necessary.
Phineas Allen, William Cooke.

346. [f.33v] *23 March 1629. Trinity House of Newcastle [to the Trinity House of Deptford]*
[The formal certificate mentioned in 345.]
Roger Holborne, Phineas Allen, William Cooke, Thomas Holborne, Robert Browne, John Harrison, George Earington, Robert Younge, Thomas Sharp, Anthony Wilkinson.

347. [f.34] *29 Dec. 1628. Trinity House to Harwich*
Summarises the petition [334], outlines the later request to reduce the charge to 6d per 100 tons [see 338], and requests a certificate. The messenger will call at Harwich when coming back from Yarmouth and Ipswich.

348. *13 Jan. 1629. Harwich. Thomas Tompson [mayor, to Trinity House]*
Masters and owners of the town agree to 347.

349. [f.34v] *24 Dec. 1628. Privy council to the port towns and London about the buoy at the Gunfleet* [Printed in *APC 1628–9*, 277–8.]

350. [*c. 28 x 30 Apr. 1629*] *Trinity House to the privy council* [*See* 333, 351–2.]
Upon their former petition [335], the privy council wrote requiring the lord mayor of London, the bailiffs of Ipswich and Yarmouth, and the mayors of Harwich, Hull and Newcastle to consult the shipowners and the masters concerned. All have returned certificates accepting the need for the new channel and agreeing to pay 6d per 100 tons or 50 chaldrons on ships trading to the north. Letters to the officers of the customs houses to enable collections to be made at London and elsewhere, as sent formerly, are requested.

351. [f.35] *30 Apr. 1629. Richard Deane, lord mayor [of London], to the privy council* [Cf Rem. vi. 175, where dated 28 Apr. 1629.]
In reply to 349, he had the letter read at a court of aldermen. A committee was named, and their certificate is enclosed [352].

352. *30 Apr. 1629. [Committee of aldermen of London to the court of aldermen. Cf Rem. vi. 176.]*
According to the order of the court of 22 Jan. they have considered the privy council letter [349] about the Trinity House petition [335], consulted shipowners and masters of the city of London, and seen the certificates from Hull and other outports. Those concerned agree to pay the proposed charge of 6d per 100 tons, provided that the channel is well

buoyed and maintained so that they no longer have to use the dangerous channel of the Spitts.
[Sir] Hugh Hammersly, James Cambell, Ralph Freeman, [Sir] Maurice Abott, Henry Garroway.
[Marginal note] From the aldermen to the lord mayor.

353. [f.35v] *8 Jan. 1629. Ipswich. Richard Fisher [to Trinity House]*
He received their letter of 29 Dec. [**341**] on 1 Jan., and delivered the enclosed letter from the council [**349**] to the bailiffs. Since then 'we' owners and masters have been consulted and have agreed. A copy of the report of the bailiffs to the privy council [**354**] is enclosed, as requested.

354. *7 Jan. 1629. Ipswich. Tobias Blosse and William Clyatt, gentlemen, bailiffs of Ipswich [to the privy council]*
Reply to **349** agreeing to the proposal [**335**].

355. [f.36] *10 Jan. 1629. Harwich. Thomas Tompson, mayor, to the privy council*
Reply to **349**, agreeing to the proposal [**335**], emphasising the danger of the channel of the Spitts to great shipping.

356. [f.36v] *24 Jan. 1629. Trinity House of Hull to the Trinity House of Deptford*
Reply to **343**, reporting that the mayor, being an elder brother, summoned the fraternity who had agreed with the proposal [**335**]. A certificate to the privy council is enclosed [**357**].
Henry Chambers, mayor; Cuthbert Tompson, Robert Raykes, Thomas Ferres, Martin Jeffarson.

357. *24 Jan. 1629. Hull. Henry Chambers, mayor, [to the privy council]*
Reply to **349**, agreeing to the proposal [**335**] on behalf of the Trinity House of Hull and of Hull seamen trading to the north.

358. [f.37] *4 Jan. 1629. Yarmouth. Benjamin Cowper and William Buttolph, bailiffs, to the privy council*
Reply to **349**, agreeing to the proposal [**335**] on behalf of the town's principal masters and shipowners.

359. [f.37v] *12 May 1629. Palace at Westminster. Order under the privy seal to Trinity House*
Trinity House have long held by patent of queen Elizabeth the office of ballastage and lastage* of ships in the Thames, usually giving annually 2 butts of wine or £50 to the lord high admiral from the office. During the lifetime of the duke of Buckingham, the rent was given to Capt. Thomas Porter in consideration of sea service to the late king. The office of admiralty is now in commission, and in view of Porter's services to James I and Charles I, the £50 is granted to him during pleasure, together with arrears since the death of Buckingham.
John Hacker.[1]

1. *Recte* Packer, duty clerk for the month (PRO, Privy Seal office, docquets, 6747).

360. [*13 x 31 May 1629*] *Covenant by Trinity House*
Under a privy seal of 12 May 1629 [**359**], the king granted to Capt.
Thomas Porter £50 a year which Trinity House usually paid to the late
lord high admiral from the ballastage office instead of 2 butts of wine.
Trinity House covenant to pay annually the £50 to Porter in 2 equal parts.

361. [f.38] *11 June 1629. Charterhouse.* [*Sir*] *Kenelm Digby* [*to Trinity
House. See* **362.**]
He thanks them for their decisions on several questions lately referred to
them and seeks another ruling upon which many will depend: what shares
in prizes are due to those who went out on his voyage in meaner places,
and afterwards were removed to better? What is his own entitlement to
shares, being commander-in-chief and authorised to constitute such
officers and to take such ships as consorts as he saw fit?

362. *27 June 1629.* [*Trinity House*] *to Sir Kenelm Digby*
In reply to **361**, those who were advanced are entitled to the shares of the
new places from the date of their advancement and prior thereto
according to their entitlement in their former posts. The entitlement of a
commander-in-chief on a warfaring voyage with several vessels under his
command is unusual, but there is one precedent. Sir James Lancaster,
having 2 ships under his command, took 'great purchase', and was
allotted the shares of 2 captains and as acknowledgement of his merit was
presented with £1,000 by the adventurers from their part of the goods.
Sir Henry Mainwairinge, Messrs Ewins, Salmon, Hockett, Browne,
Totton, Swanly, Cooke, Best, Case, Bennett, Bushell.

363. [f.38v. *? Before 3 July 1629*] *Trinity House to the king* [*See* **364.**]
The office of lastage* and ballastage of ships in the Thames has been
under the great seal of England time out of mind. Trinity House now
enjoy the office so important for navigation and preserving the Thames.
The office has never been questioned but now Miles Croxton, late a
tenant of the corporation who was dismissed for his abuse and dishonest
dealing, seeks to overthrow the office and within these few days has had
some of Trinity House arrested by the court of king's bench. He labours
to dissuade men from conforming to the office. To suppress his insolence
and prevent the inconveniences which are ready to ensue, the king is
asked to refer the hearing of the cause to one or 2 of the privy council,
which he may be pleased to do because Croxton lately petitioned the king
to the same purpose. But after the king granted a hearing by the privy
council and Trinity House had attended for some time, Croxton declined
'your majesty's grace to him in that reference'.

364. *3 July 1629. Court at Nonsuch. Order of* [*Sir*] *Sidney Montagu,*
[*master of requests*]
Reference of a petition [? **363**] to the lord privy seal, the lord high
chamberlain of England and the earl of Dorset, lord chamberlain to the
queen, or any 2 of them.

365. [f.39] *28 Oct. 1629. Whitehall. Order of the privy council*
Present: Lord keeper, lord privy seal, earl marshal, lord steward, earls of Dorset, Bridgewater and Carlisle, viscount Dorchester, lords Savile and Newburgh, Mr vice chamberlain, master of the rolls.

This day the board was informed on behalf of owners and masters of small barks and vessels trading to Calais, Rouen, and Dieppe that since the peace with France, they have been deprived of employment because French barks carry all merchants' goods to and from those places. Since it concerns the maintenance of shipping and seamen, and the petitioners and their families who are in great want, the board refer the matter to the officers and farmers of the customs, together with Trinity House.

366. [f.39v] *25 Jan. 1633. Star chamber. Order of the privy council* [*Cf* PC 2/42, p. 398.]
Present: Lord keeper, archbishop of York, lord privy seal, earls of Dorset and Danby, bishop of London, Mr secretary Windebanke.

It has been complained that Miles Croxton, tenant of Trinity House, has not paid his rent of 20 marks a year for ballastage as ordered by them on 13 Jan. 1630 [**367**]. Croxton has been called but no good reason has been found for non-payment. He is to pay the arrears amounting to £30 at Christmas at the rate of £5 a quarter and in future must pay his rent as it becomes due.

367. [f.40] *13 Jan. 1630. Order of the privy council about rent due from Miles Croxton to Trinity House for ballastage in the Thames* [Printed in *APC 1629–30*, 233.]

368. [f.40v. *? 18 Nov. 1629 x 29 Jan. 1630*][1] *Trinity House to the king*
The office of lastage* and ballastage in the Thames has been under the great seal of England time out of mind. Trinity House have held the office without molestation, paying £50 a year to Capt. Thomas Porter by order of the king. They have been at great charge perfecting the supply of ballast and the daily cleansing of the river which with engines, lighters and wharves is not less than £3,000 or £4,000. Lately John Gilbert and Abraham Johnson have each obtained a patent on pretence of having new engines for cleansing the river, but their aim is to deprive the petitioners of their right of ballast. If the grants pass the great seal, much trouble will be caused, and Porter's £50 would be 'decayed'. The king is asked to direct the lord keeper to stay the grants and to examine the case.

1. Johnson sought a patent on 18 Nov. 1629 (*CSPD 1629–31*, 100); see also **369**.

369. *29 Jan. 1630. Whitehall.* [*Lord*]*Dorchester* [*secretary of state*] *to the lord keeper*
The king does not intend to abridge former grants to the petitioners by any new patents. He is to examine the case [**368**]; meantime the new patents are not to pass the great seal.

370. [f.41] *14 Feb. 1630.* [*Sir*] *Ro. Heath* [*to Trinity House. See* **371**.]
There is likely to be a controversy between the town of Newcastle and

himself about the making of a ballast shore at South Shields. He trusts to his own judgement as to what may be done by law, but seeks their advice as to the convenience of the project. Newcastle objects that the ballast shore will hurt the town, endanger the river [Tyne], not help navigation, and make coal dearer. He has been informed otherwise. He will never desire anything for a profit which is injurious to another, much less to the public, and will not entertain anything hurtful to the town, trade, or private men. But if it is but a quarrel picked, and much more, if it will be good for the public and trade, as he is made to believe, he will not leave off. He will rely on their judgement.

371. *20 Feb. 1630. Trinity House to Sir Robert Heath*
In reply to **370**, a ballast wharf at South Shields would be of great use to trade and shipping. The only harm to the town of Newcastle would be that ships discharging ballast and loading coals at South Shields would also buy there their provisions of beer and bread etc. which used to be obtained at Newcastle. The wharf would not endanger the river but would better it because daily experience shows that the 'inning* of void places and flats in rivers' causes the stream to run straighter, so scouring the channel and gaining more water. Navigation would benefit because the deeper the water, the safer the ships. Coal would be cheaper rather than dearer because if ballast is discharged and coal loaded at South Shields, ships may make at least one, if not 2, extra voyages a year [f.41v] and so more coal will be brought to London and places on the coast, and prices reduced. So much for the objections. The weightiest argument for the proposal concerns the great ships now trading for Newcastle of which special care should be taken because of their service to the king. They are needed even in the Newcastle trade because of the enemy. If trade is in small ships, as in times past, the greatest part will be carried off to the enemy's country. The ballast wharf would much lessen the danger to great ships, always provided that the town does not interrupt the unloading of ballast at, and the bringing of coal to, South Shields. To discharge ballast at the Shields and go to town for coal would be injurious to trade.
Walter Coke, master; Thomas Best, Ro. Salmon, William Ewens, Anthony Tutchen, Jo. Totton, Jo. Bennett, Samuel Doves, Gervais Hockett, Christopher Browne, Jonas James.

372. [f.42] *26 Feb. 1630. Ipswich. Richard Fisher and others to Trinity House* [See **284–5**, **373**.]
They have had letters and messengers from Capt. James Dupper and Mr Harrison saying that if they desired waftage* for the north coast, they could have it on their first request to the lords of the council. Dupper's first letter said that if they petitioned as the Lynn men had done, 2 of the king's ships would be lent, provided that they manned and victualled the ships; the cost of even that would be met by the woodmongers and coal buyers who would be drawn to give 12d a chaldron at London. They suppose that Dupper is motivated by his own ends rather than their safety, and that in the 'long run' the 12d a chaldron would come out of the

owners' purses. Later Dupper or Harrison wrote to one of the chief magistrates of the town saying that waftage could be had at no charge to the owners if they petitioned. If that were so, they think that Trinity House would have heard of it or would have been consulted by the council, either at the same time as, or before, Dupper. If waftage can be had by petition, Trinity House are asked to frame and send a petition to them, and they will obtain as many hands to it as they can. They are loath to act without the counsel of Trinity House. The danger they now run of losing their ships will weaken their estates and strengthen the enemy.
Richard Fisher, John Carnaby, William Hammand, Edmund Morgan, Richard Bowell, Edward Peach.

373. *27 Feb. 1630. Trinity House* [*to Richard Fisher and others at Ipswich*]
In reply to **372**, Trinity House had heard nothing but sent for the master of the Woodmongers' company, the chief merchants and buyers of 'your' coal; he denied that there had been any speech with Dupper or treaty to pay 12d a chaldron for waftage* and said that a payment would not be agreed. As to the loan of 2 of the king's ships, Trinity House cannot give advice because it is a business of state. Evidently Dupper has good intelligence and is privy to the intent of the privy council. [f.42v] They agree that Dupper wants to manage the business for his own ends, because he has little to do here at home. As to the letter from Dupper or Harrison to one of the magistrates, it would be advisable to seek confirmation. If a grant is to be had, it should not be neglected but they will not draft a petition until more information is available.
Mr Coke, master; Robert Salmon, Thomas Best, Messrs Bennett, Totton, Tutchen, Case, Bell, Hockett, Browne, Doves, Tompson, Rainsborowe.

374. [f.43] *6 May 1622. Order of the privy council about the Algiers expedition* [Printed in *APC 1621–3*, 212–13. The prince of Wales is listed as present here but not in *APC*.]

375. [f.43v] *7 Apr. 1630. Certificate by Trinity House*
At his own suit and that of many shipmasters and captains trading to Leghorn, Morgan Read, an Englishman resident there who is reputed honest, suitable, and in the favour of the duke of Florence [i.e. Tuscany] is appointed consul for ships and seamen at Leghorn for so long as he is a true English subject and helps English seamen in the port of Leghorn as necessary. He is empowered to collect such fees as were paid to his predecessors, Messrs Edmondes and Hunt and Capt. Thorneton. The duke is asked to accept Read as consul.
Capt. Best, Messrs Coke, Case, Tutchen, James, Browne, Hockett, Salmon, Rainborow, Bushell, Ewins, Totton.

376. [f.44] *8 Apr. 1630. William Burrell and Henry Bowers to Trinity House*
They hold from Trinity House the office of ballastage at Greenwich, Woolwich and Erith. Their lease for the wharf and land at Greenwich has

expired and is in the possession of the earl of Arundel. They ask Trinity House to negotiate with the earl for a lease, and will honour any agreement made, provided that the rent does not exceed £50. They will take the lease from Trinity House, if the corporation sees fit.

377. [f.44v. *Before 21 Apr. 1630. Mr Pulford to Trinity House. See* **378.**]
Robert Barker, merchant of Plymouth, had commission to buy and ship to Italy 200 hogsheads of pilchards for John Barker, Andrew Charlton and Richard Longe, merchants of Bristol. He contracted on their behalf with William Rowe of 'Milbroke' [? Millbrook in Cornwall], owner of the *Merchant Bonadventure* of that port, to freight the pilchards from Plymouth to Villefranca [Villefranche-sur-mer] and Leghorn for £4 a ton. They were loaded in Nov. 1628, Barker not knowing that the ship, which was fully laden with merchants' goods, had any letters of reprisal. On the voyage to Villefranca, a Portuguese caravel, laden with sugar and other goods, which had 'spent her masts' and lay as a wreck, was taken near the North Cape and towed to Villefranca where she was sold for a great sum. The voyage to Leghorn which was the better port for the sale of pilchards was retarded by at least 20 days, and by the time of arrival it was almost mid Lent, and the market was lost. The sale of the pilchards yielded not one penny to the merchants, nor is it likely to do so. Nevertheless, the 'owners' [sic] sue for freight, and refuse the merchants any share in the prize or compensation for the loss of the market. Can owners by law or usage recover their freight and not be liable to satisfy the merchants' damages in loss of their market? Ought not the merchants by right have a share in the goods taken in the prize 'according to their tonnage'?

378. [f.45] *21 Apr. 1630. Trinity House to Mr Pulford*
In reply to **377**, the merchants are to pay the freight to the owners according to charter party, but are entitled by ancient custom of the sea to a full third of all reprisal goods, bearing one third of all charges arising thereupon.
Walter Coke, master, [Sir] John Wattes, Thomas Best, William Ewins, William Rainborow, William Bushell, Ro. Salmon, William Case, Anthony Tutchen, Gervais Hockett, John Bennett, Christopher Browne.

379. *29 Apr. 1630. [Trinity House to the lord mayor of London. Cf* SP 16/166/19 (1); *CSPD 1629–31*, 250; *Rem.*, 85–6.]
An estimate of the charge of 6 ships, each of about 240 or 250 tons and furnished with munitions and ordnance for the guard and convoy of the Newcastle trade:

	£
Pay of 6 ships at £70 per ship a month	420
Wages for 65 men per ship at 22s per man a month	429
Victuals at 22s per man a month	429
Cost per month	1,278
Cost for 6 months	7,668

For the levy of the charge they forbear, not knowing the amount of coal on which it is to be laid; neither can the coasters tell them, nor is there a general consent to the charge.

Walter Coke, Thomas Best, Robert Salmon, Jonas James [John Totton in SP], William Case, Mr Browne.

380. [f.45v] *4 Feb. 1630. Leghorn. Morgan Reade [to Trinity House]*
Captains and masters 'of our nation' coming here and finding no consul have, with the consent of the merchants, asked him to petition for a consul's patent, and have written the enclosed letter [381]. If appointed, he promises to observe their commands and give all men content.

381. [*Before 4 Feb. 1630] James Moyer, William Knight, Bence Johnson, Daniel Gatts and James Dammarell [to Trinity House. See 382.]*
Trinity House are asked to establish a consul in this port of Leghorn. The post being void and leaving no one to speak for them, 'our' nation is much slighted by the ministers of the duke [of Tuscany], and 'much exacted upon' to the prejudice of shipping coming to the port. Morgan Read is willing to accept the place, being honest and able, of good repute with the duke, with sufficient means, and much respected by shipmasters and merchants. He has promised to write to Trinity House about the post [380].

382. [f.46] *21 Apr. 1630. Westminster. Charles I [to the duke of Tuscany. Text in Latin and English.]*
By ancient custom 'our' merchants have had a consul at Leghorn for the affairs of shipping. Morgan Read, for long a merchant there, has been chosen consul and confirmed by Trinity House whom it concerns. The duke is desired to approve the election and to grant Read authority to exercise the office in shipping affairs and over 'our' pilots, officers and mariners.

383. [f.46v] *July 1630. [Trinity House] to Mr Pringoll [of the Dover fellowship of lodemanage]*
Presuming on his promise, they entreat him to be their agent for the erection of a seamark[1] on the King's Downs for leading ships through the Channel of the Gulls, the proportion of which in length, breadth and height, and everything needed for the work, they leave to him and Bartholomew Lewrence, their master workman. He is asked to oversee the work and make provision of materials while the corn is on the ground so that it can start after harvest. They will pay his costs, and now deliver £10 to him to buy materials. The farmers of the Customs House will give him authority to obtain from Mr Pertivall, their collector, any more money needed for materials and workmen's wages.

1. Described as a wall in the paper schedule of contents (see above, p. xvi)

384. [f.47–47v] *1535. An act for the preservation of the Thames* [Printed in *Statutes*, iii. 550.]

385. [f.48. *Before 6 Nov. 1630*][1] *John Browne, founder of the king's iron ordnance, to lord Vere of Tilbury, master of the ordnance*
The king has reserved all drakes* for his service. No harm will come if subjects have them, but rather the contrary, as Trinity House can testify. He is therefore asked to mediate with the king to remove the restraint for the following reasons. First, if drakes are of use in the king's ships, they are of much more use in subjects' ships for scouring the decks [with shot] against boarding, especially in small ships which are not strong enough in ordnance to entertain an enemy at a distance. Secondly, drakes are likely to be used seldom by the king's ships, but frequently by subjects'. The objection that drakes might fall into enemy hands and so be turned 'against us' may be made to any invention, and applies equally to any ordnance. Moreover for want of drakes many ships may be taken and the enemy furnished with both great ordnance and ships. Failure to use drakes for fear of being captured is unworthy of the English nation. Unless the restraint is removed, the art of making drakes will be lost.

1. cf. SP 16/175/97; *CSPD 1629–31*, 389–90, where it is attributed to 24 Nov. 1630. It was, however, mentioned on 6 Nov. (**386**).

386. *6 Nov. 1630. Lord Vere, master of the ordnance, to Trinity House about* **385** [*Cf* SP 16/175/97 (i); *CSPD 1629–31*, 390.]

387. [f.48v] *25 Nov. 1630. Trinity House* [*to lord Vere, master of the ordnance*][1]
In reply to **386**, they recommend the use of drakes* on merchant ships for the following reasons: (a) They are fit for the upper decks, even the poop and the forecastle, when great ordnance cannot be used nor a port between the lower decks opened. (b) If the enemy comes near, drakes can beat men from their high decks, preventing boarding, which great ordnance lying low cannot do. (c) Loaded with case shot, they make good work of the upper works of an enemy ship. (d) If enemies board, drakes can scour the decks from the forecastle to the poop. (e) Formerly fowlers and murderers* were used to scour the decks of boarders; drakes are much better and, loaded with case shot or bullets, are of special service at a fair distance. (f) They dispute the objection that great ordnance may do what they pretend can be done by drakes. Merchant ships cannot carry weighty ordnance on their higher decks and if great merchant ships do so, it cannot do like service, for drakes fire 2 or 3 shots to one fired by a piece of great ordnance. (g) Great ordnance need 4 or 5 men a piece; drakes need only 2, which is important for merchant ships with few men. [f.49] (h) Drakes are fit for even the smallest merchant ships, and will preserve many of them from the enemy who will be discouraged when their men are killed in every corner by fire from the drakes. (i) The use of drakes by subjects will be no disservice to the king, rather the contrary if subjects, their goods and ships are preserved. They ask him to mediate with the king to permit subjects to have drakes.

T. Best, deputy master; Sir Henry Manwaringe, Messrs Salmon, Bennett, [Walter] Coke, Totton, Tutchen.

1. cf SP 16/175/97 (ii); *CSPD 1629–31*, 390. The SP text is also signed by Robert Bell, William Case, Samuel Doves, George Hatch, Gervais Hockett and James Moyer, but not by Salmon.

388. [f.49v. *? 1631*] *Trinity House to Richard, lord Weston, lord treasurer*
About 16 years ago [on 28 Aug. 1615], the late king granted to Sir Edward Hayward, one of his cupbearers, a patent [C 66/2078, no. 11] for a lighthouse or beacon at Dungeness in Kent and for a levy (to be borne equally by shipowners and merchants) of 1d a ton upon ships, both outward and homeward bound, towards the erection and maintenance of the lighthouse. The petitioners, being mostly shipowners, are willing to pay their share in view of the benefit they receive. Nevertheless, one Mr Lamplewe, who received the allowance for keeping the lighthouse, obtained by misinformation from the late king letters which forced the petitioners to pay the whole levy from the outset, contrary to the intent of the patent. An investigation by the officers of the London Customs House is requested, and if it appears that the collection does not agree with the intent of the patent, instructions should be given for the charge to be borne equally by the petitioners and the merchants as originally intended.
[Marginal note] Petition about Mr Bullocke's lights.

389. [f.50. *c. 16 Apr. 1631*] *Trinity House to the king about ballastage* [*Cf* SP 16/188/73; *CSPD 1631–3*, 12.]

390. *16 Apr. 1631. Lord Dorchester, secretary of state, to the lords commissioners of the admiralty about* **389** [*Cf* SP 16/188/73 (i); *CSPD 1631–3*, 12.]

391. [f.50v. *? Before 23 Jan. 1631*] *Edmund [? or Edward] Needham, David Ramsey, the king's servants, and their associates to the king* [*See* **392**; **395**.]
Experience gained by travel overseas for many years enables them to cleanse the Thames of banks of sand, gravel, mud, stone and clay which the common sewers daily augment and which will lead to the ruin of the city and commonwealth. The king is asked to instruct the privy council to summon the petitioners to outline their experience and plans.

392. *23 Jan. 1631. Court at Newmarket. [Sir] Thomas Aylesburye [master of requests] to the privy council*
Reference of **391**.

393. [f.51. *9 March x 1 June 1631. Needham, Ramsey and others to the privy council. See* **394**]
According to the privy council order made after reading their petition [**391**], they set out their plans for cleansing the Thames, based on their experience overseas. With lighters made fit, labourers, shovels and

grapnels, they will scour the channels of all banks of sand and gravel which forces the tide to make new channels. Next they will trench and roll both sides of the river beginning at low water and carry their rolling to the foundations of the houses on both sides of the river and from there carry it [i.e. the soil] away to places convenient for sale so that both sides of the river will be made more sloping and deeper than the main channel, and the channel will then shoot all soil to the sides, and not from the sides to the channel. Thus the river will be always navigable. The old main channel may be kept clear with 2 dragging lighters (fitted with 2 iron rakes of 20 cwt. apiece and 2 fathoms broad, fastened at the stern with a great cable) falling down with the tide and taking hold of banks or anything remaining in the channel. When at a stay, they will bring the cable to the capstan bar and wind up the lighter till the buoy, fastened to the rake, comes home and so clears the lighter, to fall down with the tide again. All shipowners, bargemen, fishermen and watermen who trade in the river will prove that the patents granted by James I for scouring the Thames were used for private gain and stop the river, to the prejudice of city and commonwealth, so that the king may lawfully call in those patents. Reports that Needham and Ramsey were partners [f.51v] in these patents or sought to renew them are untrue. They seek to maintain the city's charter and make the river navigable. What money the lord mayor, aldermen and citizens of London, the suburbs and Middlesex can lend for this famous work will be repaid from the sale, at ordinary prices, of sand for building, gravel for ballasting ships, stones and small gravel for paving, clay for brick making, tiles, paving of houses, and earthen vessels. Money borrowed shall remain in the hands of the lord mayor, being treasurer for this business. In view of their endeavours, the petitioners request a favourable reply to the king's reference of 23 Jan. [392] so that the king may declare by letter his pleasure to the lord mayor for effecting the work and no more time be lost and money spent in soliciting this business, the petitioners having other employment overseas. If anyone be grieved by these proceedings, let him complain to the privy council and there be satisfied. They will perform what was stated in their petition to the king, the privy council, and the city of London.

394. *1 June 1631. Whitehall. T. Meautys [clerk of the privy council] to Trinity House*
Reference of **393**.

395. [f.52] *18 June 1631. Trinity House to the privy council about* **393–4** [Cf SP 16/194/28; *CSPD 1631–3*, 82. Edward Needham's christian name (Edmund in **391**) is wrongly calendared as Charles in *CSPD*. The SP text is signed by Samuel Doves, master; Anthony Tutchen, W. Bushill, John Totton, Gervais Hockett, wardens; John Bennett, William Rainborowe, William Ewen, Edward Maplesden, William Swanley, T. Best, Robert Salmon, Walter Coke, William Case.]

396. [*No date*] *Trinity House to the lord treasurer* [The petition is not entered.]

397. [f.52v. *Before 3 Aug. 1631*] *Francis Wadloe of London, merchant, to the privy council as commissioners for the regulation of the jurisdiction of the king's ecclesiastical and civil courts* [*See* **398.**]
Upon his petition the privy council ordered the plaintiff [R. Toackley, **399**] to proceed no further until the question of jurisdiction had been decided. Unwilling to be at further legal charge, he asks that the case be speedily determined on a report from Trinity House.

398. *3 Aug. 1631. Portsmouth.* [*Lords*] *Weston, Dorset, Lindsey and Dorchester* [*lords commissioners of the admiralty*] *to Trinity House*
Reference of **397** for arbitration or report so that in conference with the judges further course may be taken.

399. [f.53] *19 Nov. 1631. Ratcliff. Trinity House to the lords commissioners of the admiralty*
In reply to **398** about the case between Francis Wadloe, merchant, and Robert Toackley, mariner, they have interviewed both parties several times. The charter party shows that Wadloe hired a ship from Toackley for a voyage of between 7 and 12 months at £20 a month; he agreed to put in a crew of an able master, 7 mariners, and a boy; was to victual and pay the crew; and pay £300 if he did not deliver the ship at London at the end of 12 months, 'the danger of the seas excepted', with all provisions and tackle, reasonable use and wear excepted. Tockley covenanted that the ship would be provisioned with tackle, masts, yards, sails, anchors, cables, etc. under a like penalty. Toackley, the owner, duly provided the ship properly provisioned, and the merchant put in a crew, victuals, and his goods. Once at sea, the master and crew conspired and ran away with the ship to the north part of Scotland where they sold the goods and went to sea again. The 12 months are expired, and Toakley demands the return of the ship or the penalty. Both parties were asked to put themselves upon Trinity House. At first Toackley was willing provided that Wadloe gave security for payment of anything awarded, which Wadloe could not or would not do. At the next meeting, Toackley refused to put himself upon Trinity House. [f.53v] Trinity House find the running away of the master and crew with the ship and goods not to be a peril of the sea.
Samuel Doves, master; T. Best, Robert Salmon, Walter Coke, John Totten, Anthony Tutchen, William Bushell, James Moyer, Robert Bell, William Ransbury, G. Hatch, Jonas James, Gervais Hocket, John Tomson, etc.

400. *7 Dec. 1631. Trinity House* [? *to Sir John Coke, secretary of state. See* **405.**]
Suit [**401**] has been made to them by many merchants, captains and masters of ships trading to Genoa to allow Signor Francisco Massola, a Genoese, to be consul at Genoa only for mariners and ships. Since Massola is of good report, an able man, and in the favour of the state of Genoa, they allow him 'forasmuch as in us lies', to be consul for so long as he assists 'all our nation' there. His fee is to be 2 ducats a ship, great and small. [f.54] The state of Genoa is asked to accept him as consul.
Samuel Doves, master, etc.

401. *26 March 1631. Leghorn. Robert Sainthill and others [to Trinity House. See* **400**.*]*
Experience has shown the need for a consul of their nation at Genoa so that merchandise and shipping receive no detriment. Almost all other nations find the help of a consul to be very necessary to settle controversies and differences in accounts. No one is more fit for the post than Signor Francisco Massola, a merchant residing here who is expert in the English tongue and has long been well affected to them. The petitioners being merchants and shipmasters entreat the king or the lords of the council and the officers whom it concerns to elect him consul and give him the powers commonly granted to consuls which they have formerly petitioned on behalf of others.
Robert Sainthill, Job Throckmorton, Isaac Honiewood, Henry Draper, Henry Robinson, Tobias White, Cobham Doves, Thomas Simmber, Robert Swyer, George Bucher, Edward Abbott, Richard Rowe.

402. [f.54y] *10 Dec. 1631. Westminster. Charles I to the doge and governors of Genoa* [in Latin. *See* **400–1**.]
Commendation of Francisco Massola as consul at Genoa.

403. [f.55. *1629 x 1633*][1] *A plan for manning the navy, submitted to the king*

	Men for home service	Men for remote service
1. *Prince [Royall]*	500	
Merhonor	350	
Ann Royall } *Triumph*	300	350
2. *St George* *St Andrew* *Victorie* *Swiftsuer* *Repulse*	260	300
3. *[Constant] Reformation* *Defiance* *Vanguard*	250	280
4. *Rainbowe* } *Lyon*	240	270
5. *Wastspight* } *Nonsuch*	220	250
6. *Assurance* } *Convertine*	200	225
7. *Garland* } *Bonadventure*	170	190
8. *St Dyonis* *Antelope* *[Happy] Entrance*	160	180
9. *Drednought*	140	150
10. *Adventure* } *Mary Rose*	100	110

The number of men are sufficient for any service. Crews of ships for the constant guard of the Narrow Seas in peace may be lessened by at least 20 in a 100 below those shown.
[ff.55v–56] The quartering of men for fighting for 7 ships of several burdens and numbers of ordnance:

[(a) *Prince Royall*; (b) *St George*; (c) *Vanguard*; (d) *Assurance*; (e) *Guardland*; (f) *Drednought*; (g) *Mary Rose*. O = quantity of ordnance; M = men required to man them.]

	(a)		(b)		(c)		(d)		(e)		(f)		(g)	
	O	M	O	M	O	M	O	M	O	M	O	M	O	M
Cannons-perier*	2	6	2	4	2	4								
Demi-cannons*	6	24	4	16	2	8								
Culverins*	12	48	18	72	14	56	8	32	4	16				
Demi-culverins*	18	54	12	36	14	42	12	36	14	42	14	42	8	24
Sakers*	13	26	2	4	6	12	10	20	14	28	8	16	10	20
Port-pieces* ⎱			2											
Fowlers ⎰	4	7	2		4	4	4	4	2	2	2		2	
Falcons											2	4	2	4
Minions*			2	4	2	4					4	8	4	8
	55	165	44	136	40²	130	34	92	34	88	30	70	26	56

	(a)	(b)	(c)	(d)	(e)	(f)	(g)
Admiral and retinue	83						
Captain and lieutenant	³	2	2	2	2	2	2
Master and his mates	³	3	2	2	2	2	1
Boatswain and his company	80	46	45	35	25	24	15
Carpenter and his company	10	8	6	4	4	4	3
On the orlop*	6						
Stewards, cooks and mates or shifters	10			4			
Steward and mates		3	2		1	1	1
Cook and mate			2				
Trumpeters	10	4	4	4	4	3	
Gunner and his company	165	136	130	92	88	70	56
Powder room	20	5	5	5	4	4	3
Small arms men	100	45	45	45	35	25	16
Surgeon and his mates	6	4	3	3	2	2	2
Steerage and 'condidge'⁴	10	4	4	4	3	3	1
	500	260	250	200	170	140	100

1. Dates suggested by exclusion of the *White Bear*, sold in 1629 and completion of the *Charles* in 1633. The *St Claude* (given away in 1632) was as large as the *Mary Rose* but may have been omitted because she was a prize (Anderson, 16, 18, 20).

2. *Recte* 44.
3. Perhaps subsumed under 'Admiral and retinue'.
4. 'Condidge' derived from 'conder' – one who steers a ship.

404. [f.56v] *13 June 1632.* [*Ratcliff. Report by Trinity House. Cf* SP 16/218/47; *CSPD 1631–3*, 353.]
Their opinion was desired about the making of a ballast shore at South Shields, which is 6 miles on this side of Newcastle. [Their reasons are similar to those in **371** with the following additions.] At neap tide, great ships cannot come to any ballast shore above [South Shields] but have to await the spring tide, whereas they can always cast their ballast at this shore. If the wharf is not filled with ballast, that which is already there will next winter be washed into the river to its great detriment.
Mr Bell, master; Sir John Wattes, Capt. Best, Messrs Salmon, Cooke, Bennett, Hatch, Tutchin, Totton, Case, Moyer.[1]

1. SP text omits Bell, Wattes and Cooke but includes Christopher Browne, Samuel Doves, Jonas James, William Rainborowe and William Swanley.

405. [f.57] *25 Aug. 1632. Trinity House to Sir John Coke, chief secretary of state*
By reason of **401** signed by merchants, captains and owners of good note, Trinity House sought the appointment of Massola as consul at Genoa [**400**]. According to their former desire, they ask the king to confirm the appointment and seek Coke's furtherance therein.
Robert Bell, master; T. Best, Robert Salmon, Anthony Tutchin, Gervais Hockett, Samuel Doves, John Totton, John Bennett, William Ewen, etc.

406. *19 Sept. 1632. Order by Trinity House*
They have considered the petition of the men who mutinied in the *Mary*, Roger Marten master, and who 'set their hands in a mutinous manner to a circle' against a voyage from Gore End to the Texel in Holland to deliver the ship, which might have been very prejudicial to the merchants and owners, and prove a bad example to others. Those who set their hands to the circle shall pay out of their wages a proportionable part of the charges, past or future, of sending up the principal mutineer from the ship and committing him to the Marshalsea.
R. Bell, master; Messrs Salmon, Bennett, Tutchin, Case, Hockett, Bushell.

407. [f.57v. *20 Dec. 1632. Masters of Trinity House and others to the principal officers of the navy. Cf* SP 16/226/74; *CSPD 1631–3*, 468.]
According to warrant they have examined the 2 new ships of the king now built in dry dock at Deptford and Woolwich. The measurements and burdens, on the basis both of the old rule used by Mr Burrell in the time of the commission [of 1619 for the navy] and on that laid down by the privy council on 26 May 1628 for ships of the king and of merchants, are:

	Ship built at Deptford by Mr Goddard [*Henrietta Maria*]	Ship built at Woolwich by Mr [Peter] Pett[1] [*Charles*]
Old rule:		
Length of the keel	106 ft	106 ft 4 inches
Breadth from outside [the planks]	36 ft 5 inches	36 ft 3 inches
Draught	16 ft 6 inches	16 ft 6 inches
These figures multiplied together and divided by 100 produce in tons and tonnage*	848	848
New rule:		
Length of the keel	106 ft	105 ft 2 inches (excepting the false post)
Breadth inside the planks	35 ft 9 inches	35 ft 7 inches[2]
Depth from the upper edge of the keel to the diameter of the breadth	15 ft 8½ inches	16 ft 3 inches
These figures multiplied together and divided by 100 produce in tons and tonnage	793	810⅔

From appearances, the ships are very substantially timbered and the floor-riders, beams and knees* on the decks are of large and fit sizes and well bolted for ships of [f.58] their burdens. Footwaling clamps and the 'middle bands' [? bend* or wale for the middle deck] are of sufficient scantling and well made, the breast hooks are sufficient to strengthen the bows, and the transoms are well kneed to strengthen the sterns. The ship at Deptford lacked standers upon the gundecks and knees at the upper end of the pillars. The ship at Woolwich lacked 2 knees on the lower transoms, knees to all pillars at the lower and upper ends, and all stander knees upon both gundecks, except for 2 on the quarter deck. When these defects are made good, both ships will be very serviceable for the king.[3]

1. Phineas Pett and Peter, his son, were both concerned with her construction (Pett, 149).
2. 33 ft 7 inches in Oppenheim, 254.
3. Subscribed in SP text by John Goodwyn (master attendant), Peter Pett (? of Deptford), Edward Stevens, John Greaves, John Dearslye (shipwrights), T. Best, Robert Salmon, Walter Cooke, William Rainborow.

408. *10 Jan. 1633.* [*Masters of Trinity House and shipwrights to the principal officers of the navy. Cf. SP 16/231/23; CSPD 1631–3, 512.*]
They have considered the warrant of 2 Jan. 1633 concerning the ships at Deptford and Woolwich [*Henrietta Maria* and *Charles*]. The ship at Deptford draws 16½ ft and her ports will be about 4½ ft above water. Her ports are mostly too little; in future those on the lower gundecks should

be made bigger by '2 or 3 inches square'. Her ports are also too near each other; in ships of this burden, they should be 9 ft apart. Orlops* of ships built for the king hereafter should be flush, fore and aft (i.e. without falls). The ship at Woolwich is 'full bodied. . . . and will not easily settle into the water for at 16 foot she will be a steady ship fit for service' [sic]. Her ports will be about 4 ft above water. Ports of ships built for the king hereafter [f.58v] should be 4½ ft or 4 ft 8 or 9 inches above water. The size of the ports is right and they are 9 ft apart. The beams on both gundecks 'round* too much' by 3 or 4 inches, and this should be mended in ships hereafter. Other deficiencies are noted in the former certificate [**407**].

Thomas Best, deputy master; Robert Salmon, Walter Coke, Mr Ransbury [of Trinity House].[1]

1. SP text also subscribed by John Goodwin, Peter Pett, Edward Stevens, John Greaves, John Dearsley. Note in SP text: received on 19 Jan. concerning the ships ready to be launched.

409. [*? Oct. 1632 x July 1633.[1] Trinity House*] *to the court of requests* [*Cf* SP 16/16/164.]

According to the commission of the court of 9 Nov. last about the suit between Elias Henderson, pl., and William Jones, def., concerning payments and disbursements for building the *Mary and John* of London, they have heard the allegations of both parties and examined their witnesses according to articles provided by the parties. The account for the ship with provisions and fitted for sea came to about £1,850. At the time, the pl. presented the account to the owners [f.59] at the Mairemaide Tavern, Cornhill, where it was audited, approved and signed and the book of accounts was left with the pl. About 2 years later, when the pl. was dismissed from the ship on exception taken against him by the owners, he had made a second account showing that the ship cost more than appeared in the first account. With John Barker, his father-in-law, as his assignee, he commenced his suit, alleging himself wronged by the first account. His assignee presented the second account to some of the owners and Mr [Anthony] Haviland, deceased, gave him £10 and Mr [Thomas] Woodgate £12 to be free of trouble, as testified on oath. No other owner gave more than their part of the original £1,850. The first account with the alleged error wronging the pl. cannot be produced by him, but depositions show that it was left with him after clearing. If it were produced, the case would be clear. They consider that the account was left with the pl. because the custom is to leave all accounts with the master in case the part-owners want an account of expenditure and of money received for freight; and that the first account was only £1,850 for the ship wholly furnished. No wrong can be proved or recompense [f.59v] given until that account is examined.

Capt. Best, deputy master; Robert Salmon, Walter Coke, William Case.

1. On 25 June 1632, the court of requests ordered the def. to appear before the second day of Michaelmas term to explain why a commission should not be established to resolve the dispute (PRO, court of requests, order books, vol. 61). See also **419**.

410. *23 Feb. 1633. Ratcliff. Trinity House to the earl of Pembroke* [*Cf* Scott, ii.371.]
They have considered his letter about fishing, especially in view of the king's zeal for the work. They will adventure £50 a year with him and yearly assign 2 men to serve on committees.
Thomas Best, deputy master, Walter Coke, Robert Salmon, William Case, John Bennett.

411. [f.60] *9 March 1633. Trinity House to Mr Harwood, mayor of Poole*
Nicholas Howard and Peter Talbott of Purbeck came today to complain about the mayor, stating that Howard's brother, Peter Baker, taken by the pirates of Algiers in the ship with Mr Mott, had been redeemed by Howard and his friends for £77, but that Baker, on coming home, had visited the mayor and Mr Robarts several times in vain to obtain something towards the cost. If Howard's allegation is true, there is just cause of complaint to the lord keeper against Harwood; if not, the parties deserve punishment. Talbott seeks a contribution towards the release of his brother who is still in Algiers, which if Harwood can assist, course will be taken for the rest.
Capt. Best, Messrs Tutchen, Totton, Cooke, Hockett.

412. *7 Sept. 1633.* [*Trinity House*] *to the mayor and aldermen of Poole* [*See* **411.**]
They have received a letter from women of the town whose husbands are captive, but Trinity House are replying to the mayor and aldermen because the letter was written by the town clerk, presumably at the direction of the mayor and aldermen. In a letter of 24 Apr. the writers explained that they had attended the lord keeper who had told them to instruct the mayor and aldermen to appoint a person or persons to deal with the business and who, together with the writers, was to attend him next term. A reply dated 10 June was received but nobody has come this term, nor has a letter been sent to the lord keeper or to themselves. If the present letter is that of the mayor and aldermen, any default is theirs, because had they attended the lord keeper, the business would now be ended. They are ready to accompany the mayor and aldermen to the lord keeper, and there should be no delay lest the women become better informed and complain not of the writers but of the mayor and aldermen.
[Marginal note] The women can be acquainted with this letter. 7 Sept. 1633.

413. [f.60v] *1 Dec. 1632. Mary Burell, Edward Eltonhead and Ralph Eltonhead to Trinity House*
They are tenants for the office of ballastage at Greenwich, Woolwich and Erith. Their lease of the wharf and land at Greenwich belonging to the earl of Arundel has expired. They ask Trinity House to negotiate with the earl for a 15 year lease of the ballast wharf at Greenwich, the ballast way, the ballast pit, the ballast field of about 3 acres, 2 other fields, each of 5 acres lately bought by the earl from Clement Lyneere, the old ballast pit of one acre, the stable yard of half an acre, a field of 2 acres encompassed

by the highway, and a corner of the great mead of wet ground containing a road adjoining the wharf. They will pay whatever rate is negotiated, provided that it is no more than £50 a year. Subject to that proviso, they will accept whatever is agreed and will take a lease either from Trinity House or the earl, whichever Trinity House prefer.
Witnesses: Lancelot Johnson, Jo. Best, etc.

414. [f.61] *30 March 1633. Report by Trinity House*
They consider the proposition to build houses on the Bridge to be inconvenient to the river because the soil from many or all those houses, of which there is a great quantity, is thrown into the river, thereby increasing shoals, sands and banks and the river will be less capable for the great trade and traffic to London. If it is objected that the houses are of long standing, and the question asked what damage had been done to the river, they say that every shoal and bank from the Bridge to Blackwall had been nourished thereby, but it was not noticed in former ages when ships were small, drawing little water. Ships for the service of the king and the city are now larger with a greater draught, whereby there is more danger from shoals. The river, which they dare presume is the greatest for navigation in the known part of the world, decays yearly. Within their memory the Pool near St Katherine's and Wapping was 12 or 13 ft at low water, and is now at most 8 or 9 ft; at Limehouse, formerly 15 or 16 ft, now 12 or 12½ ft; at Blackwall, 18 or 19 ft, now 13 or 14 ft. If special care is not taken to prevent the casting of soil into the river, it will grow unnavigable within 6 or 8 miles of London, except by boats, with evil consequences. The building of houses would also require the best and largest timber in the land, of which there is already great want for building ships of the king and of merchants. The king's officers, especially the shipwrights, can vouch for this. It would be better to have no houses or buildings on the Bridge than there to be a lack of timber for building ships. Experience has lately shown the danger of fire, which is a threat to the city.[1]
Thomas Best, deputy master; Messrs Salmon, Coke, Totten, Bushell, Tutchin, Benett, Ewins.

    1. A fire beginning on 9 Feb. had destroyed 41 houses on the Bridge (*Rem.* 35; D. Davis, *A history of shopping* (1966), 110).

415. [f.61v] *30 March 1633. Trinity House to Sir Henry Martin* [*admiralty court judge*]
Cases of Hollander captains dishonouring the king and abusing subjects:
(a) In 1614, Mr Trenchfield, master of the *Delight*, and Mr Blith, master of the *Centurion*, met Capt. Mole with 3 of the States' ships off the South Cape, and they had to take in their flags or else fight, which they refused to do being richly laden. (b) Mr Walter Coke has divers times had to take in his flag on the Barbary coast. (c) In Feb. 1618, Mr Anthony Wood, master of the *Royal Exchange*, and Mr Walter Whitinge, master of the *Dorcas*, met Capt. Quass with 6 States' ships off Cape Gata, 50 leagues within the Straits, who ordered them to strike their flags 'for the Lords the States'; had they declined he would have fought them and they were

richly laden. (d) In 1618, Mr Page was at Gibraltar in the *Marigould* of London with divers English ships from Malaga under the command of the town when Capt. Quass entered the road with 6 ships. The *Marigould* was flying her flag 'in top' [at her topmast]. Quass sent his lieutenant in a pinnace to order the flag to be taken in, which Page refused to do, saying that he was as free to wear his king's colours as Quass was to wear the States'. When the wind came fair, the whole fleet set sail and came to sea, but Page, being threatened, dared not wear his flag any more. Whenever the States' ships meet any merchant ships, they make them take in their flags, in contempt of the king.

Thomas Best, deputy master; Messrs Salmon, Coke, Totten, Bushell, Tutchin, Benett, Ewins.

416. [f.62] *22 May 1633. Trinity House to Mr Secretary Coke about a ballast wharf at South Shields* [*Cf* SP 16/239/23; *CSPD 1633–4*, 66. The SP text is signed by Robert Bell, master; Anthony Tutchen, Samuel Doves, John Totton, T. Best, William Rainborowe, William Ewen, Gervais Hockett, Robert Salmon, John Bennett, Christopher Browne, and William Case.]

417. [*After 22 May 1633*] *Trinity House to Sir Robert Heath*
They thought it good to send him a copy of their letter [**416**] to Mr Secretary Coke for his better satisfaction.

418. [f.62v] *8 June 1633. Trinity House* [*? to the committee for Providence Island. Cf Calendar of State Papers Colonial 1574–1660*, 161, 166.]
They have had Mr Punt and the purser before them several times about the expense of the victuals. Whereas the proportion of victuals for passengers was for 12 weeks, they were victualled for 7 or 8 days more. There were victuals for 20 weeks for the crew, but the voyage lasted 26 weeks before the men were discharged. The expense of the victuals for the extra time they 'set against the lessening of his [? Punt's] full proportion'; the small difference in balance they pass by. 'For the master his directions in the expense of the victuals' they find not much amiss, 'but little regarded'. It could not be otherwise because the defects of the master caused the 'disgovernment' in the men. Yet it may be turned to good account in future voyages by making better choice [of master] and employing Trinity House for advice. The master admits his abuse of Mr Hailhead and blames it on his own 'choler and discontent'. He says that it has taught him a lesson and will admit his fault before the addressees. He blames his carriage towards the crew on their want of duty, mutinous stubbornness and ill language. Trinity House, however, attribute it to his lack of discretion in command and 'too much forgetfulness of himself and too little esteem of his men'. That which concerns the purser is 'little worth', only they wish the addressees a better steward hereafter. Nevertheless, since the master pays to the negligent servant no less than to the good, so must both the master and the purser be paid their wages. Trinity House will be ready to rebut the slander that the addressees had failed to victual the ship.

419. [f.63] *13 July 1633. Award [by Trinity House. See* **409.**]
The suit in the court of requests brought by Ellis Henderson against
William Joanes about errors in the account for building the *Mary* [*and*]
John of London, together with all other differences between them, was
by their mutual consent referred to the writers for arbitration. Henderson
shall pay £7 16s to Joanes within 30 days in full settlement of a bill for £14
15s which Henderson owes to Joanes, on payment of which Joanes is to
deliver the bill to Henderson; no error is found in the account for building
the *Mary* [*and*] *John*; both parties are to pay their own legal charges; and
all actions are to cease.
Capt. Best, Messrs Coke, Rainborow, Salmon, Case, Bell.

420. [f.63v. *19 July x 2 Aug. 1633*] *Ken. Edisbury, Den. Fleming and
Phineas Pett* [*principal officers of the navy*] *to Trinity House* [*Cf CSPD
1633–4*, 147; **421.**]
The lords commissioners of the admiralty have instructed them to survey
the king's 2 ships building at Woolwich and Deptford [*Unicorn* and
James]. Both ships being well advanced, any defects should be amended
before the decks are laid. They have been ordered to take some of Trinity
House, the king's masters attendant [see **475n**] and master shipwrights as
assistants, and to report on what needs to be done before the ships are
completed. Trinity House are to choose 3 elder brothers, who should
include Capt. Best and Mr Rainsborow, to attend a meeting at Woolwich
at 9 a.m. on Thursday. The ship at Deptford will be inspected in the
afternoon.

421. [f.64] *2 Aug. 1633. Masters of Trinity House, masters attendant and
shipwrights* [*to the principal officers of the navy. Cf* SP 16/244/23(1);
CSPD 1633–4, 172.]
They have surveyed the ships building for the king at Woolwich and
Deptford. The dimensions of the ship at Woolwich [*Unicorn*] are: length
by the keel, 107 ft; breadth from outside to outside [the planks], 36 ft 4
inches; breadth between the planks, 35 ft 8 inches; depth from the upper
[edge] of the keel to the diameter of the breadth, 15 ft 1 inch; depth of the
keel, 1 ft 8 inches; depth from the upper edge of the keel to the upper
edge of the deck, 17 ft 10 inches; draught of water amidships, 16 ft 3
inches, at which draught she will be port free 5 ft. The dimensions of the
ship at Deptford [*James*] are: length by the keel, 110 ft; breadth from
outside to outside [the planks], 37 ft 6 inches; breadth between the
planks, 36 ft 10 inches; depth from the upper edge of the keel to the
extreme breadth, 16 ft 2½ inches; depth of the keel, 1 ft 9 inches; depth
from the upper edge of the keel to the lower edge of the ports, 22 ft 2
inches; draught of water amidships, 17 ft 2 inches, at which draught she
will be port free 5 ft. The timbers are of sufficient size and scantling with
convenient scarfing*. The quality of the timber and planks is good,
especially in the ship at Deptford which cannot be better, while that used
in the ship at Woolwich is as good as could be got in the New Forest. The
workmanship is sufficient. [f.64v] The orlops* lie at a convenient height;
the beams 'round* well'; both are flush fore and aft. The ports are not yet

cut out but are marked out about 9 ft apart. They and the master shipwrights consider that the first 2 ports, both fore and aft, should be 2 ft 6 inches broad, and the remainder should be 2 ft 2 inches square between the timbers. They agree with the outstanding work as proposed by Mr [Peter] Pett and Mr Boates. Both will be very serviceable men-of-war. William Rainborow, Walter Coke, Anthony Tutchen [of Trinity House], William Coke,[1] Thomas Awstin [masters attendant],[2] Edward Steevens, Henry Goddard, John Graves, Ro. Tranckmore, John Ducy, John Southern, John Taylor [shipwrights].[3]

1. Also an elder brother by 1633 or soon afterwards (*THD*, 71).
2. Cf Pett, 166; **475**, **480**.
3. For Steevens, Graves and Taylor, see **280**; for Goddard, cf Oppenheim, 208; for Tranckmore, cf *CSPD 1627–8*, 166; for Ducy (or Ducie) and Southern, cf SP 16/304/19.

422. [f.65] *July [1633] Negropont, aboard the galley Patron Reall. Thomas Spaight [to an unidentified addressee. Cf CSP Ven. 1632–6, 129, 144; **423**.]*

On coming into the Arches [of Pelagos], they sent a boat to sea which brought word that corn was plentiful everywhere, but especially at Volos, whither they sailed. Having been there for 5 days, and having been promised a sale, the Turks betrayed them at the agreed time, but only 2 were taken and 3 killed in the ambush. They tarried several days, trying in vain to redeem the captives. They then sailed to 'Zetourn' [? Zituni, now Lamia], where none dared to sell them corn. After 10 days, having got 700 'killoes',[1] they came to the Gulf of Salonica where they agreed with a Turk for '6,000 killoes at 62½ per killoe'. While this was being loaded, boats were sent to fetch more. They went from there to Cassandra Gulf, loaded about 6,000 'killoes' at Paliuri, and decided to stay there for fear of the galleys. Contrary to expectations, however, the galleys approached them on Whitsunday [9 June 1633] determined to despoil them by fair means or foul. They had a present for Capt. Bushawe and saluted him but, without one word or sending to them, he assaulted and, it being calm, boarded them. The fight lasted for more than 2 hours and Bushawe did not leave until he had fired the *Hector* and, half an hour later, Spaight's ship too. Twenty of the crew were slain and 70 men made slaves, including himself and Messrs Harris, Wylds and Duckmanton. He beseeches the addressee to secure the release of himself and the others, for he was taken in his service. Spaight, together with his father and mother, will contribute towards the ransom. His pen cannot express his miserable condition, chained as a rower, and fed on bread and water. They are to be taken to 'Stambolo' to be seen by the grand signor, and God knows their fate thereafter. He does not doubt that Sir Peter Wych [ambassador in Turkey], with a letter from the addressee, will be very effective. This letter is written in a dark hole.

P.S. 'They have done more than they can answer. We laded our corn for Venice from whence we came, and were thither bound per a Voizo [? Vijose in Albania] right to Constantinople, that we passed the time till new currants'. Those who he knows were saved include: George Lamden, Robert Stanherd, John Comfort, Messrs Wyld, Parr and

Harris, —Morice, Goodman Wylde, Messrs Parratt, Lacken and Nunnes, Philip Legon, John Preston, Thomas Handly, —Pitcher, —Cadwell, —Duckmantine, —Chilbourne, —Organy, —Orwell, —Pacey, Edward Lambe, Zachary Champion, George May, Christopher Lutcombe, Christopher Bowman, William Trenchfeild.

P.S. 'We carried our corn from Venice and came to pass the time till lading new currants which have advice to Stambolo.'

1. 8⅔ killow of corn at Constantinople was equivalent to one London quarter (L. Roberts, *Merchants mappe of commerce* (1700), 271).

423. [f.65v. *? Aug. x Nov. 1633*][1] *Trinity House to the king*
They petition on behalf of Richard Harris, William Wylds, and 70 Englishmen taken by the Turks with the loss of the *Hector* and *William and Ralph* of London. Last March the ships sailed from Venice into the Arches [of Pelagos] which owes obedience to the grand signor, who is in amity with the Venetian states, to await the 'reculta' [i.e. harvest] for new currants. In June they began trading with the Turks at Paliuri in Cassandra Gulf lading corn for Venice. Capt. Bushawe, sailing from 'Stambolo' with a fleet of 60 galleys, came into the port on Whitsunday and, without parley, contrary to the custom of the sea, suddenly assaulted and boarded the ships. After a bloody fight in which 20 were killed, he set fire to both ships and took the surviving 70 in chains in the galleys. The Turks had no just cause and acted contrary to the law of arms. Much misery will be caused to wives and children and many able men will be lost to the king. Their fight against such a mighty armada was the wonder of Christendom. The king is asked either to send a letter to the grand signor, or to instruct his ambassador to seek justice and secure the release of the seamen and compensation for the loss of the ships.

1. News of the fight had reached England by Aug. and instructions were sent to the English ambassador in Nov. (*CSPD 1633–4*, 189–90; *CSP Ven. 1632–6*, 144).

424. [f.66] *5 Oct. 1633. Trinity House to Sir John Wostenholme*
In reply to his enquiry about the command of the fort of Glückstadt in the river of Hamburg [the Elbe], they are well acquainted with the river and its navigable channels. The distance between the fort and ships as they pass is less than the range of a saker* shot. Ships would therefore be under the command of the fort which has ordnance of the greatest force, namely whole and demi-cannon*. Ships could not pass without desperate danger. Besides the northeast side of the channel lies in the land of the king of Denmark from Brunsbüttel to 'Copper Church', which is 3 miles above the fort. The king could plant cannon to command navigation in the river for most of the way. As soon as is convenient, they will provide a draught [i.e. plan] of the river, showing the fort and channel and the distances from land to land.

425. [f.66v. *12 Oct. 1633*] *Trinity House* [? *to Secretary Coke. Cf* SP 16/247/70; *CSPD 1633–4*, 244; **492.**]
Neglect of the responsibilities of the office of ballastage will cause grave inconveniences. Those seeking to ballast are wholly incapable of carrying

out these responsibilities. (a) There must be a sufficient number of wharves at convenient places on the sides of the river. (b) Enough ballast must be available at these wharves to meet all requirements. (c) As much gravel, sand and rubbish as possible should be taken out of the river from shoals and places of danger. (d) Sufficient great and small lighters need to be available to take the ballast to wharves and ships. Gravel and sand must lie on the wharves for long enough [cf **492**] to dry so as to be suitable for all ships, especially those which carry cloth and other dry goods which must have dry ballast since otherwise the merchant will suffer damage which the shipowner has to make good.[1] (e) Ballast lighters must be measured and their ballast-carrying capacity clearly marked so as to prevent abuse, and to set down a reasonable price [see **492**] for every kind of ballast according to quality. (f) Ships must be assigned to the right place for ballast. (g) There must be no cause for complaint by subjects of a lack of ballast or of just weight. If ballast is not available, the employment of ships will be hindered and merchants and owners will suffer prejudice. The lack of ballast for a day or 2 can cost £6, £7, or £8 a day, depending upon the number of the crew.[2] (h) They have had the office of ballastage for 120 years and have always fixed prices without complaint. These idle fellows know nothing of ballastage, much less about the Thames, its dangers and places from which it is fit or unfit to take up gravel. Furthermore Trinity House have for long provided all things necessary for the execution of the office of ballastage and the cleansing of the Thames, and have never been reproved. They are ready to prove this to the king or to the privy council. [f.67] The provisions for the ballastage office have cost them and their assignee, Mr William Burrell, lately deceased, about £3,000. To change the execution of the office after 100 years will confound the work and prejudice subjects and navigation. Mr attorney [general] has already given the legal view and he should also consider the question of convenience.

P.S. £50 a year is paid to Capt. Thomas Porter out of the rent due to the king, by order under the privy seal.

1. This sentence is written in the margin and omitted in the SP text.
2. From here to the end is erased in the Trinity House, but not the SP text.

426. [*c. Nov. 1633*] *Trinity House to Sir Henry Martine* [*admiralty court judge. Cf* HCA 3/34, f. 370.]
According to his reference of 27 July last about the difference of account between John Bennet, pl., late master of the *Grace* of London, and Edward Beane, John Victers, Robert Burdett and John Deasrsly [sic], part-owners of the ship, both parties have appeared and the account drawn up and audited by their nominees. The owners owe £113 2s 6d [or £173 2s 6d] to Bennett, who has been much wronged and prevented from getting his due and maintaining his wife and family.

427. [f.67v] *11 Nov. 1633. Trinity House to the mayor* [*of Poole. See* **411–12**.]
They have received his letter of 'the 20th present' [sic] and copies of his former letters which they had already had. At the end of this term, they

intend to tell the lord keeper what they have done: the number of shires committed to their trust with the money collected, charges arising, and who have been redeemed, and so accordingly to the mayor's part, insofar as he tells them. Whereas he conceives that they wanted him to come to perfect the business, it was the lord keeper who expected some of the alderman last term. As to the extraordinary charges in his account, they do not consider that all is due from the 'poor remains' of the captives' money. William Raineborow, master.

428. *6 Nov.* [? *1633*] *Certificate by the merchants who loaded goods in the Providence of Bristol* [*See* **429.**]
The *Providence* of Bristol, Samuel Andrewes master, recently sustained great damage in her late voyage from London to Bristol in cutting down her masts by the board and otherwise in a storm to save the ship and her goods. The undersigned [not entered] who are merchants, laders of the ship, are content to include these losses in a general average*, and to pay their part according to the law and custom of merchants.

429. *30 Nov. 1633. Trinity House to Mr Hollworthy*[1]
In answer to his enquiry, their opinion is that a ship with all her furniture is liable to an average*. As to whether the goods in a ship which has received damage are liable to average, their opinion is that damage to goods is not to be made good by way of average, but the damaged goods are to be included in the average according to their value.

1. ? Richard Holworthy, on whom see P. McGrath, *Merchants and merchandise in 17th century Bristol* (Bristol Record Society, 1955), 145.

430. [f.68] *12 Dec. 1633. Trinity House to Dr Reeve*[1]
In reply to his letter of the 5th about 'loadsmonye' [cf **312**] taken by a new court of law at Dover, this is what they call the pilot's wage for taking a ship in or out of port. What a corporation receives for 'loadsmony (as you call it)' is the 1s in the pound levy on the earnings of pilots for admitting and appointing pilots. No man can be pilot to take charge of a ship unless appointed by a corporation. The money is used to relieve the poor of the corporation. Taking 'loadsmony' does not tie a pilot, court, or corporation to make good damage which happens under the hand of the pilot. There never was such a precedent, nor would there be a pilot in the world if it were so. The fee is £2 for piloting a small ship from London to the Downs, £3 for a large one, and £5 for the largest, while the value of the lesser ship and her goods will be £20,000, sometimes £30,000, and the greater sort £50,000, £70,000 or £100,000. What justice there would be in making a pilot liable for such losses is left to his judgement. They never have heard of such a law, nor will, they presume. Skill avails a pilot nothing without the blessing of God. For a pilot to be deprived of his best anchor and cable is a custom of the lords of the Cinque Ports, but Trinity House know not by what law and it seems 'to smite where the Lord hath wounded'. As for the abuse of the people, if the report of the master is true, it is barbarous.

1. Perhaps the author of 'Historia navalis' (cf *CSPD 1629–31*, 145).

431. [f.68v. *Before 22 Feb. 1634*] *Trinity House to the lords commissioners of the admiralty* [*See* **432**; *cf* SP 16/228, f.117v; *CSPD 1633–4*, 470.]
They have had the sole execution of the office of lastage* and ballastage for 100 years, for these 38 or 40 years under the broad seal. Lately the king has confirmed the grant under his privy seal, reserving a rent of £50 a year assigned to Capt. Thomas Porter. Lastly in 2 references the king has declared his intention not to abridge their rights. Nevertheless, the attorney general, on information and considering only the legal point, has preferred a *quo warranto* action against the corporation in the court of king's bench, being of opinion that the right of sole ballastage does not belong to them. The commissioners are asked to consider the point of convenience and how prejudicial would be the 'promiscuous' ballastage of ships, with nobody answerable for misdemeanours. The commissioners know how it concerns the reputation of the petitioners that the office be executed without prejudice to the river.

432. *22 Feb. 1634. Whitehall.* [*Lords commissioners of the admiralty*] *to the attorney general* [*Cf* SP 16/228, f.117v; *CSPD 1633–4*, 470; **431.**]
He is desired to stay further proceedings on the *quo warranto* brought against the petitioners about ballastage until he has spoken to the writers and further order given.
[Lords] Lindsey [omitted from SP text] and Dorset, [Sir] John Cooke, [Sir] H. Vane, [Sir] Francis Windbancke.

433. [f.69. *? Before 6 Dec. 1634*] *Trinity House to the lords commissioners of the admiralty about Humphrey Streete and the ballastage office* [*Cf* SP 16/278/15; *CSPD 1634–5*, 344. The SP text is annotated in a contemporary hand as received on 6 Dec. 1634 and is ascribed by *CSPD* to that date.]

434. [f.69v] *19 Dec. 1633. Admiralty court order to Sir John Wentworth, Francis Brewster and Henry North, esquires, Thomas Trenchfeild, 'Charles' [? recte Christopher] Browne and George Hatch, mariners*
The bailiffs, commonalty and adventurers in the fishing trade at Dunwich, Southwold and Walberswick in Suffolk have complained that Sir John Rowse, for private gain, has lately made heading banks and 2 sluices whereby the ancient, previously navigable, channel belonging to the towns is blocked not far above the mouth of the haven. The haven and harbour are much decayed and likely to be stopped, impoverishing the inhabitants and prejudicing the king's service and customs. In the star chamber on 29 Nov., the privy council ordered Sir Henry Martin, admiralty court judge, to institute an enquiry by some members of Trinity House, together with some gentlemen of Suffolk with no interest and not living nearby. Martin has decreed a commission to them accordingly to view the haven, channel, headings and sluices, and to make a report to the admiralty court, to be presented to the star chamber board by the beginning of next term.
Thomas Wyann, deputy register.

435. [f.70] *17 Jan. 1634. Sir John Wentworth, Francis Brewster, Henry North, Thomas Trenchfeild, Christopher Browne and William Ewen to the privy council about the threat to the fishing trade at Dunwich, Southwold and Walberswick [Cf SP 16/260/28(1); CSPD 1633–4, 453–4. CSPD does not list the signatories or mention that the sluice had been built near the site of a mill which the father of Sir John Rowse, who had died 30 years since, had built on the stream.]*

436. [f.70v] *8 March 1634. Trinity House to the principal officers of the navy*
According to the order dated 29 Jan. 1634 they have consulted sailmakers whose opinions are enclosed. Mildewing of sails can only be lessened if shipmasters take care to open the sails often to dry, air and cool them. Sails left furled for long become heated, which mildews them more than lying wet. 'Buckt cloth double' [? cloth steeped or boiled in an alkaline dye] is too weighty, boisterous and unmanageable. But for double sails for great ships good 'warpt' cloth is best.

437. [f.71] *4 March 1605. Certificate by Thomas Milton and others*[1]
They were summoned before Sir Julius Caesar, admiralty court judge, and empanelled as a jury to set down how far the king's chambers, havens, or ports on the coast extend. They comprise all the coast within a straight line drawn between each headland of England. [The headlands are listed, together with the distances and bearings, one from another, starting with Souter Point and ending with Holyhead.] A plat is enclosed [not entered].
Thomas Milton, William Bigate, John Burrell, William Joanes, Peter Hilles, Michael Edmonds, James Woodcott, Thomas Best, William Ivy, John Skynner, John Wyldes, Henry Hancken, William Case.

    1. Cf SP 14/13/11; *CSPD 1603–10*, 202. The jury were probably elder brethren of Trinity House (cf Monson, iii.209).

438. [f.71v] *24 Jan. 1634. Edward Steevens and other shipwrights [? to the principal officers of the navy. See **421**.]*
According to 'your' warrant of 19 Dec. [not entered], they have surveyed the 2 new ships built for the king in dry dock at Deptford and Woolwich, and have calculated the burdens according to the old rule and that laid down by the privy council on 26 May 1628.

	Ship built at Woolwich by Mr Boate [*Unicorn*]	Ship built at Deptford by Mr [Peter] Pett [*James*]
Old rule:		
Length by the keel	107 ft	110 ft
Breadth outside [the planks]	36 ft 4 inches	37 ft 6 inches
Draught	16 ft 3 inches	17 ft 2 inches
These figures multiplied together and divided by 100 produce in tons and tonnage*	841	944

	Ship built at Woolwich by Mr Boate [*Unicorn*]	Ship built at Deptford by Mr [Peter] Pett [*James*]
New rule:		
Length by the keel	107 ft	110 ft
Breadth inside the planks	35 ft 8 inches	36 ft 10 inches
Depth from the upper edge of keel to the diameter of the breadth	15 ft 1 inch	16 ft 2½ inches
These figures multiplied together and divided by 100 produce in tons and tonnage	767	875

The frames, mould, workmanship, the sizes and scantlings of the timbers, the binding within and without board, and the quality of the materials in the scarf* riders, beams, knees*, etc. is good. The decks of the ship at Deptford go flush fore and aft, as does the lower gundeck of the ship at Woolwich, but a rise is cut in the fore part of the gunroom in the upper gundeck. In future, both gundecks should be flush, as they have certified formerly. The ports of both ships will lie about 5 ft from the water and are 8 or 9 ft apart or under in the case of the ship at Woolwich, and 9 ft in that of the ship at Deptford. The ports are of a convenient depth and breadth. Both ships will be very serviceable royal men-of-war.
Edward Steevens, John Ducy, John Southerne, John Graves, John Dearsly, Robert Tranckmore.[1]
[Note at end] The certificate following [? **439**] was written under this, and both were presented as one.

1. For Dearsly see **280**; for the others see **421**.

439. [f.72. *14 Jan. 1634. Trinity House to the principal officers of the navy. Cf* SP 16/273/27; *CSPD 1634–5*, 185.]
They were required this day for the king's service to give their opinions of the 'reasons abovementioned' [not entered]. Nine of the 10 ships built in the time of the late commissioners of the navy [appointed in 1619] were cast in the 2nd and 3rd ranks of the king's ships. The 4 new ships built at Deptford and Woolwich within this last 2 years are likewise of much greater burden than those mentioned in the propositions of the commissioners. It is concluded that the reasons of the 'masters' for increasing the cables in the new ships by one inch for mooring in habour and for service are very fitting, but for the old ships mentioned in the propositions, to which 'divers of us' then subscribed, cables of the scantlings then set down will suffice.
Anthony Tutchen [omitted from SP text], William Rainborowe, Thomas Best, Robert Salmon, Walter Coke.

440. *4 June 1634. Trinity House to the same*
Following a warrant dated 31 Dec. they viewed and certified concerning the 2 new ships of the king then in dock at Woolwich and Deptford

[*Unicorne* and *James*]. Now that the *Unicorne* does not prove answerable to their opinion, they acknowledge their error, which proceeds from their not weighing well the overbuilding of the ship, which is the only cause of her tenderness. They were not alone in this error because many others of good judgement have also failed in their opinion of her.

441. [f.72v. *Before 23 Apr. 1634*] *John Hide and others* [*to Trinity House. See* **442**.]
Being lately at Genoa, they had needed a friend on divers occasions as they were strangers and repaired to Francisco Massola their consul who had renounced the task. Signor Phillippo Barnardi befriended them and considering the need for so able a protector in future, they recommend Barnardy as consul. He is honest and able, has a great affection for England, having long been there, and knows the language and customs of the English.
John Hide, Nicholas Hilson, Robert Nethersall, John Hall, Reynold Newe, John Gargardnall.
[Marginal note] The merchants' letter to the company on behalf of Barnardy as consul.

442. *23 Apr. 1634. Certificate by Trinity House*
Upon the suit of merchants, captains and masters trading to Genoa, they appointed Francisco Massola, a Genoese, to be consul for so long as he aided the English nation there, but now they have been credibly informed that he has renounced the consulship. Phillippo Barnardy having been recommended in his stead [f.73] Trinity House, insofar as in them lies, appoint him consul for so long as he provides assistance. His fee is to be 2 ducats a ship, great or small. The state of Genoa is asked to accept him as consul.

443. *29 March 1634.* [*Commissioners of the admiralty to Trinity House seeking an opinion on a petition by Capt. Thomas Porter and Capt. Hawkeridge* (**444**) *about pilotage. Cf* SP 16/264, f.2; *CSPD 1633–4*, 528.]

444. [f.73v. *? Before 12 Feb. 1634*] *Capt. Thomas Porter and Capt. William Hawkeridge to the king* [*See* **443**; **445**.]
Strangers daily enter the king's ports for trade and succour and sound the harbours and entry places on the coast of England, Scotland and Ireland, the Thames only excepted, which has made them as skilful as 'our best pilots' and has caused much mischief and misery. Thus in 1631 Turkish pirates landed at night at Baltimore in Ireland, sacked the town, and carried away 109 persons whom they sold as slaves in Algiers, which they would not have dared, had they not known the haven. The mischief is because there is no restraint on foreigners entering without native pilots, as is the rule in Spain, France, the 'Two Countries', Denmark etc. where native pilots have to be employed and pilotage paid. To keep foreigners at the like distance and to employ aged seamen unfit for long voyages, the king is asked to ordain that no stranger shall enter in or out without a pilot under penalty. In view of their services and the late great losses of

Hawkeridge, the king is asked to empower the petitioners to appoint pilots in England, Wales and Ireland [sic], the Thames excepted, and to take such fees from strangers for their services as are granted to like officers by foreign princes.

445. *12 Feb. 1634. Court at Whitehall.* [*Sir*] *Sidney Montague* [*master of requests*] *to the lords commissioners of the admiralty*
Reference of [? **444**].

446. [f.74] *26 Apr. 1634.* [*Trinity House to the lords commissioners of the admiralty. Cf* SP 16/266/39; *CSPD 1633–4,* 570.]
In reply to **443**, they oppose the grant of a patent to prevent strangers from entering the ports and harbours of the kingdom without pilots for these reasons: (a) Apart from the Thames, Bristol, Hull, Lynn and some other petty places, the harbours are open and free from danger. Corporations of seamen exist at Newcastle, Hull and Dover, charged by their charters to provide pilotage. Yarmouth is a limb of the Cinque Ports to whom pilotage belongs. (b) It would be a needless charge and give much discontent to strangers, and might endanger the king's subjects to have a like charge put on them in all foreign countries. (c) Strangers were never subjected to pilotage, those few places formerly mentioned excepted, nor has there been such a proposal previously.[1] The king's subjects pay pilotage only at Venice in Italy. In all other places within the Straits, in the ports of Spain, Holland, and Denmark, they are free, although anyone can have a pilot if he wishes. (d) Ports are open to receive all navigation in all countries. God forbid that the ports of the king's dominions should be shut up, as they will be if pilotage is made compulsory. Since pilots are not required, ships often enter for shelter and to safeguard lives and goods when it is not possible to obtain pilots. (e) Whereas the 'petitioner' [sic] conceives that the Turkish action at Baltimore was caused by their knowledge or that of a Christian stranger, this was not so. The Turks took a fisherman not far away and made him guide them into the port, promising to set him free, which they did. (f) Since ports in all countries are known to those seamen who trade in them, knowledge [f.74v] of English ports which have so great a trade cannot be clouded. (g) The petitioner conceives that if strangers had to have pilots, they would be kept ignorant, but a mariner once brought in and out of a port is there made a pilot forever.[2]

1. There had been a proposal in 1582 (*THD*, 121–2).
2. Signatures in SP text: William Raineborowe, T. Best, Walter Coke, Samuel Doves, Robert Bell, William Ewen, William Swanley, Jonas James, George Hatch, Robert Salmon, William Case, James Moyer, W. Bushill, Anthony Tutchen, John Totton, Gervais Hockett, Robert Kitchen, John Bennett, Christopher Browne.

447. [f.75. *Before 23 Apr. 1634*] *Patrick Kirwane and Thomas Lynch, merchants of Ireland, to Trinity House* [*See* **448**.]
They request an opinion on the following 2 cases: (a) Two merchants freighted a ship from Ireland to London and back again and let 6 tons in her by charter party. The ship reached London, discharged her lading,

and began to relade. Goods came so fast from the 2 principal merchants and strangers, that when the servant of the merchant who had freighted the 6 tons arrived, there was space for only 4 tons. Nevertheless, he came with the other 2 tons within the time specified in the charter party. When the master refused to accept them, he brought them ashore and ventured them in another ship without the consent of his own master or the other freighters. Who is to bear the loss of these 2 tons? (b) Mr Kirwane freighted a 60 ton ship for £120 for a voyage from Ireland to Bilbao and loaded 20 tons of salmon. His factor, Mr Lynch, seeing the ship ready to part not half loaded, put another 10 tons aboard without the consent of the principals. What freight should be paid?

448. *23 Apr. 1634. Opinion by Trinity House*
Their opinion on these cases propounded to them today [**447**] is: (a) The servant of the third merchant took the 2 tons of goods ashore again without protesting against the master and principal factor according to law. Although he offered to lade in due time and according to the charter party, since he had direction from neither the principal freighter nor the master to ship the goods in another vessel, the third merchant must bear the whole loss of the 2 tons loaded by his servant. (b) In the second case, the factor is to pay to the principal or first merchant a proportionate part of the freight, i.e. £20.
William Rainborow, master, John Bennett, Anthony Tutchin, William Ewens, Thomas Best, William Bushell.

449. [f.75v] *24 May 1634. Trinity House to the privy council supporting the building of a quay and dry dock at 'Dunham Bridge' [Downham Bridge on the Orwell near Ipswich] in Suffolk [Cf SP 16/268/59; CSPD 1634–5, 38. The SP text is signed by William Rainborowe, master, Anthony Tutchen, John Totton, Gervais Hockett, Samuel Doves, James Moyer, William Case, T. Best, Robert Salmon, Walter Coke.]*

450. *4 June 1634. Certificate by Trinity House*
Sir William Curteene, merchant of the city of London, has made suit to them about the need for a consul for ships and seamen at Trapani in Sicily and has sought their allowance of Henry Dyke, a merchant, to be settled there as consul. They are credibly informed by Curteene that Dyke is of good report and an able man, being already consul there for the Dutch. Insomuch as in them lies, they appoint Dyke consul for so long as he helps 'our nation'. His fee is to be 2 ducats a ship, great and small. The viceroy of Sicily is entreated to accept him as consul.

451. [f.76] *7 June 1634. Trinity House to Sir Robert Heath*
In answer to his letter about the king's pleasure for ballast in the Tyne, they recommend an order entered in the register of the council. All men can, and many will, then take copies to answer exceptions. Whereas he desired them to find a man to seize the ballast and receive the money, if there is anything else needed, they will do their best therein.

452. [f.76v] *4 June 1634. Masters of Trinity House and shipwrights [to the principal officers of the navy. Cf SP 16/269/42(1); CSPD 1634–5, 66.]*
According to the warrant dated 24 May they have been aboard the king's ship, the *Unicorne*, now at Chatham, and on conference with her principal men they conclude that she is unfit to bear sail because she has too little breadth and too much height. To remedy these defects and for the grace of the ship, the following work is required: (a) Since she is too high for her breadth, her upper works need to be taken down to the level of the upper edge of the ports in the waist of her upper gundeck, and the upper deck taken away, leaving a large quarterdeck and forecastle. The great cabin floor should go flush with the middle deck, the roundhouse floor 'settled' 18 inches, and the roundhouse made a convenient height to make her 'shipp shapen'. The step of the mizen should be brought down to the lower gundeck and the friezes, spirket wales and gunwales on the forecastle removed. The timbers and work in the waist and on the quarterdeck should be made as light as possible. (b) It is fit to girdle her with 8 strakes of wales and plank, the thickest being 5 inches, 'to continue the breadth one foot higher than now it is, and to bring on a wale to finish it under the ports'. The total cost of the work, timber, planks, pitch, tar and ironwork and the workmanship of carpenters, caulkers, joiners, carvers and painters, would be £500.
William Raineborow, Anthony Tutchen, John Totton, James Moyer [of Trinity House], Edward Steevens, Henry Goddard, Peter Pett [? nephew of Phineas Pett], John Graves, Robert Tranckmore [shipwrights].[1]

1. For Steevens and Graves, see **280**; for Goddard and Pett, **407**; for Tranckmore, **421**. SP describes Steevens as of Trinity House.

453. [f.77] *30 May 1634. Mincing Lane [London. Sir] Henry Palmer and Ken. Edisbury [principal officers of the navy] to Trinity House and Shipwrights' Hall*
The lords commissioners of the admiralty directed the writers to survey the king's new ships now building in dry dock at Deptford and Woolwich [*Leopard* and *Swallow*] before the deck beams or planks are laid to enable the remedy of any defects which cannot be so well done when they are fully built. At least 3 from both Trinity House and Shipwrights' Hall are required to set aside all other business and assemble at Woolwich on next Monday morning, 4 June,[1] to survey the materials and workmanship, and to prevent ill quality in the laying of her orlops*, the contriving of her ports and the rounding* of her gundecks. The ship at Deptford will be surveyed similarly in the afternoon.

1. Sic. 4 June was a Wednesday.

454. [f.77v. *16 June 1634. Trinity House and Shipwrights' Hall to Sir Henry Palmer and Kenrick Edisbury, principal officers of the navy. Cf SP 16/269/96(1); CSPD 1634–5, 82.]*
In reply to **453**, they have surveyed the 2 ships building for the king at Woolwich and Deptford. The dimensions of the ship at Woolwich [*Leopard*][1] are: length by the keel, 93 ft 8 inches; breadth from outside to

outside the timbers, 32 ft 8½ inches; depth from the upper part of the keel to the diameter of the breadth, 12 ft 1½ inches; depth of the keel, 1 ft 7 inches; rake of the stern, 31 ft 3 inches;[2] rake of the stern post, 4 ft 6 inches; the flat floor about 13 ft (it could not be exactly measured); draught amidships, 12 ft 9 inches, at which draught the master shipwrights may lay the orlops* so as the lower edges of the ports are 5 ft 9 inches from the water. The dimensions of the ship at Deptford [*Swallow*][1] are: length by the keel, 95 ft 6 inches; breadth from outside to outside the timbers, 32 ft; depth from the upper edge of the keel to the diameter of the breadth, 11 ft 7½ inches; depth of the keel, 1 ft 8 inches; rake of the stern, 27 ft 9 inches; rake of the stern post, 4 ft 8½ inches; the flat floor about 13 ft (it could not be exactly measured); draught amidships, 12 ft 3 inches, at which draught the master shipwrights may lay the orlops so that the lower edges of the ports are 5 ft 9 inches from the water. [f.78] Their timber, material and workmanship are sufficient; only part of the oak plank is green and of insufficient length. As to their upper works, what is to be done for rounding* of the beams, laying the orlops flush fore and aft, and making the ports, they leave to the king's directions but they wish the master shipwrights to take great care in building the upper works as snug and as light as may be.

Walter Coke, Robert Salmon, William Rainborow, Anthony Tutchen [of Trinity House], Edward Steevens, John Taylor [shipwrights, see **280**] Thomas Hawkins [? shipwright].

1. Cf Oppenheim (p. 254) and **467**.
2. 31 ft 7 inches in SP text.

455. [f.78v] *1 June 1634. Court at Greenwich. Order of the privy council* [*Cf* PC 2/44, 24–5.]

Present: the king, archbishop of Canterbury, lord keeper, archbishop of York, lord treasurer, lord privy seal, duke of Lennox, marquess [of] Hamilton, earl marshal, lord chamberlain, earl of Dorset, earl [of] Bridgewater, viscount Wimbledon, lord Newburgh, Mr treasurer, Mr comptroller, Mr vice chamberlain, Mr secretary Coke, Mr secretary Windebanke.

Upon consideration of a complaint by the mayor and burgesses of Newcastle that the ballast shore lately built at South Shields on the Tyne by Sir Robert Heath, lord chief justice of common pleas, would prejudice shipping, navigation and the river, the care of which had been entrusted to them by the king, and upon hearing both sides with their counsel, it was ordered that: (a) the ballast shore be finished and backed with ballast to make it fit for the saltworks which are begun there for the king's service in the first place; (b) seamen shall be free to cast their ballast there if they wish, but not forced to do so; (c) the town of Newcastle and the hostmen are not to hinder seamen indirectly by refusing to transport coal in keels to the ships which cast their ballast at Shields. The king reserves the ordering of the ballast shore so that navigation and shipping benefits, no loss of customs and other duties occurs, and the town suffers no loss of trade [f.79] or the river any hurt.

456. [*? 8 June 1634*] *Watermen's company to the privy council about the employment of watermen at sea* [*Cf.* SP 16/269/52; *CSPD 1634–5*, 69–70.]

457. [f.79v] *8 June 1634. Thomas Meautys, clerk of the privy council, to the lords commissioners of the admiralty requesting an opinion on* **456** [*Cf* SP 16/269/52(1); *CSPD 1634–5*, 70.]

458. *30 June 1634. Lords commissioners of the admiralty to Trinity House about* **456** [*Cf* SP 16/264, f.27; *CSPD 1634–5*, 98. **458** subscribed by lord Cottington, Sir Henry Vane, Sir Francis Windbanck and the earl of Lindsey.]

459. [f.80–80v] *9 July 1634. Trinity House to the lords commissioners of the admiralty about* **456** [*Cf* SP 16/271/46; *CSPD 1634–5*, 138–9. *CSPD* does not mention the distinction which Trinity House drew between 'we that are owners and masters of ships' and 'those men that be masters mates, gunners, carpenters and boatswains'. The SP text is signed by Walter Coke (described as deputy master in **459**), Anthony Tutchen, Jonas James, George Hatch, Thomas Trenchfeild, T. Best, James Moyer, John Totton, Robert Salmon, Christopher Browne.]

460. [f.81] *25 Oct. 1634. Certificate by Trinity House*
At the instance of the bearer, David Davison, ropemaker of Wapping, they certify that it is much better for the spinning of yarn for all sorts of cordage to be done under cover than in the open air. Yarn spun in the open air is subject to moisture in the air, dew and rain. If there is moisture in yarn made into cordage, the cordage soon rots endangering ships of merchants and of the king. Even the best hemp, when spun moist or wet, will rot. To spin and make cordage under cover is not a new device but ancient in all countries, as in Muscovy, Prussia, Holland, Poland, Lübeck and Hamburg.
Walter Coke, deputy master, etc.

461. *29 Oct. 1634. Trinity House to the lord privy seal*
They have seen the engine model which Mr Needham and his 'second', Mr Browne, have made for cleansing the Thames and have seen it work. It is of no use to the river but a 'mere fancy or toy fallen from an idle head'. The reasons are too tedious to trouble him with, but can be given if desired.
Walter Coke, deputy master, etc.

462. [f.81v. *? After 5 May 1634. A project. See* **463.**]
Provision has been made by statute [2 Richard II, stat. 1, c. 4] for mariners to be retained in the king's service under his admiral or lieutenant, but there is no other provision for retaining them for the service and defence of this kingdom. Mariners at sea or in foreign parts not under the admiral or his lieutenant are neither bound to return, nor restrained from serving foreign princes. The king thereby loses the

service of expert and courageous seamen whose names are not made known. Despite laws against the transportation of ordnance, there is no means of discovering the names of those who transport it. Merchants, masters, owners and governors load as much ordnance as their ships will bear, and return scarce half or quarter, having sold the rest at great profit. The master of the ordnance of the Tower takes notice only of the ordnance which is exported from the port of London, and takes bonds only for the ordnance imported but there is no provision for discovering what becomes of the ordnance afterwards. At no other port is there any regulation of ordnance at all. Nor is there a register of seamen leaving and returning and no officer is appointed for these purposes. The course hereafter propounded would prevent these evils and also the illegal export of wool, fuller's earth, hides, leather and other prohibited goods allegedly sent to another port in the kingdom but really carried overseas. [f.82] Since his accession the king has created a new office for the entry of passes to ascertain the names of all subjects leaving the realm, their places of abode, estates, degree, destination and intended date of return so that the king can recall them if he requires their services.[1] A similar register of seamen, ordnance and prohibited goods would provide the king with information about the number and quality of seamen and would prevent illegal practices. Prohibited goods would be listed and bonds taken against their export without licence as laid down by former proclamation [? of 30 Sept. 1632 (*Proc.* i.196)]. The creation of an office and register at London and all other ports, creeks and havens of England and Wales is requested. Details would be kept of each ship departing, her burden, captain, master, governors, owners, officers, seamen and passengers, her guns, muskets and other munitions, [f.82v] and of prohibited goods carried, and on her return of any discrepancies in personnel or ordnance, and where prohibited goods had been landed. A copy of the entry would be given to the master, owner, or chief officer of the ship before departure. The books of entry and the register should be delivered once yearly to the king's remembrancer in the court of the exchequer, as is done by the customer and comptrollers of the port of London. On pain of forfeiture, ships should be prohibited from leaving port for Newfoundland, the North Sea or any other place, and the crew forbidden to disperse or unload on return before the entries are made and an oath administered. Since many ships go out of one port and return to another where there would be no record of their departure, officers should not grant clearance before an oath has been taken, and an entry and copy [f.83] made. The copy is to be shown to the authorised officer, and an explanation given of discrepancies under oath. The master of the ordnance of the Tower [of London], saving his privileges, and the authorised officers are to take care that these provisions are not breached. It is requested that those whom the king appoints as keepers of the register and as clerks should receive for taking bonds and making the entries and copies a fee of 2d a head for captains, governors, masters and officers, and 1d for mariners, ships' boys and passengers for voyages abroad, payable both outwards and homewards, and half these amounts for voyages to ports in England and Wales, and 1d a ton on ships entering and leaving for voyages abroad, and a farthing for voyages to ports in England and Wales. [f.83v] These dues would be paid only by the king's subjects and on ships belonging to the king's subjects. Payment would be made by the master or owner before departure and on return, on pain of the same forfeiture.

1. ? The grant of 25 May 1630 to Patrick Craford and Matthew Birkenhead (cf C 66/2537, no. 7) or of 21 Jan. 1636 to Thomas Mayhew (*CSPD 1635–6*, 175).

463. [*? After 5 May 1634*] *Report by Trinity House*
They report their opinions of **462**. No better provision can be made than that which already exists. The new office would maintain many idle fellows and damnify many thousand honest men, enthralling all merchants, owners and masters. To await the pleasure of this 'great officer', thereby losing their tide, fair wind and weather would delay all ships. The projector argues that there is no provision for registering seamen but is ignorant of 'our customs' because no ship can be cleared in the customs house and searchers' office until the number of the crew is given in a note signed by the master or purser, whereby the number of seamen at sea can always be known. Besides, every 4 or 5 years, the lord admiral takes a muster of seamen, so that a new office is not needed for this business. As for seamen who run away from ships overseas and enter the service of foreign nations, the projector offers no remedy. Great disorder exists among seamen at home, since for every 500 who take press money, only 200 or 300 appear despite all the wit of the king's officers. Besides, the late proclamation [of 5 May 1634 (*Proc.* i.200)] against runaways abroad and the orders of Trinity House based on the civil law render offenders liable to loss of wages and, if they come home later, to imprisonment either by the judge of the admiralty or by Trinity House. As to ordnance, the projector acknowledges divers laws to prevent transportation but says that there is insufficient provision to discover the names of the transporters. This savours of silliness, for once transportation is discovered, the names of those responsible cannot be hidden. The master and crew will reveal the names of the owners of the ordnance and who hired the ship. If discovered abroad, every customs house will say for 12d when it was landed, and the name of the ship and master. Besides, in every port and creek of the realm, the customs house is like the eye of Argus, ever vigilant and prying. [f.84] Further, ordnance cannot be taken aboard any ship without a warrant from the lord high admiral to the master of the ordnance, who must first take bonds for its safe custody at all times. When a ship returns from a voyage, the ordnance is inspected by officers appointed by the master of the ordnance as appears by order of 24 June 1619 [order no. 11 in **464** is then quoted] which was sent by the privy council to Trinity House with command to perform it. Failure to do so would render the corporation liable to condign punishment. The matter of the illegal export of prohibited goods is for the gentlemen of the Customs House to answer. As to the dues being a small charge on subjects, the annual yield would be £5,000 or £6,000, a grievous burden upon navigation.

464. [f.84v] *24 June 1619. Order by the king to the privy council to prevent the illegal transport of iron ordnance* [*Cf* SP 14/109/109; *CSPD 1619–23*, 55.]

(1) Since the only furnaces for casting iron ordnance are in Sussex and Kent, the one market for buying and selling it shall be at the 'further Tower Hill', London, commonly called East Smithfield, which is to be free for all founders of iron ordnance, merchants and others, as accustomed. (2) Iron ordnance is only to be landed at Tower wharf, as accustomed. (3) Iron ordnance is only to be proved at Ratcliff fields, as accustomed. (4) Iron ordnance is to be shipped only at Tower wharf. The lieutenant of the Tower is to assist in the removal of ships which hinder the loading and unloading of iron ordnance there. (5) Iron ordnance is only to be shipped from London because of great abuse in stealing and shipping away ordnance, principally in the outports. (6) Furnaces for manufacture may only be built in future by licence of the king on the advice of the lord admiral and the master of the ordnance. (7) No founder is to sell iron ordnance unless it bears his name (or at least 2 letters of it), its weight and year, so as to ensure that each piece is of the right weight and no more. [f.85] (8) The master of the ordnance is to take bonds of £1,000 from founders, with the condition that they must provide him annually with details of iron ordnance manufactured, the number, height, weight and nature, and to whom it was sold; that the ordnance will be delivered only to the market place at Tower Hill; and that they will obey the other orders. (9) Iron ordnance is only to be shipped from the port of London. Shipping from all ports and creeks of Sussex, i.e. Lewes, 'Michinge',[1] Newhaven, Brighton, the old and new Shoreham and their members and elsewhere forbidden. The master of the ordnance or his deputy is to take bonds of £500 and £1,000 from principal searchers and other officers to enforce this regulation. (10) If any licence is granted by the king and council for export to foreign princes and others, it is first to be registered with the master of the ordnance who is to take bonds to ensure that the provisions of the warrant are not transgressed. (11) When any new ship is to be supplied with ordnance, certificate is to be brought from Trinity House to the lord admiral testifying the burden of the ship and the quantity and quality of the ordnance required. The lord admiral will signify his approval to the master of the ordnance who is to take bonds from the master and one owner to ensure that the ordnance is for the defence of the ship and is not to be sold. The bonds are to be [f.85v] for 4 years unless the ship is sold or there is a change in the master or owner. (12) The master of the ordnance shall cause the letter of the lord admiral, or a copy, to be returned to the searchers' office in the Customs House with 'test' that bonds have been taken. The searchers are to certify the same to the collectors outward. The ancient fee of 6d a ship for viewing the ordnance on her return is to be paid, and searchers and collectors are to 'confer' their books once a quarter.[2] (13) Bonds are to be certified to the court of exchequer as by law they ought. No action is to be taken to execute them unless the master of the ordnance certifies that they are forfeit, or upon manifest testimony of the same. (14) The customer, with the consent of the vice admiral or his deputy dwelling

there, or the farmer's deputy is to take bonds in the outports. If a ship in the outports is to be supplied with new ordnance, the ordnance must be bought at the market at Tower Hill as aforesaid, and bonds are to be taken by the master of the ordnance as for the port of London. (15) For every new ship which is to be furnished in the outports, the burden of the ship and the ordnance required is to be certified to the lord admiral who will signify his approval to the master of the ordnance and he will take bonds as for the port of London. Copies of bonds are to be sent to the customer and searcher of the outport who are to keep registers as in London. Letters are to be written to the outports to this effect. (16) Only the accustomed fees are to be taken and new ones are not to be exacted.

1. Just west of Newhaven and south of Piddinghoe (C. Saxton, *An atlas of England and Wales* (1936 ed.).)
2. The SP text has an erased note stating that forfeited bonds are to be returned to the king's remembrancer, with testimony that they were forfeit.

465. [f. 86. *After 25 March 1634] A note of the dues received for Winterton light in the port of London and in the outports from 26 March 1629 to 25 March 1634*

(a) Port of London:

1629 [−30]			1630 [−1]			1631 [−2]			1632 [−3]			1633 [−4]		
£	s	d	£	s	d	£	s	d	£	s	d	£	s	d
173	9	8¹	84	3	2	65	1	10	62	3	6	66	16	2
53	18	0	69	4	0	75	7	0	101	3	9	93	18	9
58	8	6	115	0	4	70	0	2	87	3	11	88	3	0
129	10	8	106	15	0	51	12	2	121	11	6	121	8	7
43	18	4	120	18	4	94	13	10	134	0	4	161	16	0
101	14	0	43	5	2	13	2	10	66	4	8	22	15	6
53	9	5	94	2	4	71	5	9	71	6	4	105	19	0
44	19	10	14	12	0	28	2	11	62	0	0	37	0	9
31	0	2	47	10	10	37	3	4	39	7	10	43	7	11
17	0	4	6	5	8	5	19	10	19	1	4	17	18	3
23	12	8	20	16	0	26	7	5	32	9	2	15	17	5
10	2	8	38	9	4	70	19	11	59	0	2	45	3	2
641	4	3²	761	2	2	669	17	0³	855	12	6	820	4	5⁴

(b) Outports and 'crossers of the sea in the port of London':

1629 [−30]			1630 [−1]			1631 [−2]			1632 [−3]			1633 [−4]		
£	s	d	£	s	d	£	s	d	£	s	d	£	s	d
18	11	6	70	0	0	11	6	1	14	2	0	14	1	5
19	13	6	20	11	7	15	1	10	34	5	0	8	2	3
50	0	0	12	11	5	5	1	0	20	0	0	64	1	3
20	2	3	1	2	6	12	5	0	58	12	9	31	2	0
50	0	0	60	0	0	1	1	7	2	11	8	50	10	3
4	5	0	4	15	9	36	3	0	30	0	0	16	8	6
32	6	0	16	11	10	1	3	0	4	2	6	88	0	0

(b)—cont.

1629 [−30]			1630 [−1]			1631]−2]			1632 [−3]			1633 [−4]		
£	s	d	£	s	d	£	s	d	£	s	d	£	s	d
10	17	10	18	16	2	43	13	6	40	0	0	4	1	4
5	0	0	32	14	11	36	13	6	43	17	5			
			20	0	0	40	19	8	19	3	11			
			3	0	0	7	14	3	53	10	0			
						29	19	0	24	12	5			
						30	17	4	13	10	7			
210	16	1	260	4	2	271	15	9[5]	358	8	3	272	17	0[6]

Total for the year:

£852 0s 4d	£1,021 6s 4d	£941 12s 9d	£1,214 0s 9d	£1,097 1s 5d[7]

Total for coasters in the port of London for 5 years, £3,748 0s 4d; cost of collection, £374 16s; balance, £3,373 4s 4d; total receipts from the outports and the 'crossers of the sea' in the port of London, £1,378 1s 3d; total receipts, £4,751 7s 5d;[8] less one eighth of the total, £593 18s 2d; balance, £4,157 7s 5d; cost of the maintenance of the service at £160 a year for 5 years, £800; 'so resteth clear per annum one year with another for 7 parts of 8' is £671 9s 5d, £3,357 7s 5d.

1. Presumably monthly totals.
2. *Recte* £741 4s 3d.
3. *Recte* £609 17s.
4. *Recte* £820 4s 6d.
5. *Recte* £271 18s 9d.
6. *Recte* £276 7s.
7. *Recte* £1,096 11s 6d or £1,093 1s 5d.
8. *Recte* £4,751 5s 7d.

466. [f.86v] *3 Dec. 1634. [Sir] Henry Palmer and Ken. Edisbury [principal officers of the navy to Trinity House. See **467**.]*
The carpentry in the 2 new ships of the king [*Leopard* and *Swallow*] now in dry dock is complete. The king's master shipwrights at Chatham and Shipwrights' Hall have been asked to meet Palmer and Edisbury at Deptford at 9 a.m. on Tuesday 9 Dec. to resurvey the hulls and give an opinion on the materials, workmanship, burden and properties of these ships. Some principal men of their brotherhood should be chosen to observe the building, the rounding* and laying of the gundecks, the distances between, and the sizes of, the ports, the placing of cook rooms, storerooms and bulkheads, and to assess the draught and the burden in tons and tonnage*, and the suitability of the ships for the service of the king.

467. *10 Dec. 1634. [? Trinity House and the shipwrights to Sir Henry Palmer and Ken. Edisbury]*
In reply to **466** they have surveyed the 2 new ships of the king in dry dock at Deptford and Woolwich and have calculated the burdens according to the old rule and that laid down by the privy council on 26 May 1628.

	Ship built at Woolwich by young Mr [Peter] Pett [son of Phineas] [*Leopard*][1]	[f.87] Ship built at Deptford by Mr Peter Pett [nephew of Phineas] [*Swallow*][2]
Old rule:		
Length by the keel	95 ft	96 ft
Breadth from outside to outside [the planks]	33 ft 8 inches	32 ft 10 inches
Draught	13 ft 6 inches	12 ft 9 inches
These figures multiplied together and divided by 100 produce in tons and tonnage*	575	536
New rule:		
Length by the keel	95 ft	96 ft
Breadth inside the planks	33 ft	32 ft 2 inches
Depth from the upper edge of the keel to the diameter of the breadth	12 ft 4 inches	11 ft 7$\frac{1}{2}$ inches
These figures multiplied together and divided by 100 produce in tons and tonnage	515	478

The frames, workmanship, the size and scantling of timbers, the goodness and strength of materials in the scarf* riders, beams, knees*, etc., and the rounding* and laying of the gundecks, together with the siting of cooks' rooms, storerooms and bulkheads is good. The distances between the decks is 6 ft 6 inches. The lower edges of the ports will be 5 ft from the diameter of the breadth. The ports are 8 ft 8$\frac{1}{2}$ inches apart in the case of the ship at Woolwich, and 8 ft generally in that of the ship at Deptford. The ports in both ships are 2 ft 1 inch from the orlop*, and the sizes 2 ft 4 inches fore and aft, and 2 ft 2 inches in depth. Both ships are suitable for the service of the king.

1. & 2. Evident from the dimensions in Oppenheim, 254.

468. [f.87v. *? Before 2 Oct. 1634*] *Thomas Smith, receiver general of the duchy of Cornwall, to the king about ballastage in the Thames* [*Cf* SP 16/275/11, annotated as received on 2 Oct. 1634; *CSPD 1634–5*, 224, which ascribes it to that date. *CSPD does not mention Smith's account of an offer by the city to pay 2d for every ton of sand and gravel taken from the Thames.*]

469. *2 Oct. 1634. Sir Thomas Aylesbury, master of requests, to the attorney general seeking advice on* **468** [*Cf* SP 16/275/11(1); *CSPD 1634–5*, 224–5.]

470. *11 Dec. 1634. Order of* [*Sir*] *John Bankes* [*attorney general. Entry deleted.*]

He appoints 9 a.m. on Wednesday 17 Dec. to hear this business [? **468–9**]. All concerned are to attend his chambers in Gray's Inn.

471. [f.88–88v] *1535. An act for the preservation of the Thames* [Printed in *Statutes*, iii.550.]

472. *31 Jan. 1635. Trinity House to Sir Thomas Roe*
In reply to his letter there is no remedy. The tower [? a Forelands lighthouse] is Sir John Meldrome's for £250 'present pay' at sealing of the deed.
Walter Coke, deputy master; Capt. Best, Mr Rainborowe, Capt. Browne, Mr Totten, Mr Tutchin, etc.

473. [f.89. *? Before 2 Feb. 1635*] *Trinity House to the king about Sir John Meldrom's proposed lighthouses at the North and South Forelands* [*Cf* SP 16/283/1, annotated March 1635; *CSPD 1634–5*, 497, ascribing it to 2 Feb. 1635. The Trinity House text states that a similar petition was sent to the council. SP 16/89/27, ascribed incorrectly in *CSPD 1627–8* (p. 494) to 1627, is a further copy.]

474. [f.89–89v] *9 Feb. 1635. The king to Sir John Meldrom empowering him to erect lighthouses at the Forelands* [*Cf* SP 16/283/26; *CSPD 1634–5*, 505.]

475. [*Before Apr. 1637*] *Shipmasters and others to the king* [*Cf* C 66/2764, no. 59; *THD*, 210.]
A great number of men and ships have been lost at Orfordness in Suffolk because of the dangerous sands and cliffs on that coast. They ask for authorisation of a watch house with fires kept there continuously at night, similar to those elsewhere. A charge of a halfpenny a ton on ships passing by that place would be fitting.
John King, master of the *John and Barbary* of Ipswich, Isaac Bromell, master of the *Ensurance* of Harwich, Stephen Callmege, master of the *Elizabeth*, George Mullett, master of the *Blossome*, George Lawes, master of the *Neptune*, Henry Rivers, master of the *William and Francis* of London, John Laurlstond of North Shields, master of the *Pationesses* of Shields, John Wilds, master of the *Unity* of Manningtree, John Martrey, master of the *Prudence* of London, Edward Rand, master of the *Dolphin* of Newcastle, Thomas Rickaby, master of the *Neptune* of Bridlington, mark of William Cason, master of the *Ann and Ann* of London, mark of Anthony Groome, master of the *Mary* of London, Samuel West, master of the *Talbott* of London, [f.90] John Horner, master of the *Nathan* of Ipswich, Thomas Chapman, master of the *Content* of Ipswich, John Bell, master of the *William* of Newcastle, James Shrive, master of the *Mary Ann* of Ipswich, mark of John Coles, master of the *Hermite* of Woodbridge, Robert Partridge of Woodbridge, master of the *Centurion*, mark of George Clarke, master of the *White Lyon* of London, John Niddock, master of the *Exchange* of Harwich, John Westwood, master of the *Jonas* of Lynn, mark of John Whaly the elder, a

great owner of Woodbridge, Robert Clarnly, the *Ann and Samuell*, owner of divers ships at Ipswich,[1] John Tillott, master of the *John and Dorothy* of London, John Moore, master of the *Robert and Ellen* of London, mark of George Battell, master of the *Amity* of Woodbridge, John Wright, master of the *Lilly* of London, Henry Harrison, master of the *Appletree* [of] London, Edmund Levar of Ipswich, Humphrey Mason, master of the *Endevor* of Aldeburgh, James Beetes of Aldeburgh, Anthony Taillor, master of the *Presala and Thomasin* of London, Richard Skinner, master of the *Recovery* of Ipswich, Stephen Greenwich, master of the *Greenwich* of Ipswich, Anthony Woodward, master of the *George* of Woodbridge, mark of George Leafe, master of the *Unicorne* of Aldeburgh, Humphrey Witoh, master of the *Protection*, mark of Godfrey Tilman, master of the *Litle David*, Frank Knall of Trinity House, Henry Ford, master of the *Rosemary*, Thomas Cletcher, master of the *Releefe* of Ipswich, [mark of] Henry Askettle, master of the *Margarett and James* of London, James Ricrost, 'pilot for the coast by the Trinity Houses', [mark of] Charles Hawkins, master and brother of Trinity House, Peter Lunt, master of the *Peter Bonaventure* of London, William Partrich of Woodbridge, James Talbott, master of the *Luffuld Mary* of Ipswich, John Caboern, master of the *Ann* of London, Robert Wright, master of the *Rebecca* [of] Newcastle, William Copland, master of the *Mathew* of London, Peter White, one of the 4 masters,[2] Nicholas Skinner of Rye, Francis Scurtes of Aldeburgh, Stephen Richard of London, Peter Logie, James Daling, William Kay, George Dinling, Andre [sic] Alexandre, Edward Thurston, John Mavon of Newcastle, Thomas Haliwell of Sandwich, [f.90v] Reuben Broade of London; John Allen, William Stanford, Robert Redmer, Robert Baker, William Smith, John Fowler, Robert Engle, Robert Fish, Robert Hill, William Walborne, Robert Dennis, Francis Fuller, Christopher Bregwell, Nicholas Wyatt, Adam Mells, Robert Baker, Robert Meddowes, John Sayaward, John Bledor, John Swan, Walter Aklenne, John Dobes, Thomas Dunn, John Arnold, Thomas Cheney, Thomas Wilche, Henry Lambe, Christopher Dunne, Nicholas Robertes, John Troudell, John Baxter, Richard Blogd, John Rolleson, Robert Duck, Thomas Browne, Robert Smith, William Faune, James Crages, Henry Pelcher, William Lockett, John Fish, Oliver Sharpe, Peter Gunwell, all of Yarmouth; John Webb, Phoenix Worde, Daniel Hercoy, Thomas Aldermaine, Henry Groome, all of Rotherhithe; Nicholas Kirk, William Tomlinson, Thomas Barnard, Robert Marison, William Rookes, all of Hull; Roger Crepen, John Hume, Robert Mells, all of Sandwich; John Gobson of Rochester; William Shank, Robert Ripen, James Chevin, all of Aldeburgh; John Harrison, mark of Cuthbert Sharper, both of Newcastle; James Gibbs of 'Burrowstones' [? Borrowstounness]; William Bagg of Ipswich; Thomas White, James Marle, Edmund Woodgreene, Richard Gakope, Robert White, John Kiddy, Tristram Stephens, William Keyte, William Caller, Richard Tutter, Edward Donfeld, all of Dover; Richard Stimsen, George Richardson, mark of Thomas Botte, Christopher Browne, John Denton, Thomas Forth, Nicholas Samson, the mark of John Arnold, the mark of Thomas Poters.

[Marginal note] Petition of Sir John Meldrome to the king [cf *THD*, 210].

1. 'At Ipswich' may also refer to Whaly.
2. The masters attendant or principal masters (cf Monson, iii. 393–4).

476. [f.91] *28 Feb. 1635. Ratcliff. Trinity House [to the fellowship of lodemanage at] Dover*
From a letter of 23 Feb. sent by Mr John Pringle to his kinsman, Mr John Tompson,[1] the addressees are understood to have been informed by Mr Williams of the Dover fellowship of the plan of Sir John Meldrome for lighthouses at the North and South Foreland and to have desired to know how far Meldrome had proceeded. On a petition to the king in the names of shipmasters, inhabitants of Sandwich, Dover and 'Norgate' [? Margate], together with chief pilots of the king's navy, Meldrome obtained a grant to erect the lighthouses. As soon as Trinity House heard of Meldrome's proceedings they petitioned the king without delay certifying that neither the corporation nor the masters attendant [see **475**] had had any notice of the grant nor had their approbation been given, 'the like we did conceive of you'. Thereupon the king temporarily stayed proceedings, but they do not know how soon they will be called to give their reasons for opposing the grant. Since the addressees do not agree with the project, they are asked to write as soon as possible giving their reasons. The levy is to be 2d a ton per voyage, as appears in the enclosed copy of the warrant which would prove a great grievance to navigation, besides other bad consequences. Those who set their names to the petition are unlikely to contribute much to the levy. The mayor of Sandwich and the 2 Randes of Deal are the principal signatories of the petition, and there are 50 or 60 others whom they do not know.
Robert Salmon, Thomas Best, Walter Coke, Samuel Doves, John Totton, Jonas James.

1. ? The elder brother, or the Mr Tompson 'my lords secretary' mentioned in **499**.

477. [f.91v] *3 March 1635. Trinity House of Dover [sic (see **283**) to the Trinity House of Deptford]*
Their letter [**476**] and the enclosed petition were received by which they were fully informed. The mayor and jurats of Dover wrote last week to the lord warden touching the dangers to these parts and to the kingdom if lighthouses are erected at the Forelands, viz. the danger to the state, increased charges for merchants and mariners, and that in time of hostility the lights would enable enemies to land on the coast and anchor in the Downs and in places nearby. In a chase at night, the lights would bring ships into the Downs where the ships of the king and of merchants lie at anchor, and these might be boarded at night without any resistance, and set on fire. It may be said that the lights will not be kept in times of hostility, but meantime they will acquaint strangers with the coast 'that they may go through by their depth as well as our ships'. In the late hostility with France, the lord warden took care to order the cutting down of all stairs and passages in the cliffs. The lights would therefore be more advantageous to an enemy than beneficial to the kingdom. The writers

have not given an opinion on, or approbation of, the lights and are abused in the report and the petition. They hear that a bond of £1,000 has been given to Sandwich, freeing the inhabitants from paying the charges. As for Deal, the addressees know that there is no shipping to be charged. Many more who set their names to the petition are believed to have no shipping or understanding in sea affairs, and have acted without regard to the state or shipping. If a further certificate is needed, 100 masters and owners will set their hands to the same.

Joseph Loper, master; Ralph Pascall, John Valie, John Pringle, Thomas Teddeman, Edmond Woodgreene, Edward Wenwright.

[Marginal note] Received on 5 [March].

478. [f.92] *11 March 1635. Sandwich. Matthew Peke, deputy mayor, [? to the mayor of Dover. See **477**, **479**.]*

'Loving friend and conbrother',

In reply to his letter he is unacquainted with the matter but has conferred with Mr Verall, the town clerk, who intends to be with the addressees tomorrow, and leaves a further declaration to him.

479. *11 March 1635. Dover. Certificate by Francis Verall, town clerk of Sandwich [See **477–8**.]*

He well remembers that lately Mr Paule and Mr Spycer of London sealed a bond of £1,000 to the mayor and jurats of Sandwich, with condition that the masters of ships of Sandwich and its 'limbs' should not pay any charge for the intended lights at the North and South Foreland. The bond was left with the mayor of Sandwich.

Certificate that Henry Bull was a witness to the bond.

480. [f.92v. *25 March 1635*] *Trinity House [to the lords commissioners of the admiralty. Cf* SP 16/285/41; *CSPD 1634–5, 599.]*

It is their duty to give a relation of, and their exceptions against, the proceedings of Sir John Meldrome for lights at the Forelands. In his petition to the king, Meldrome states that Dover, Sandwich, Norgate [? Margate] and other ports, with the 'chiefest' pilots of the navy royal were suitors for the lights. Rather Meldrome was the suitor. Neither he nor his agents came to Dover, as appears by a letter [? **477**] from the corporation there. He and his agents could not get a signature at Sandwich, where he was the suitor, but when he gave a bond of £1,000 to free the town and its limbs from the charge, the mayor and all other men of the town and its ports were willing to subscribe. Trinity House and all owners and seamen of London and the Thames would be ready to sign if freed of the charge. As for the chief pilots of the navy, the principal pilots are the king's 4 masters [see **475**]. Of these, William Cooke and Peter White have certified orally before Trinity House that they oppose the project, and they certify that Mr Austen is of their opinion; the fourth, Mr Goodwyn, is at Portsmouth. As for knights and gentlemen (sea captains), nothing need be said because they will acknowledge that they cannot take the places of masters or pilots, neither know they the channels, depths and dangers, and how to avoid them. The reasons why these lights would not be a safeguard against the dangers of the Goodwin Sands are: (a) The distance between the lights at South Foreland and the danger of the Channel of the Gulls is at least 10 miles, at which distance the lights could not be seen and therefore could not be of use. (b) The lights at North Foreland cannot be useful for the Channel of the Gulls because the leading mark for channels must be on the same point of the compass from the ship 'as will carry you through'. [f.93] The lights at North Foreland 'when we shall come to the entrance of the Gulls will be 4 points differing from the point or lying of the channel' and, therefore, are of no use for avoiding the dangers of the Goodwin Sands. (c) The lights at the South Foreland are of no use for ships out at sea, because landmarks and soundings are more certain than lights. (d) If lights at the Forelands were of use, the writers who daily adventure their estates there would be most forward to obtain them. There are other objections too tedious for the board. If the king wishes there to be lights, the levy should be proportionate to the costs of erection and keeping, which would be one quarter of the levy of 2d per ton proposed by Meldrome for laden ships. Trinity House would provide lights for ½d a ton, if the king wishes. The danger of the Goodwin Sands is no greater than they have been since time out of mind. Trinity House have never known any ship to be lost for want of lights. Ships are cast away there when driven from their anchors by storms which lights could not prevent.

481. [f.93v] *1 May 1635. Whitehall. Privy council to Sir Thomas Pellam, bart., Sir Thomas Sackvill, knight of the Bath, Sir Edward Burton, Robert Foster and John Fagg, esquires, Giles Waters, mayor of Winchelsea, Thomas Trenchfeild, George Hatch and Anthony Tutchin of Trinity House, Mark Thomas and John Nowell, jurats of Rye, or any 4 of them* [Cf PC 2/44, p. 551.]
Enclosed is a petition to the board from the jurats and inhabitants of Rye, complaining that the inning* of divers land endangers the harbour and causes its decay; that without speedy remedy it will become unusable by shipping; and that the inhabitants, being mostly merchants and mariners, will then have to find a new place of habitation. All of which is certified under the hands of most of the petitioners. Although the petitioners would not presume to present untrue information on such a public matter, for better satisfaction the addressees should visit the harbour on 19 May and certify the condition of the harbour to the board and what can be done to effect a remedy. They are also to order those who meddled with any inning of land to proceed no further.
Archbishop of Canterbury, lord keeper, archbishop of York, lord privy seal, lord Cottington, Mr comptroller, Mr treasurer, Mr secretary Coke, Mr secretary Windbanke.

482. [f.94] *20 May 1635. Rye. [Sir] Edward Burton, John Fagg, Thomas Trenchfeild, Anthony Tutchin, George Hatche, Giles Waters, Mark Thomas and John Nowell to the privy council.*
In reply to **481**, they have inspected the harbour at Rye and find it much

decayed, as stated in the petition. The inning* of saltmarshes within the harbour against the channel to Winchelsea by Richard Milles, mayor of Rye and tenant of the earl of Thanet, Peter Farneden and Anthony Norton, gentlemen, and Thomas Peacock was almost complete. Other saltmarshes lying against the channel within the harbour running to Tillingham were being inned by Thomas Shreele. The completion of these works would have been very hurtful to the harbour, and they ordered the works to be stopped and the innings to be opened. They also viewed the harbour called the Camber which used to be a succour for ships and barks of good burden in stress of weather, and found it utterly decayed owed to the inning of great quantities of saltmarshes up the Weyneway channel[1] within the last 40 years, partly within the last 6 years, by Sir Henry Gilford and George Curtis, gentleman. Henry Peck, esquire, has inned saltmarshes against the channel to Winchelsea within the last 20 years. Gilford has done likewise on the other side of the channel within the last 40 years. William Sheppard, esquire, deceased, inned part of St Mary Marshes[2] now belonging to the town of Rye. Joseph Benbricke, jurat of Rye, has done likewise within the last 40 years. Sheppard inned saltmarshes against the channel to Tillingham within the last 40 years. All these works have conduced to the decay of Rye harbour. The stop made by the commissioners of sewers 12 years since across the indraught near Old Woodruffe[3] about 4 miles up the channel from Rye has swarved [i.e. silted] the [f.94v] channel from the indraught to and below the sewers of White Kempe and the Five Waterings towards Rye. The groins set alongside the channel to Winchelsea and in the harbours and creeks of Rye are a danger for navigation and a means to gather 'swerne' [silt] there. They are credibly informed that Rye is decayed and impoverished, with fewer merchants, seamen and fishermen than formerly because of the decay of the harbour and of fishing; that the inhabitants cannot improve the harbour or keep it in its present state; and that in short time without help it will be lost.

1. The mouth of Weyneway creek was east of Rye, on the south side of Guldeford level (BL, maps 5460 (31)).
2. Immediately northwest of Rye (cf *Sussex Archaeological Collections*, xcviii (1960), 125).
3. ? Woodruff, now a hamlet half a mile north of Fairfield.

483. [f.95] *18 May 1635. Court at Greenwich. Order of the privy council* [*Cf* PC 2/44, p. 572.]
Present: the king, archbishop of Canterbury, lord keeper, archbishop of York, lord privy seal, duke of Lennox, marquess [of] Hamilton, earl marshal, lord chamberlain, earls of Dorset, Bridgewater, Carlisle and Holland, lord Cottington, Mr treasurer, Mr secretary Coke, Mr secretary Windebancke.

Ships coming from sea are not to pass Gravesend with ordnance loaded with bullets. Those leaving the port of London are not to load ordnance until they reach Gravesend. When ships going to and from London fire their ordnance as they pass the king's court at Greenwich, the ordnance is

to be aimed at the side of the river opposite to that on which the palace stands.
W. Trumball.

484. *30 May 1635. Memorandum*
Shipmasters warned about the 'warrant aforesaid' [**483**]: Thomas Johnson, John Hemings, Roger Martin, Rowland Langram, Nicholas Isaac, Lawrence Moyer, Edward Johnson, John Severne, Nicholas Barnes, Richard Russell, Thomas Davis, Edmund Grove, Walter Mayniard, John Lymbrey, George Bodham, Robert Hackwell, John Tanner, John Jaye, Nicholas Hilson, Thomas Gibbs, John Babb, Andrew Batten, Benjamin Cranley, Peter Swyer, Thomas Hughes, George Downes, John Baker, Joseph Baker,—Cole,—Barker,—Gayner, John Piggott,—Flowers, John Blake, Nathaniel Goodladd, Robert Swyer, Anthony Thorne, Anthony Cole, John Webb, Nathaniel Case, John Jones, John Thomas, Thomas Nicolles, Jeremy Blackman, Richard Wight, [f.95v] John Seayres, Brian Harrison, Richard Fernes, Christopher Fothergill, George Watkins, John Martin, John Hall, John Grant, William Jenkins, John Plumley, John Smith, Robert Bowers, John Whetston, Thomas Babb, Thomas Baxter, John Ellison, John Smith, Robert Toackley, Robert Page,—Smith, Diggory Man, Edmund Bostock, James Gray, James Bacon, Thomas Punt, Edmund Ellison, John Goodladd, John Lowe, William Munt,—White, Richard White.

485. *6 June 1635. Trinity House to Sir Henry Martin* [*admiralty court judge*]
Philip White has certified that Martin requires their opinion as to whether the laying of chains for mooring ships in St Katherine's pool in the Thames, between Horseydown stairs and St Saviour's dock, will prejudice the river or ships passing by. Their opinion is that it will not. Mooring ships with anchors and cables was always dangerous for barges, light horsemen and wherries, especially at low tide, because the channel is narrow and ships' cables lying high and the upper arm of anchors being dry, casualties happened. Mooring with chains will prevent the danger because the chains lie very low under water, and the anchors to which they are fastened have no upward arm. Besides, cordage which daily grows scarcer will be saved.

486. [*f.96. Before 3 Oct. 1635*][1] *Trinity House to the privy council*
Some 20 years ago, at the request of Sir Edward Haward, merchants, owners and masters signed an agreement for building and maintaining a fire light at Dungeness with a charge of 1d a ton upon ships and goods benefiting thereby, payable on return, the owner paying half. Haward then obtained letters patent from the late king with provision contrary to the agreement of 2d a ton (1d outwards, 1d homewards), being double the amount formerly agreed. At first payment was refused but the contention and delay was too great a charge upon the owners who were thereby forced to pay according to the patent, being 4 times the agreed amount, since merchants pay no part. The king's pleasure of late was to

renew the patent, and their suit is that the patentee should receive what was agreed, namely 1d a ton payable on return, the merchant paying half. The petitioners would erect and maintain the light for 1d a ton.

1. Before the agreement of 3 Oct. 1635 under which the merchants agreed to pay half (PC 2/45, pp. 142–3).

487. [f.96v. *? Nov. 1634 x June 1635*][1] *Trinity House to the king*
They apologise for troubling the king about ballastage, he having in 2 references of their petitions [see **492**] declared his intention not to abridge their rights by any new grant. Yet if the king leaves them, the ballastage office will be taken from them and the corporation will suffer loss of their ancient privileges, although by special order under the privy seal they pay Capt. Thomas Porter £50 a year for the enjoyment of the office and are willing so to continue. The suitors to the king for the office are Mr Webb, secretary to the duke of Lennox, and Mr Barnett, secretary to lord Carlisle, who are incapable of the business which they cannot perform without much offence to merchants, owners and shipmasters. The king is asked to continue to settle the office on the corporation as it has been for over 100 years, still under the lord admiral.

1. In the undated SP 16/309/6, Humphrey Streete, an associate of Smyth, states that in the preceding June Smyth sought a patent; that since no progress was made, Barnard (i.e. Barnett) and Webb offered to help in Oct.; that in Oct. Smyth made another petition which was referred to the attorney general; and that later Barnard and Webb petitioned on their own behalf. Smyth's Oct. petition was probably that of Oct. 1634 (cf *CSPD 1634–5*, 224). If so the date of SP 16/309/6 is Nov. 1634 x June 1635 and the date of **487** is similar.

488. [f.97. *9 May x 3 Oct. 1635*] *Trinity House to the privy council about the dues for Dungeness light* [*Cf* SP 16/296/65; *CSPD 1635*, 362–3, attributed to Aug. 1635. In substance the text is similar to **486**.]

489. [f.97v] *28 Aug. 1635. Order by the admiralty court*
Many suits have been begun in the admiralty court by merchants and freighters against shipowners, masters and mariners touching damage to goods after the ship is safely arrived in her port of discharge and the goods delivered into lighters to be carried ashore. There is an erroneous opinion that owners, masters and mariners are responsible until the goods are put ashore, and are liable for damage to goods between ship and shore, resulting in many suits against them, whereby they are discouraged, navigation is disturbed, and the suits are fruitless to the merchants who began them. On the advice of Sir Henry Martin, the admiralty court judge, the king declares that by the law and custom of the sea, after a ship is moored as close as is safe to the place where the goods are to be landed, the liability of the owners, master and mariners ceases as soon as the lighter appointed by the merchant or freighter to collect the goods is free of the tackle of the ship. [f.98] Similarly they are not liable while the goods are in transit from the shore to the ship.

Mariners often dishonestly hire themselves to several masters at the same time, thereby disappointing some masters who have then to seek new mariners when their ships are ready to sail and the wind is fair.

Mariners proved guilty of this offence before the admiralty court judge shall be committed to prison for one month. Masters, upon notice that a mariner was previously hired by another master, shall discharge him and not suffer him to go to sea upon pain of paying 20s a week for use of the poor during the time he is aboard.

Whereas much damage has been caused by fire to ships and merchants' goods because of the heating of tar and pitch aboard ships in the Thames, the practice is hereby prohibited upon pain of forfeiture of £5 for the use of the poor. Great seal of the admiralty affixed.

Thomas Wyan, deputy register.

490. [f.98v] *28 Aug. 1635. Promulgation of an admiralty court order*
Order made in the third session, Trinity term, 1631. Complaint is made daily to the admiralty court judge by ship masters and commanders employed in voyages overseas that mariners are so disobedient and mutinous that they cannot bear the command. Mariners conspire to depose a master who does not conform to their wishes and put another of their choosing in his place. Voyages are hindered and many times overthrown, to the loss of the employers and the discouragement of commanders. Such insolences commonly spring from one evil spirit who, once he has drawn matters to a head, shelters himself under their common answer of 'one and all', or by writing all names in a circle so that the ringleader who put his name first cannot be detected. To avoid such evils, it is ordered that any mariner who uses the pernicious phrase 'one and all' or who signs his name in a circle shall not only lose his wages but shall be noted for principal mutineer and severely punished.

The judge decreed this order to be 'established' on the Exchange. The great seal of the admiralty court is affixed in testimony.

Thomas Wyan, deputy register.

491. [f.99] *19 Sept. 1635. Trinity House to Mr Hawker of Challock*
His courteous letter was received long since but was not answered because it was thought that he would visit them, nor did they know how to send by post to him until yesterday. If he can come to London, they will meet him, given notice, and, they believe, content him. If not, on receipt of his letter, they will give him a fair return. He should be well advised in cutting down his trees which are a special mark not only for the king's ships but also for 'all the prime merchants' ships of this kingdom'.

P.S. It was almost a month after the date of his letter before it came to their hands.

492. [f.99v. *? 12 Oct. 1633 x 24 June 1636*][1] *Petition by Trinity House*
If the duties of the ballastage office are neglected, evil consequences will follow. [The first 7 duties listed in **425** then follow, but it is here stated that it takes 10 or 15 days for ballast to dry before it can be used as dry ballast and that the prices of 12d a ton for merchant ships and 4d for colliers are 'according to present time and former custom'. f.100] In his references of 29 Jan. 1630 and 16 Apr. 1631 made at Whitehall, the king declared his intention not to abridge the rights of Trinity House by any new grant.

They have enjoyed the office under the lord admiral for 100 years, providing all things necessary for ballastage and ensuring fair quantities and prices for purchasers. The profits amount to only £140 a year, from which £50 is paid to Capt. Thomas Porter by an order under the privy seal [see **359**]. The rest of the money has been employed to relieve poor, lame and impotent seamen, their wives and children, and to pay for repairing wharves and other charges which have already cost £1,000 or £1,200. They have never been charged with injustice or negligence. They crave the help of the addressee.

1. ? After **425** and prior to the ballastage grant to Thomas Smyth and others of 24 June 1636 (C 66/2740, no. 19).

493. [f.100v] *3 Oct. 1635. Agreement by Trinity House about the dues for Dungeness lighthouse* [Contained in order of the privy council (cf SP 16/299/39; *CSPD 1635*, 420; PC 2/45, pp. 142–3). The names appended to the SP text, not listed in *CSPD*, are John Tatam (Totton in PC 2/45), Thomas Best, Robert Salmon, Walter Cooke, John Bennett, George Hatch, William Case, Anthony Tutchin, William Ewen, James Moyer, Gervais Hocket, William Goodlad.]

494. *9 Oct. 1635. Order of the privy council ratifying an agreement between Trinity House and William Bullocke* [**493**] *about Dungeness lighthouse dues* [Cf SP 16/299/39; *CSPD 1635*, 420; PC 2/45, pp. 142–3. Those present at the meeting, not listed in *CSPD*, were the archbishop of Canterbury, lord keeper, lord privy seal, earl marshal, lord Cottington, Mr Secretary Windbancke.]

495. [f.101. *Before 23 Dec. 1635*][1] *Trinity House to the privy council*
They are credibly informed of certain gentlemen who are suitors to the king for the sole making of salt and that foreign salt might be prohibited or a heavy imposition placed on it. Their duty is to certify the prejudice that will ensue to king and country. The merchant ships of the kingdom are not matched by those of any other king. Most of them are employed for the Straits and are freighted here at home only for the outward voyage. Owners expose themselves to fortune for homeward freight but are encouraged by the certainty of salt if better employment fails. The prohibition of, or a heavy duty on, foreign salt will result in the unemployment of a third of the best merchant ships, prejudicing the honour and profit of the king, for if shipping declines, so will trade and customs duties. If salt cannot be carried homewards, outward freight will not defray the cost of the voyage and it will not be undertaken. Furthermore, on voyages abroad, ships are often employed by the French, Italians, Turks and Jews, whereby double gain is won; £4,000–£10,000 is made thereby, and is used to buy commodities for import. Customs duties on these imports will return a better account than can be raised by any imposition on salt.

1. Cf. SP 16/308/11; *CSPD 1635–6*, 44. ? Associated with the petition of Sir Richard Brooke and others for the patent granted on 23 Dec. 1635, or an abortive project of 1630 (E. Hughes, *Studies in administration and finance, 1558–1825* (1934), 83–103; *Select*

charters of trading societies, 1530–1707, ed. C. T. Carr (Selden Soc. 1913), pp.
lxxiii–lxxiv, 142–8).

496. [f.101v. *Before 10 Jan. 1636*] *Trinity House to the privy council* [*See*
497.]
Last year their lighthouses were taxed towards the setting forth of the sea
army: 10s for the 2 lighthouses in Suffolk, and £10 for the 2 in Norfolk.
Such an assessment was never known before, but they forbore to trouble
the privy council because they had been taxed before they had knowledge
of it. But now being informed that the sheriffs will, or already have, taxed
the lighthouses again, they crave exemption. No gain is made from the 4
lighthouses and 3 buoys because receipts are only £164 a year, and costs
are £147, the remaining £17 being used with a greater sum to relieve the
poor of the corporation.

497. *10 Jan. 1636. Privy council to the sheriff of Suffolk* [*Cf* PC 2/45, pp.
349–50.]
With regard to the enclosed petition [**496**], although lighthouses should
not be exempted from assessment for ship money when there is private
benefit, in this case it appears by examination that the public charge for
the common good equals the profit from the lighthouses in Norfolk and
Suffolk and the remaining £17 is employed for charitable uses. Therefore,
the lighthouses should not be assessed unless it can be shown that there is
a private benefit.
Archbishop of Canterbury, lord keeper, marquess [of] Hamilton, earl
marshal, lord Newburgh, Mr comptroller, Mr Secretary Cooke, Mr
Secretary Windbancke.

498. [f.102] *16 Jan. 1636. Letter from Trinity House*
Such is the work of the addressee that any man who is a lover of the
navigation of the kingdom, and especially themselves, will further the
business. Their ships trading to the river of Bordeaux will contribute
proportionately as do other ships when the business[1] is effected.

> 1. ? A project against Turkish pirates (cf C. D. Penn, *The navy under the early Stuarts*
> (1920), 246).

499. *1 March 1636. Ratcliff. Trinity House to Mr Pringle* [*See* **476.**]
The enclosed petition by the parishioners of 'Margarett' [St Margaret at
Cliffe][1] maligns Trinity House which they take ill although they intend to
further the business by all possible means. The petitioners have charged
them with giving an assurance of success or that Trinity House would bear
the cost but although they have encouragement no such assurance was
possible. Let the parishioners do their part and Trinity House will not fail
in theirs. First let them send the justices' certificate which the
parishioners formerly sent, and which the man whom they employed, 'or
you Mr Prindle', carried home or left with Mr Tompson,[2] my lord's
secretary; nothing can be done without it. Also they must send a man or 2
to accompany them to the lords [privy council or admiralty commission-
ers] with money in their purses to pay charges, not those of Trinity House

who will pay their own and doubt not but to prevail. Pringle should show the parishioners this letter to let them know that they are accused of slackness in having slept so long in repairing the house of God. He is entreated to set them forward and especially to obtain a certificate like the previous one subscribed by as many justices and gentlemen as possible. Trinity House will reimburse him. He is asked to reply soon. John Totten.

P.S. He is asked to move his corporation to write to Trinity House about the need to repair the church and its value as a seamark, especially for the king's ships.

[Marginal note] To Mr Pringle about the repair of 'Acliffe' church.

1. The paper schedule of contents (cf above, p. xvi) states mistakenly that it relates to the repair of the church steeple at Margate.
2. ? The John Tompson of **476**. 'My lord' may be the earl of Suffolk, lord warden of the Cinque Ports.

500. [f.102v] *5 March 1636. Order by Trinity House*
About a month ago, Capt. Bushell [? the elder brother] and Capt. Driver referred their differences to Trinity House for settlement. After hearing allegations and witnesses they order that Driver pay Bushell £6 13s 4d in full settlement.

[Signed] T. Best, Robert Bell, William Rainborowe, Samuel Doves, William Case, John Totten, Anthony Tutchen, Gervais Hockett, George Hatch, John Bennett, William Ewen.

[Note] It is £6 13s 4d J.B. [? Josias Best].

[**501–23** are entered at the back of the volume beginning at f. 77.]

501. [f.77] *21 Jan. 1632. Certificate by Trinity House*
Peter Leonard wishes to erect a new wharf at St Saviour's mill on the south side of the Thames, straight eastwards from a jetty head on the west side of the mill-dam to his new wharf lately erected. At his request, Trinity House have surveyed the place and certify that it would be very useful for shipping and likewise for the land provided that it extends no more than 20 ft into the Thames 'from the old wharf, and so to be carried straight from the aforesaid wharf to the westward of the mill-dam to the new wharf already erected to the eastward'. [ff.77v and 78 are blank]

502. [f.78–78v *bis*] *10 Nov. 1626. Order of the privy council about export of fish in strangers' ships* [Printed in *APC 1626*, 362–3.]

503. [f.79. *Before 29 Sept. 1630*] *Trinity House to the privy council about exports of fish in strangers' ships* [Cf *APC 1630–1*, 83–4; SP 16/257/29; *CSPD 1633–4*, 367, where it is incorrectly ascribed to 1633.]

504. [f.79v] *30 Sept. 1630. Privy council to the bailiffs and aldermen of Yarmouth about exports of herrings in strangers' ships* [Printed in *APC 1630–1*, 84–5.]

505. [f.80–80v] *29 Sept. 1630. Order of the privy council about exports of fish in strangers' ships* [Printed in *APC 1630–1*, 83–4.]

506. [*29 Sept. 1630 x 28 July 1631*] *Trinity House to the lord treasurer* [*See* **508.**]
The privy council order of 29 Sept. 1630 [**505**] prohibited the export in strangers' ships of herrings from Yarmouth and of pilchards and Newfoundland fish* from the western parts, requesting the lord treasurer to take notice and to give directions accordingly to the officers and farmers of the customs and others concerned. The petitioners ask for letters to that effect addressed to the officers of the customs at Yarmouth, Dartmouth, Plymouth and other western parts. Otherwise they seek his permission to petition the privy council for these letters.

507. [f.81. *1 Oct. 1630 x 28 July 1631*] *Trinity House to the privy council* [*See* **508.**]
On their petition of Sept. 1630, the privy council prohibited the export of herrings from Yarmouth and of pilchards and Newfoundland fish* from the western parts except in native ships [**505**] and wrote with a copy of the order to the bailiffs of Yarmouth. Despite receipt of the order, 6 or 8 strangers' ships were freighted with herrings at Yarmouth, and divers strangers' ships were laden with pilchards and Newfoundland fish in the western parts. The privy council are asked to ensure the execution of the order.

508. *28 July 1631. R. [lord] Weston [lord treasurer] to the officers of the customs at Plymouth, Yarmouth, Exeter, Poole, Southampton and their members concerning the implementation of the privy council order of 29 Sept. 1630* [**505**] *against the export of fish in strangers' ships* [*Cf* SP 16/197/44; *CSPD 1631–3*, 123.]

509. [f.81v. *? c.1631. Notes about fish exports. See* **506–8**, **510–12**.]
(a) A ton of pilchards exported by strangers in strangers' ships produces only 5s customs and nothing on return. (b) A ton of pilchards exported by native merchants in native ships yields no customs outwards but 40s on return. (c) Similarly herrings and Newfoundland fish* produce 8 and often 9 or 10 times as much. (d) Besides, subjects enjoy great gain by carrying fish. (e) A ton of pilchards laden in strangers' ships pays 5s customs but if transported by native ships the proceeds will be £20 per ton which employed on Italian commodities will yield 40s customs, 8 for one in 6 or 8 months, and if laden at Zante, Zephalonia or Candy will yield at least 20 nobles customs in 10 months. (f) Every ton of Newfoundland fish laden by strangers pays 10s customs. If transported by natives, the proceeds in Spain will normally buy 2 butts of wine, which pays £3 customs.

510. [f.82] *7 Sept. 1631. Whitehall. Order of the privy council* [*Cf* PC 2/41, p. 165.]
Present: lord keeper, lord treasurer, earl of Dorset, viscounts Dorchester and Falkland, lord Cottington.

Shipowners and other subjects using the fishing trade in the western parts have petitioned that the officers of the western ports be authorised to permit strangers to buy and transport pilchards and other fish in their own ships as they had done time out of mind, despite the privy council order of 29 Sept. last [505]. The petitioners conceive that it was not the privy council's intention to hinder customs and the fishing trade in those ports. It is ordered that 3 of the western merchants who are here about the Spanish business,¹ together with 3 from Trinity House, should attend the next meeting of the privy council so that further order may be given.

1. The western merchants were probably resisting the revival of the Spanish company (cf *CSPD 1631–3*, 135, 159, 176).

511. [f.82v] *28 Oct. 1631. Whitehall. Order of the privy council* [*Cf* PC 2/41, pp. 212–13.]
Present: lord keeper, lord privy seal, earl marshal, lord chamberlain, earls of Dorset, Exeter and Kellie, viscount Falkland, bishop of London, lord Newburgh, lord Cottington, Mr treasurer, Mr vice chamberlain, Mr Secretary Coke.
The board today considered the petition of the bailiffs and burgesses of Yarmouth in Norfolk showing that herrings were so plentiful this year that they had on their hands 2,000 lasts* more than were needed for the provisioning of the kingdom, which will perish unless exported in strangers' bottoms because the Turkey company who trade in that commodity have not taken them up within the time set down in former orders. The board, knowing the importance of the herring fisheries for the town and for the maintenance of many thousands of persons, as a nursery for seamen and for the increase of navigation, license the export of 1,000 lasts in strangers' bottoms. This favour is not to be expected hereafter. The lord treasurer is asked to give directions accordingly.

512. [f.83] *4 Nov. 1631. Whitehall. Order of the privy council*¹
Present: lord keeper, lord treasurer, lord privy seal, lord high chamberlain, earls of Salisbury, Exeter and Bridgewater, viscounts Dorchester and Falkland, lord Newburgh, lord Cottington, bishop of London, Mr treasurer, Mr vice chamberlain, Mr Secretary Coke.
An order similar to **511** in respect of Newfoundland fish* and pilchards taken on the western coasts.

1. Cf PC 2/41, pp. 224–5. The PC text shows that the earl marshal was also present.

513. [f.83v] *Feb. 1632. Ratcliff. Trinity House to the lord keeper*
They certify him upon the petition of Mr Wilde, merchant of London. Because of the want of words in the brief, Thomas Scott, master of the ship, and John Bonner, his mate, are not to benefit from the collection but Trinity House consider that the intention was that Scott and Bonner should benefit like the others who were taken with them. Were it not that the town of Poole was associated with Trinity House in the brief, they would have ordered that Scott and Bonner should receive their part. The lord keeper is asked to order Trinity House to that effect.
Robert Salmon, Walter Coke, Samuel Doves, Thomas Best, etc.

514. [f.84] *7 March 1632. Ratcliff. Trinity House to the privy council*[1]
According to the privy council's order of 29 Feb. 1632 they have considered the business. The petitioner has misunderstood the business and misinformed the board. Only part of the collection has been received. Whereas he pretends that Trinity House have received more than enough to meet his demand, the truth is that others will have nothing if he has all, which would not answer the trust which the lord keeper has reposed in Trinity House and the town of Poole. When the whole collection is in, both corporations must agree on how to provide for the redemption of 41 men (22 from Poole and only 19 from London). The 2 corporations agreed at the outset on the areas in which each would collect, with the proviso that when the money was collected, it should be put together and then shared out in accordance with the tenor of the brief. Trinity House therefore cannot meet the demands of the petitioner. They will pay him for the 5 men whom he redeemed when the business is concluded.
Robert Salmon, T. Best, Walter Coke, etc.

1. Cf SP 16/214/15; *CSPD 1631–3*, 284. The SP text is signed by Salmon, Best, Bushell, Rainborowe, Trenchfeild and Tutchen.

515. [f.84v] *7 March 1632. Ratcliff. Trinity House* [*? to Sir Edward Nicholas, secretary of the admiralty commissioners*]
The trees which they, on behalf of seamen trading to Newcastle etc., wish to be kept as seamarks stand in Shotley and belong to the heir of Sir Henry Felton, whose lady recently married Mr William Brookes. She has the wardship of her son. The trees are of great consequence for the safety of ships and men and the addressee is asked to take such course as is necessary for their preservation.
Samuel Doves, master, etc.

516. [f.85. *Before 15 Apr. 1632. Sir*] *John Woltenholme to Trinity House* [*See* **517.**]
Mr Secretary Cooke and the other commissioners for the king's service request Trinity House to consider the following questions and give their answers in writing before 15 Apr.: (a) How many ships should be employed against the pirates of Algiers? (b) What burdens should the ships be, and what ordnance should they carry? (c) What crews should the ships have, and what will be the charge of wages, victuals and munitions? (d) Should the ships be bought here or built for the service, and what will be the charge? (e) What will be the monthly charge for these ships, employed for one year?

517. [f.85v] *16 Apr. 1632. Ratcliff. Trinity House to Sir John Wolstenholme*
In answer to **516**: (a) For the expedition against Algiers, 8 ships are required, 4 of 500 tons, 4 of 400 tons. The ships of 500 tons should be 100 ft long by the keel, 33 ft at the beam, 33 ft rake fore and aft, and the depth from the beam to the ceiling* should be $12\frac{1}{2}$ ft. The ships of 400 tons should have proportionable dimensions. (b) 'Either of these ships' fully

157

furnished will cost £6,000. (c) Each ship should have a crew of 140. The monthly cost of wages, at 24s a man, will be £168, and that of victuals at 22s will be £154, a total of £322, or £3,864 a year. (d) Each ship should have 28 pieces of ordnance (10 whole culverins*, 10 demi-culverins*, and 8 sakers*) and 40 muskets. The cost of these will come within the £6,000. (e) Their opinion is to build, not buy.

Samuel Doves, master; Henry Manwaring, Robert Salmon, William Bushell, John Bennett, Thomas Best, John Totton, Anthony Tutchen, William Ewen.

518. [f.86. *? 1634*] *A plan for the disposition of 250 men in a king's ship having 40 pieces of great ordnance*[1]

Disposition of the crew: captain and lieutenant, 2; master and his mate, 2; surgeon and his mate, 2; carpenter and his company, 6; steward and his mate, 2; cook and his mate, 2; trumpeters, 4; steerage and 'condidge' [see **403**], 4; boatswain and his company, 40; gunner and his company for the great ordnance and the powder room, 136; 'muskets constant' [small arms company], 50; total, 250. Besides the 50 'muskets constant', the boatswain's company and trumpeters will employ 20 or 25 more, making a total of 70 'small shots'.

Disposition of the men assigned to the gunner for the ordnance, powder and powder room:

	Pieces of ordnance	Men
Gunner's room	4	20
From thence to the mast	6	20
From thence to the 'bittes'[2]	8	24
The 'chase below' [chase-ports*]	4	16
The half deck	6	16
The waist	8	22
The forecastle	4	12
The powder room		6
	40	136

1. Cf SP 16/279/27; *CSPD 1634–5*, 384, where it is attributed to 1634. Discussed in Oppenheim, 263.
2. A post for fastening cables. Riding bitts may be meant, i.e. the chief bitts used for fastening cables when the ship is at anchor.

519. [f.86v. *Before 3 Nov. 1632. Proposals presented by Capt. Kirk*[1] *to Trinity House. See* **520**.]

The charges for a ship of 250 tons, victualled for 7 months and manned by 70 men to bring home 100 soldiers from the fort at Quebec in the river of Canada, are calculated as follows: victuals for 70 men for 7 months at 20s a man per month, £490; harbour wages, half wages, and victuals in the Thames, £120; master's cabin, £10; 2½ months victuals for 100 soldiers, £250; customs on goods and other charges at Customs House and in the Thames, viz. lighterage, wharfage, cartage, warehouse room, etc., £100; insurance of the ship and goods, and interest paid, being all spent for Monsieur Decane,[2] £150; powder, shot and munitions of war, £30; wages for 70 men and officers for 7 months, £700; ship's freight at £100 a month, £700; total, £2,550.

1. Probably David Kirke (*DCB* i.404–8).
2. ? Emery or Guillaume de Caen, both of whom were involved in handing back Quebec to France in 1632 (ibid i.159–61).

520. *3 Nov. 1632. Report by Trinity House*
Capt. Kirk presented this estimate [**519**] and said that the lord treasurer required their opinion upon it. The charges for the ship, men and victuals are fair. With regard to the amounts provided for customs on goods, petty charges, insurance of the ship and goods, and interest, since these are affirmed by Capt. Kirk, Trinity House will not dispute them.
Robert Bell, master; T. Best, Robert Salmon, John Bennett, Walter Coke, William Rainborow, William Case, Anthony Tutchin, Gervais Hockett.

521. [f.87. ? c. *March 1633*] *Estimate for ships suitable for employment against the men-of-war of Algiers* [*See* **522.**]
Eight ships of about 400 or 500 tons, each with a crew of 140, making a total of 1,120 men are required. The cost of wages and victuals, together with the charges of the ship at £3 10s a month per man, amount to £3,920 a month or £47,040 a year. The cost of each ship per month at £168 and that of the men at 46s a month apiece would come to £2,576, making [an annual] total of £47,040. The cost of 1,120 men at 50s a month for wages and victuals would be £2,800. Eight ships at the rate of £140 a month per ship would cost £1,120, making a total monthly charge of £3,920 or £47,040 annually.

522. *22 March 1633. Estimate for ships suitable for employment against the men-of-war of Algiers* [*See* **521**, **523**.]
Eight ships of 400 or 500 tons, each having a crew of 140, makes a total of 1,120 required. Their cost at 50s a man per month for wages and victuals would be £2,800. The freight of 8 ships at £140 apiece per month would be £1,120. The total monthly cost would be £3,920, and the annual cost £47,040. Two small pinnaces of about 80 tons, each with 60 men at 50s per man for wages and victuals, would cost £150 a month. Pay for 2 vessels is £50 a month. The total monthly cost would be £200, or £2,400 annually. The total cost of the ships and the pinnaces would be £49,440.

523. [f.87v. ? c. *March 1633*] *Estimate for 8 ships to serve against the pirates of Algiers* [*See* **521–2.**]
Eight ships of about 400 tons, each with about 140 men, will need 1,120 men. Wages and victuals at 45s each will cost £2,520 a month. Freight of the ships at £160 a month will cost £1,280 for the 8 ships. Total cost per month will be £3,800 and per year £45,600.

GLOSSARY

average	Apportionment between shipowners and freighters of loss caused by intentional damage to a ship or her cargo in order to save the ship (e.g. cutting away masts or jettisoning cargo).
bend	The transverse section of a ship; or the outermost timbers of a ship's side.
cannon-perier	Medium shotted, short range gun of up to 8 inches calibre, and firing about a 24 pound shot.
ceiling	Inside planking of a ship laid across the floor and carried up the sides of the hold to the level of the beams.
chase-ports	Gunports at the bow or stern of a ship.
culverin	Light shotted, long range gun, of around 5 inches calibre, and firing about a 17 pound shot.
demi-cannon	Large calibre (6 inches) gun of medium range and length, firing a shot of over 30 pounds.
demi-culverin	Light shotted, long range gun, of about 4 inches calibre, and firing about a 9 pound shot.
doll	Dolium, or ton.
drake	Never very accurately described when it was in general use, but it seems to have been a term used to describe both guns lighter and shorter than those standard to their calibre, and those which were taper bored.
entry	Attestation of a ship's papers before customs.
inning	Reclaiming marsh or flooded land.
knee	A timber of naturally angular shape used to strengthen and support a ship's timbers at points of intersection.
last	A last of herrings was 12 barrels; of red fish and pilchards, 10,000–12,000 fish.
lastage and ballastage	Both words can mean the material used for ballast (i.e. sand, gravel, etc.), and the toll levied to supply it.
minion	Light shotted, long range gun, of about 3 inches calibre, and firing up to about a 5 pound shot.
murderer	Breech loading anti-personnel gun.
Newfoundland fish	Cod.
orlop	Strictly speaking, the lowest deck, but the term was used to describe all except the weather deck.
pipe-stave	Board used for making casks.

160

port-piece	Short range gun, firing a shot of up to 10 to 12 pounds.
round	A beam which rounds well having a sufficient curve to give a proper camber to the deck.
saker	Light shotted, long range gun, of about 3 inches calibre, and firing about a 5 pound shot.
scarf/scarfing	The joint by which two pieces of timber are joined into a continuous piece.
sharp	A term used to describe a ship having a narrow or wedge shaped bottom.
tons and tonnage	Tons gave the cargo capacity of a ship expressed in tuns of wine which could be carried in the hold; the addition of one third for tonnage gave the rough equivalent of modern gross tonnage (i.e. total cubic capacity).
waft/waftage	Convoy.

INDEX

Arabic numerals refer to serial numbers and not to pages; Roman numbers refer to pages in the Introduction. Two (or more) persons of the same name are grouped together unless there is ready evidence to separate them. Where more than eighteen mentions of an elder brother of Trinity House occur in the Transactions, only the first and last references are given together with the total number of mentions (e.g. seventy-five mentions, 52–410). Entries concerning cargoes, occupations, ordnance and ships are grouped together under those headings. Places in or near London have been grouped under London.

The following abbreviations have been used
    DFL   member of the Dover fellowship of lodemanage
    EB   elder brother of Deptford Trinity House
    HTH   member of Hull Trinity House
    NTH   member of Newcastle Trinity House
    YB   younger brother of Deptford Trinity House
A dagger (†) indicates a royal ship.

Abbot
  Edward, 401
  George, abp of Canterbury, 61, 68, 70, 93, 110, 229
  Maurice, kt, 352
Acton, George, 235
Acworth, Edward, 228
Adams (Adhams, etc.)
  Adam, 27–9
  John, 334
  Robert (EB), 81, 149, 222, 226, 250
Addison (Adyson)
  John, 16
  Thomas, 228; pilot, 16
admirals, 403
admiralty, commissioners of, 359, 390, 398–9, 420, 431–3, 443, 445–6, 453, 457–9, 480, 499, 515; see also Bertie, Robert; Carleton, Dudley; Cook, John; Sackville, Edward; Weston, Richard; Windebank, Francis
admiralty, high court of, xiv, 148, 178, 252, 272, 434, 489–90
  judge of, 207, 463; see also Caesar, Julius; Dun, Daniel; Martin, Henry; Treaver, Richard
  marshal of, see Smith, Solomon

  register and deputy register of, see Wyan, Thomas
admiralty, lieutenant of, 462
Adriatic Sea (Gulf of Taranto, Gulf of Venice), 9, 13
Affield, John, 84
Africa, North (Barbary), xv, 45–6, 111, 140, 158, 160, 173, 182, 185–6, 213, 415
'akall' (cable), 49
Aklenne, Walter, 475
Alberson, Nelles, 239
Alborow, —, lighthouse keeper, 326
Aldeburgh, Suffolk, 84, 237, 253, 269–70, 475
Aldermaine, Thomas, 475
Aldgate, Christopher, 235
Alexandre (Allexander)
  Andrew, 475
  William, 4
Alexandria, Egypt, 165
Algiers, North Africa, 148; consul at, 9; league with, 290; merchants at, 166; pirates of, 24, 148, 167, 198, 215, 267, 269, 411; prisoners at, 24, 166, 186, 202, 205, 216–19, 266–7, 269, 411, 444
Alicante, Spain, 160, 165, 168
Allen (Alyne)

162

163

165

Index

Gakope, Richard, 475
Galant, Thomas, 84
Gardener
    Edmond, junior, 112; shipmaster, 159
    Edward, 228
    Rev. R[ichard], 67
Gargardnall, John, 441
Garroway, Henry, kt, 352
Gaskein, Joel (HTH), 163
Gata, Cape, Spain, 24, 111, 140, 259, 415
Gataker, Rev. Thomas, 246
Gattes, Daniel, of London, 334; 381
Gayner, —, shipmaster, 484
Gdansk (Danzig), Poland, 111, 140, 253
Geare (Geer, Gere, etc.), Michael (EB), sixty-two mentions, 29–326
Genoa, Italy: consul at, 400–2, 405, 441–2; doge of, 402; English at, 400–1, 405, 441–2
Germany, xiv, 120; see also East Country
Germin (Jermyn), Thomas, kt, vice chamberlain, 455, 511–12
Geslyn, Thomas, 84
Gibbon (Gibbens, etc.), John, 228; shipowner, 307; shipowner and master, 315
Gibbs (Gibbes)
    James, 475
    John, 228
    Thomas, 228; shipmaster, 484
Gibraltar, Strait of (Strait of Morocco; Straits), 21, 159, 165, 173, 415; see also Mediterranean
Gilbert, John, 368
Gilderser, Richard, 334
Gilford, see Guildford
Glückstadt, Germany, 424
Gobson, John, 475
Goddard, Henry, 407, 421, 452
Godfrey
    Edward, 152
    Thomas, 152
Goeree, South Holland, 301
Gold, John, 253
Goldinge, Robert, 39
Goldmer Gat, Thames Estuary, buoy at, 332–4
Gollsound, John, 253
Gonston, see Gunstone
Goodlack, —, merchant, 35
Goodlad (Goodlard, etc.)
    John (EB), 3
    John (YB), 82; (? another), xv, 316–17, 484
    Nathaniel, 484
    Robert (YB), 82; 168
    William (d.1613, EB), 3, 21, 29–30, 33; (? another, the elder, shipmaster), 32
    William (c.1590–1640, EB), 238, 262,

315, 493; 228; shipowner, 307; (? another, of London), 334
Goodwin (Goodwyn), John, 282; master attendant, 407–8, 480; (? another), 228
Goodwin Sands, 480; South Sand Head, 182
Goonstone, see Gunstone
Goose, William, 228
Gore End, Kent, 406
Goslin, Wolston, 334
Goston, Francis, navy commissioner, 191–2
Gounston, see Gunstone
Grain, Isle of, Kent, 152, 155
grand mogul, 7
Grant (Graunt)
    John, 112, 228; shipmaster, 484
    Robert (YB), 82
Gravelines, France, 249
Graves (Greaves)
    Jo., of Limehouse, 45
    John, of Stepney, 151; shipwright, 280, 407–8, 421, 438, 452
Gravesend, Kent, 59, 149, 186, 483
Gray
    Cuthbert, 50–3
    James, 484
Greece, 422–3
Greene (Grene)
    —, 306
    Edmond, 334
    Henry, 23
    William, 228; of Wapping, 278; shipowner, 307
Greenhithe, Kent, xii, 330–1
Greenland, 111, 140, 168, 179, 335
Greenwich, Stephen, 475
Greenwood, —, collector of dues, 172
Greville (Gryvell), Fulke, kt, later lord Brooke, 159; chancellor of the exchequer, 93
Griffen, Thomas, 186
Griffith, George, 268
Grimble, John, 334
'Grimbsbyes Sound', Scilly, 225
Groome
    Anthony, 475
    Henry, 475
Grove
    Edmond, 228; of London, 334; shipmaster, 484
    William, 228
Guiana or Guinea, 39
guilders, 239–40
Guildford (Gilford), Henry, kt, 482
Guinea, 16, 111, 140, 173; see also Guiana
Guldeford level, Sussex, 482
Gulls, Channel of, 480; seamark for, 383
Gunfleet, Thames Estuary, buoy at, xiii, 332–58
Gunner, John, 334

171

lord high admiral (lord admiral), 178, 184, 188, 193, 199, 207, 359, 462–4, 487, 492; *see also* Howard, Charles; Villiers, George

lord keeper, *see* Bacon, Francis; Coventry, Thomas; Williams, John

lord privy seal, *see* Howard, Henry; Montagu, Henry

lord steward, *see* Herbert, William

lord treasurer, 396; *see also* Cecil, Robert; Cranfield, Lionel; Howard, Thomas; Montagu, Henry; Sackville, Thomas; Weston, Richard

Love, Thomas, kt (EB), 97, 131–2, 137, 139, 141, 148, 154, 157–60, 165–6, 198, 212, 229, 250; Capt., 215

Low Countries (Two Countries), 444

Lowe
Barnabas, 253
John, 228, 334; shipowner, 307; shipmaster, 484; (? another), 228
Robert, 334
Susan, 84
William, 84, 228

Lowestoft, Suffolk, 226, 258; buoys, beacons and lighthouses at, 172, 256–7, 319

Lübeck, Germany, 281, 460

Lucas
—, collector of dues, 172
Peter, 239

Lugo, Cape, *see* Lagit, Kep-i-

Lullton, Aden, 39

Lunne, Esther, 274

Lunt, Peter, 475

Lutcombe, Christopher, 422

Lydiard, *see* Hillyard

Lyell, James, 253

Lymbrey, John, 484

Lyme Regis, Dorset, 267

Lynch, Thomas, 447–8

Lyneere, *see* Laniere

Lynn, King's, Norfolk, 177, 180, 237, 253, 269, 475; customs at, 256–7; pilotage at, 446; Trinity House collector at, 177

Mace, William, 277

Madeira, 140

Madison, —, of Newcastle, 200

magistrates, 499

Maidstone, Kent, assizes, 155

Maillim, Henry, 253

Mainwaring (Manneringe, Manwaringe, etc.), Henry, kt (EB), 289, 362, 387, 517

Majorca, 165, 173

Malaga, Spain, 30, 158, 165, 182, 185, 415; wines of, 137, 165

Malbie (Malbey, etc.), Thomas (EB), 40–1, 47, 66, 79, 122, 139, 172–3, 177, 183, 190

Mallet, William, 112

malmsey, 21, 137

Malym, Richard, 112

Man
Diggory, 484
Edward, 5
Elizabeth, 5
John, 153

Manacle rocks, near Falmouth, 195

Manchester, earl of, *see* Montagu, Edward; Montagu, Henry

Manderstian, Seryes, 253

Mandeville, visc., *see* Montagu, Edward; Montagu, Henry

Manneringe, *see* Mainwaring

Manningtree, Essex, 475

Mansell (Mansfeld), Robert, kt, 186, 324

Manwaringe, *see* Mainwaring

Maplesden
Edward (EB), 221–2, 236, 249–50, 280–1, 395
'William' (? Edward), 251

Mar, earl of, *see* Erskine, John

March
James, 46
Richard, 45

Margate (Norgate), Kent, 214, 476, 480, 499

Marison, Robert, 475

Marle, James, 475

Marsh, Peter, of Stepney, 151; of Wapping, 278

Martin (Marten, Martyn)
Henry, kt, admiralty court judge, xiii, 138, 175, 178, 203–4, 207, 272, 286–9, 295–6, 321–2, 328–9, 415, 426, 434, 485, 489–90
John, shipowner, 50–3; of London, 334; shipmaster of London, 484; (? another, of Ipswich), 12; (? another, gunner), 239
Roger, 406, 484
Thomas, 228, 306; of London, 334

Martrey, John, 475

Marychurch, Thomas, 253

Mason
Humphrey, 475
John, 228
Moses, and Elizabeth, his wife, 67

Masse, John, 334

Massola, Francisco, 400–2, 405, 441–2

Masters, Ambrose, 334

Matham, Peter, 253

Mathew (Mathues)
Bennet, 23
Peter, and Robert, his brother, 213

183

185

189

LONDON RECORD SOCIETY

The London Record Society was founded in December 1964 to publish transcripts, abstracts and lists of the primary sources for the history of London, and generally to stimulate interest in archives relating to London. Membership is open to any individual or institution; the annual subscription is £5 ($12) for individuals and £8 ($20) for institutions, which entitles a member to receive one copy of each volume published during the year and to attend and vote at meetings of the Society. Prospective members should apply to the Hon. Secretary, Miss Heather Creaton, c/o Institute of Historical Research, Senate House, London, WC1E 7HU.

The following volumes have already been published:

1. *London Possessory Assizes: a calendar*, edited by Helena M. Chew (1965)
2. *London Inhabitants within the Walls, 1695*, with an introduction by D. V. Glass (1966)
3. *London Consistory Court Wills, 1492–1547*, edited by Ida Darlington (1967)
4. *Scriveners' Company Common Paper, 1357–1628, with a continuation to 1678*, edited by Francis W. Steer (1968)
5. *London Radicalism, 1830–1843: a selection from the papers of Francis Place*, edited by D. J. Rowe (1970)
6. *The London Eyre of 1244*, edited by Helena M. Chew and Martin Weinbaum (1970)
7. *The Cartulary of Holy Trinity Aldgate*, edited by Gerald A. J. Hodgett (1971)
8. *The Port and Trade of Early Elizabethan London: documents*, edited by Brian Dietz (1972)
9. *The Spanish Company*, by Pauline Croft (1973)
10. *London Assize of Nuisance, 1301–1431: a calendar*, edited by Helena M. Chew and William Kellaway (1973)
11. *Two Calvinistic Methodist Chapels, 1743–1811: the London Tabernacle and Spa Fields Chapel*, edited by Edwin Welch (1975)
12. *The London Eyre of 1276*, edited by Martin Weinbaum (1976)
13. *The Church in London, 1375–1392*, edited by A. K. McHardy (1977)
14. *Committees for Repeal of the Test and Corporation Acts: Minutes, 1786–90 and 1827–8*, edited by Thomas W. Davis (1978)
15. *Joshua Johnson's Letterbook, 1771–4: letters from a merchant in London to his partners in Maryland*, edited by Jacob M. Price (1979)
16. *London and Middlesex Chantry Certificate, 1548*, edited by C. J. Kitching (1980)

17. *London Politics, 1713–1717: Minutes of a Whig Club, 1714–17,*
    edited by H. Horwitz; *London Pollbooks, 1713,* edited by W. A.
    Speck and W. A. Gray (1981)
18. *Parish Fraternity Register: fraternity of the Holy Trinity and SS.
    Fabian and Sebastian in the parish of St. Botolph without Aldersgate,*
    edited by Patricia Basing (1982)
19. *Trinity House of Deptford: Transactions, 1609–35,* edited by G. G.
    Harris (1983)

All volumes are still in print; apply to Hon. Secretary. Price to individual
members £5 ($12) each; to institutional members £8 ($20) each; and to
non-members £10 ($25) each.